THE
OXFORD BOOK OF
VERSE
1945–1980

D. J. Enright is well known as both a poet and a critic. He has taught literature in Egypt, Europe, and the Far East, and was Professor of English at the University of Singapore from 1960 to 1970. His novels include *Academic Year* (1955, reissued by OUP 1985) and his newest book of poetry is *Collected Poems 1987*. In addition he has edited *A Choice of Milton's Verse* (Faber, 1975), *The Oxford Book of Death* (1983, reissued as an Oxford Paperback 1987), and *Fair of Speech: The Uses of Euphemism* (1985). *The Alluring Problem: An Essay on Irony* was published in 1986. In 1981 he received the Queen's Gold Medal for Poetry.

THE
OXFORD BOOK OF
VERSE
1945–1980

Chosen by
D. J. ENRIGHT

OXFORD UNIVERSITY PRESS

Oxford University Press, Walton Street, Oxford OX2 6DP

Oxford New York

Athens Auckland Bangkok Bombay
Calcutta Cape Town Dar es Salaam Delhi
Florence Hong Kong Istanbul Karachi
Kuala Lumpur Madras Madrid Melbourne
Mexico City Nairobi Paris Singapore
Taipei Tokyo Toronto

and associated companies in
Berlin Ibadan

Oxford is a trade mark of Oxford University Press

Introduction and compilation © D. J. Enright 1980

First published as 'The Oxford Book of Contemporary Verse' in 1980
and simultaneously in a hardback edition
Reissued as 'The Oxford Book of Verse, 1945–1980' in 1995

British Library Cataloguing in Publication Data

Data available

ISBN 0–19–283188–7

9 10 8

Printed and bound in Great Britain by
Biddles Ltd, Guildford and King's Lynn

CONTENTS

STEVIE SMITH

Born in Hull in 1902 as Florence Margaret Smith. She lived in London from the age of three onwards, and was educated at the North London Collegiate School. Worked for Newnes Publishing Company, 1923–53. Published *Novel on Yellow Paper* in 1936, and two other novels. Her poems were often accompanied by her own drawings. Received the Queen's Gold Medal for Poetry in 1969. She died in 1971.

EARLE BIRNEY

Born in 1904 in Calgary, Alberta. Educated at Universities of British Columbia, California in Berkeley, and Toronto. His picaresque novel of wartime, *Turvey*, was published in 1949. Has twice received the Governor-General's Award for Poetry. A freelance writer and lecturer since 1968, he has travelled widely in South America, Australasia, Africa and the East.

CONTENTS

A. D. HOPE

Born in Cooma, New South Wales, in 1907. Educated at Sydney University and Oxford. He was Professor of English at the Australian National University, Canberra, until 1969 and then Library Fellow till 1972. He has written on poetry and Australian literature.

NORMAN MacCAIG

Born in 1910 in Edinburgh and educated at Edinburgh University. He was a schoolmaster in Edinburgh between 1934 and 1970, and until recently Reader in Poetry at the University of Stirling. With Alexander Scott, he edited *Contemporary Scottish Verse 1959–1969* (1970). He received the Queen's Gold Medal for Poetry in 1986.

ELIZABETH BISHOP

Born in Worcester, Massachusetts, in 1911. Educated at Vassar College. She lived in Brazil for sixteen years, and has translated contemporary Brazilian poetry. Lectured at Harvard University. She received the Pulitzer Prize in 1956 and her most recent collection, *Geography III*, won the 1976 Poetry Award of the National Book Critics Circle of America. She died in 1979.

CONTENTS

ROY FULLER

Born in 1912 in Failsworth, near Manchester. Served in Royal Navy. He worked as solicitor to a building society until retirement in 1969, when he became a director. He was elected Professor of Poetry at Oxford, 1968–73, and received the Queen's Gold Medal for Poetry in 1970. He has published novels, criticism, memoirs, and fiction and verse for children. He died in 1991.

R. S. THOMAS

Born in Cardiff in 1913. Educated at University College of North Wales, Bangor. He was ordained priest in 1937, and served as Vicar of St Hywyn, Aberdaron, with St Mary, Bodferin, from 1967 until retirement in 1978. Awarded the Queen's Gold Medal for Poetry in 1964. He has compiled selections of George Herbert's and Wordsworth's verse.

JOHN BERRYMAN

Born in 1914 in McAlester, Oklahoma. Educated at Columbia University and Cambridge. He taught in various American universities, notably the University of Minnesota, 1954–72. Wrote a biography of Stephen Crane (1950), a novel, *Recovery* (published in 1973), and essays on literature, some of which are collected in *The Freedom of the Poet* (1976). He died in 1972.

CONTENTS

RANDALL JARRELL

Born in Nashville, Tennessee in 1914. Educated at Vanderbilt University. He served in the U.S. Army Air Corps, and taught at Kenyon College, Sarah Lawrence and the University of North Carolina. Published a novel, *Pictures from an Institution*, in 1954, several collections of criticism, and books for children; also translations of the Brothers Grimm and (in 1976) of Goethe's *Faust, Part One*. He died in 1965.

C. H. SISSON

Born in Bristol in 1914. He was educated at the University of Bristol and in France and Germany, and worked in the Civil Service until 1973. He has published novels, criticism, translations of Horace, Lucretius, La Fontaine, Dante, and Virgil, and (in 1959) *The Spirit of British Administration and Some European Comparisons*.

GAVIN EWART

Born in London in 1916. Educated at Wellington College and Cambridge. He has worked for the British Council, as an advertising copywriter and, since 1971, as a freelance writer and part-time teacher. He edited *Forty Years On: An Anthology of School Songs* (1964).

CONTENTS

CHARLES CAUSLEY

Born in 1917 in Lauceston, Cornwall. Served in Royal Navy. He taught in his native town for many years, and has worked as a full-time writer since 1976. He received the Queen's Gold Medal for Poetry in 1967. He has edited anthologies and written verse for children.

ROBERT CONQUEST

Born in Malvern in 1917, and educated at the University of Grenoble and Oxford. He worked in the diplomatic service 1946–56, and has since held fellowships at the London School of Economics and at American universities and institutions. He edited the 'Movement' anthology, *New Lines* (1956), and has published two novels, science fiction anthologies, and books on Soviet affairs.

ROBERT LOWELL

Born in Boston, Massachusetts, in 1917. Educated at Harvard, Kenyon College and Louisiana State University. He taught in the Universities of Iowa, Boston, and Harvard, and at the University of Essex. He published adaptations of Racine: *Phaedra* and Aeschylus: *Prometheus Bound*. He lived in England from 1970 until his death (in New York) in 1977.

CONTENTS

JOHN HEATH-STUBBS

Born in 1918 in London. Educated at Oxford. He was Visiting Professor of English at Alexandria University, 1955-8, and at Michigan University, 1960-61, and Lecturer at the College of St Mark & St John, London, 1963-72. He has published plays, criticism, and translations of Leopardi, Hafiz, and Omar Khayyam. He received the Queen's Gold Medal for Poetry in 1973.

D. J. ENRIGHT

Born in Leamington, Warwickshire, in 1920, and educated at Cambridge. He taught for twenty-five years, mainly in the East, and then worked in publishing in London. Has written criticism, novels, translations of Japanese poetry, and a partial autobiography, *Memoirs of a Mendicant Professor* (1969), and edited *The Oxford Book of Death*, 1983.

HOWARD NEMEROV

Born in New York City, 1920. Educated at Harvard. He taught in several universities, including Bennington College, 1948-66, and from 1969 in Washington University. He published three novels and a critical book, *Figures of Thought* (1978). He won the Pulitzer Prize and a National Book Award in 1978. He died in 1991.

CONTENTS

GEORGE MACKAY BROWN

Born in Stromness, Orkney, in 1921, and educated at Newbattle Abbey College and Edinburgh University. He lives in Orkney, and has written plays, short stories and novels, and stories for children.

RICHARD WILBUR

Born in New York City in 1921, he grew up in New Jersey. Educated at Amherst College and Harvard. He has taught at Harvard, Wellesley College, and Wesleyan University. Awarded the Pulitzer Prize in 1957. He has published adaptations of plays by Molière and lyrics for a comic opera based on Voltaire's *Candide*.

KINGSLEY AMIS

Born in South London in 1922. After army service he took a degree at Oxford. Taught at University College, Swansea, for twelve years, and was a Fellow of Peterhouse, Cambridge, 1961–3. He has published eighteen novels since his first, *Lucky Jim* (1954), critical works, and a survey of science fiction, *New Maps of Hell* (1961). He edited *The New Oxford Book of Light Verse* (1978).

CONTENTS

DONALD DAVIE

Born in 1922 in Barnsley, Yorkshire, and educated at Cambridge. He has taught at Trinity College, Dublin, at Cambridge, and the University of Essex, as Professor of English at Stanford University, California, and now at Vanderbilt University. He has published criticism, adaptations of Mickiewicz, and translations of Pasternak, and *A Gathered Church*, a study of the literature of Dissent, 1978. He edited *The New Oxford Book of Christian Verse*, 1981.

PHILIP LARKIN

Born in Coventry, Warwickshire, in 1922, he held posts in libraries from 1943 onwards, and was Librarian of the University of Hull until his death in 1985. Awarded the Queen's Gold Medal for Poetry in 1965. He published two novels, *Jill* (1946) and *A Girl in Winter* (1947), jazz criticism, and literary criticism *(Required Writing*, 1983), and compiled *The Oxford Book of Twentieth-Century English Verse* (1973). He died in 1985.

VERNON SCANNELL

Born in 1922 in Spilsby, Lincolnshire. Educated at the University of Leeds. Formerly amateur and professional boxer. He was a schoolteacher between 1955 and 1962, and since then has worked as a freelance writer and broadcaster. He has published novels, autobiography, and a book on the poetry of the Second World War, *Not Without Glory*, 1976.

CONTENTS

DANNIE ABSE

Born in Cardiff in 1923. Educated at the University of South Wales, King's College, London, and Westminster Hospital. He works part-time as a doctor in a London chest clinic. He has published three novels, several plays, including *Pythagoras* (1979), and an autobiography, *A Poet in the Family* (1974).

ANTHONY HECHT

Born in 1923 in New York City, and educated at Bard College and Columbia University. He served with the U.S. Army in Europe and Japan, and has taught at several universities, since 1967 at the University of Rochester. His second book of poems, *The Hard Hours* (1967), won the Pulitzer Prize. He has co-translated Aeschylus's *Seven Against Thebes*.

LOUIS SIMPSON

Born in Jamaica in 1923, and educated at Columbia University. Took U.S. citizenship and served as combat infantryman. He has worked in publishing, and taught at the University of California, Berkeley, and since 1967 at the State University of New York. He was awarded the Pulitzer Prize in 1964. *A Revolution in Taste*, studies of modern poets, appeared in 1979.

CONTENTS

PATRICIA BEER

Born in Exmouth, Devon, in 1924. Educated at Exeter University and Oxford. She has taught in universities in Italy and England, and is now a full-time writer living in London and Devon. She has published an account of childhood, *Mrs Beer's House* (1968), a study of women characters in nineteenth-century women's novelists, *Reader, I Married Him* (1974), and more recently a novel.

JAMES K. BAXTER

Born in 1926 in Dunedin, New Zealand, and educated at Otago University, Dunedin, and Victoria University, Wellington. He worked as a labourer, a schoolmaster, a journalist and a social worker, and published numerous plays and essays on poetry and New Zealand poetry in particular. He died in 1972.

CHARLES TOMLINSON

Born in Stoke-on-Trent in 1927, and educated at Cambridge and the University of London. Since 1956 he has taught at the University of Bristol, with visits to American universities. He is a painter, and has collaborated in translations of Tyutchev, Vallejo, and Machado. He edited *The Oxford Book of Verse in English Translation* (1980).

CONTENTS

THOM GUNN

Born in Gravesend, Kent, in 1929. Educated at Cambridge and Stanford University, California. He has lived in San Francisco since 1954, and taught at the University of California, Berkeley, between 1958 and 1966. He is currently a freelance writer. He has edited selections from Fulke Greville and Ben Jonson. *The Occasions of Poetry: Essays in Criticism and Autobiography* was published in 1982.

PETER PORTER

Born in 1929 in Brisbane, Australia. He has lived in London since 1951, and worked as a reporter, a bookseller, a clerk and (for ten years) in advertising, and is now a freelance writer and broadcaster. He has written three radio plays, edited a choice of Pope's verse and a selection from Thomas Hardy's, and published a volume of 're-creations', *After Martial* (1972).

A. K. RAMANUJAN

Born in 1929 in Mysore, South India, and educated at the University of Mysore and Indiana University, Bloomington. He taught in India between 1950 and 1958, and now lives in Chicago, teaching Dravidian Studies at the University of Chicago. He has translated classical Tamil love poems and religious lyrics from the medieval Kannada.

CONTENTS

TED HUGHES

Born in Mytholmroyd, West Yorkshire, in 1930. Educated at Cambridge. He has worked as a rose gardener, a night watchman and a reader for the Rank Organization. In 1956 he married the American poet, Sylvia Plath, who died in 1963. Has written plays and poems for children, edited selections from Emily Dickinson and Shakespeare, and adapted Seneca's *Oedipus*. He received the Queen's Gold Medal for Poetry in 1974, and was appointed Poet Laureate in 1984.

DEREK WALCOTT

Born in St Lucia, West Indies, in 1930, and educated at the University of the West Indies. He has taught in America, and several of his plays have been performed in London and New York. He lives in Trinidad, working as a reviewer, an art critic and director of the Trinidad Theatre Workshop.

GEOFFREY HILL

Born in 1932 in Bromsgrove, Worcestershire, and educated at Oxford. He was visiting lecturer at the University of Michigan 1959–60, became Professor of English Literature at the University of Leeds, and is now University Lecturer in English at Cambridge. His version of Ibsen's *Brand* was performed and published in 1978 and *The Lords of Limit: Essays on Literature and Ideas* appeared in 1984.

CONTENTS

PETER REDGROVE

Born in Kingston, Surrey, in 1932. Read Natural Sciences at Cambridge. He has worked as a scientific editor and journalist, and lectured in America, and is currently Resident Author at Falmouth School of Art. A novelist and playwright, he has also written (with Penelope Shuttle) a book on the psychology of menstruation, *The Wise Wound* (1978).

JON STALLWORTHY

Born in London, in 1935, of New Zealander parents, and educated at Rugby and Oxford. He worked for Oxford University Press, was Anderson Professor of English at Cornell University, New York, and is now Reader in English Literature at Oxford. He has published a biography, *Wilfred Owen* (1974), and edited Owen's poems, collaborated in translations of Polish and Russian poetry, and compiled *The Oxford Book of War Poetry* (1984).

SEAMUS HEANEY

Born in County Derry, Ireland, in 1939. Educated at Queen's University, Belfast, where he later lectured. He has also taught in the University of California, Berkeley, and Carysfort College, Dublin. Since 1982 he has been Visiting Professor at Harvard. *Preoccupations: Selected Prose 1968–1978* appeared in 1980.

CONTENTS

DEREK MAHON

Born in Belfast in 1941, and educated at Trinity College, Dublin. He has lectured at the Language Centre of Ireland in Dublin, and at the New University of Ulster, Coleraine, and currently lives in Cork. He has translated Nerval and Molière, and edited *Modern Irish Poetry* (1972).

DOUGLAS DUNN

Born in 1942 in Inchinnan, Renfrewshire, Scotland. Educated at the Scottish School of Librarianship and the University of Hull. He worked as a librarian in Ohio, 1964–6, and at the University of Hull, 1969–71. He lives in Fife, as a freelance writer. He has edited selections from Byron and Delmore Schwartz, and published a collection of stories, *Secret Villages* (1985).

INTRODUCTION

Much as he might prefer to, it is hardly permissible for an anthologist to evade all mention of the principles on which his choice of poets or poems is based. I am obliged to admit that I have chosen poets whom I esteem and whose staying power is attested to by the collections they have published in the period under survey—and then as many of them as could be given a reasonable representation in the available space. Writers flourishing in the 1930s or characteristic of that decade fell outside my brief, as I saw it; and the under-40s are thinly represented. Increased life-expectancy is reflected in literary development (at least one hopes it is only that), and while young poets of substantial published achievement are in short supply these days, there are rather more older ones in evidence than used to be the case.

I have included American poets, not because I believe that contemporary American poetry is bigger and better than British (though it does incline to be more extreme, at all extremities), but because it would have been painfully impoverishing and therefore absurd to exclude them. And I have included Commonwealth poets, not for the sake of ingratiation (though the Commonwealth still strikes me as meaning more to us culturally than 'Europe' ever will), but because to debar them from an anthology of contemporary verse in English would be perverse. I trust it will not sound presumptuous in any personal sense to cite the words of Arthur Quiller-Couch, introducing the *Oxford Book of English Verse 1250–1900*: 'Nor have I sought in these Islands only, but wheresoever the Muse has followed the tongue which among living tongues she most delights to honour.'

I have drawn freely, aiming to 'represent' poetry rather than the countries which make up the English-speaking world. While I hope (I certainly believe) that there is considerable diversity of matter and manner here, I have not gone out of my way to achieve geographical sweep. There is a sense in which I have selected, or often selected, poems which seem to me representative of their authors—poems in which the writers are doing best what they characteristically do—but for obvious reasons the characteristic of length, the long poem or sequence, could not be entertained. Quiller-Couch remarked that the best is the best, even though a hundred judges have declared it so. While in the nature of the undertaking I have not been faced by a judicial bench of those proportions, I have tended where no great effort was required to avoid the more frequently anthologized poems, not to make way for 'the second-rate merely because it happened to be recondite', but because there were sufficient others which I found at least equally good.

These 'principles', or some of them, serve to differentiate this book from Philip Larkin's *Oxford Book of Twentieth-Century English Verse*, a selection which, besides covering a wider time-span, excluded American and (virtually) Commonwealth writers, but took in a much larger number of poets, many of them sparsely represented. Commenting on this in his preface, Mr Larkin referred to the class of poems 'judged by me to be worthy of inclusion without reference to their authors'. He had been prompted, he said, to the conclusion that 'once the anthologist has to deal with poets born after 1914 his loyalty turns perforce to poems rather than to individuals'. I have not myself found this to be overwhelmingly the case: some individual poets impress me as distinctly better than others, and by virtue of the individual poems they have written. However, while the reading involved in the task of selection was vastly pleasurable, I found the final juggling much less so. It is common among reviewers of anthologies to complain, often with some justification, 'If A and B are in, why are Y and Z out?' (And Y and Z will have sharper cause to complain.) Yet if Y and Z are in, neither they nor A or B will get much of a showing. It was at this stage that I envied Mr Larkin his generous terms of reference—though even *he* left some people out.

Proust remarked that, like microbes and corpuscles, theories and schools devour one another and by their warfare ensure the continuity of life. I doubt, though, that the present is a time for schools or manifestos, whether grandly or modestly styled. 'Acmeists', 'Imagists', 'Parnassiens', 'Symbolists', 'Projectivists'—these days the words ring out like great ancient bells, in a secularized city. The group most frequently referred to in Britain during recent decades, and more often than not with only moderate enthusiasm, was 'the Movement' (a title, not invented by its members, whose simplicity suggests either considerable potency or abject poverty), and the most notable thing about it, except as concerns sociologists and culture-historians in search of a footnote, was the nonchalance with which, after a brief cohesiveness, its members went their separate ways. The best movement is one that doesn't move far in the same direction.

I notice, incidentally, that the present book contains poets who were associated severally with the New Apocalypse, with the Movement, which was explicitly anti-Apocalyptic, and with the Mavericks, an alliance formed in opposition to the Movement. True, these poets are decidedly unalike—if they were not, they wouldn't all be here—but their differences are scarcely to be defined or appraised by reference to the platforms on which they once assembled.

To say this is not to cast aspersions on that age-old congeniality of feeling and purpose which brings writers, and particularly young ones, together. A cold wind blows through the world of the arts, where supply is eternally in excess of demand, and one finds shelter where one may. Nor am I recommending any variety of Noble Savagery or Doing-your-own-thing. The latter is a contemporary phenomenon worth noting as one of several factors in the weakening of poetry as a public affair. A lot of interest is shown in poetry today, compared with the recent and probably the remoter past, but not very much of it is disinterested. That is, there is little respect for poetry as distinct from admiration for oneself for writing it: indeed, poetry is seen as something that is written, not something that is read.* This phenomenon—does it arise in progressive or indolent classrooms? Is it an aspect of our distaste for élitism and specialization? Or a sign that, when religion has materialized itself into thin air and creeds are shaken and traditions dissolved at a rate unimagined by Matthew Arnold, people turn to pen and paper for consolation and sustenance? —is as barely credible as (something to which any poetry editor will testify) it is widespread. Here are writers who have spared themselves the discomforts attendant on what W. Jackson Bate has termed 'the remorseless deepening of self-consciousness before the rich and intimidating legacy of the past' through the simple expedient of ignoring

---

* Poetry is such a fearfully personal business that it is often hard to discern, at higher levels of skill than those alluded to here, where devotion to the art ends and self-promotion (of a curious sort, some may think) begins.

the past. What then deepens is another sort of self-consciousness, and it is sad to think of people as exclusively each his own poet, moving in a cloud of their own breath.

The writing of verse as a self-administered form of therapy is of course traditional and helpful, being both cheaper and often more effective than other methods. Its true sponsor is the National Health Service rather than the Arts Council, and it is only exceptionable when mistaken for poetry as a mode of communication with other people on matters of mutual consequence. One form of Noble Savagery—'O for a life of Sensations rather than of Thoughts!'—has demonstrated its appeal, chiefly for the young and for busy people who look for quick returns: the type of writing which, abandoning the ancient poetic habit of making connections between one thing and another as either vulgar or old-hat or 'academic', gives itself up to unconnected whimsies, velleities or spasms. At its best D. H. Lawrence, who did it best, characterized the genre as 'the poetry of that which is at hand', 'the insurgent naked throb of the instant moment' where 'there is no perfection, no consummation, nothing finished'. The genre can have its successes—we should never forget that, as W. H. Auden put it, 'Parnassus has many mansions'—but in the main it is more accurately described by another phrase lifted from Lawrence: 'the living plasm vibrates unspeakably'. Such writing has been praised for being *groping and semi-articulate, like us*, as though poetry is merely to repeat and condone our weaknesses.*

Proust also remarked that a work in which there are theories is like an article on which the price-tag has been left. The alignments so prominent in other spheres of activity, it seems to me, are best avoided or at least played down in the arts. A conscious 'programme' can be crippling: in as far and for as long as he can, the poet best remains unattached, he finds his own way or is led into it by a multiplicity of circumstances ranging from the happily 'accidental' through the unplumbably deep-seated to the most deliberate experimentation. We are in a region where one is tempted to say there are no laws. But there are: their presence is only to be inferred from what

* On the connection between the squabbling camps of 'pop spontaneity' and 'academic complexity', those puny present-day exemplars of the *naiv* and the *sentimentalisch*, see Anthony Thwaite, 'The Two Poetries', *The Listener*, 5 April 1973.

we can tell is an offence against them, or what we recognize as a triumphant observance. Writing is full of unwritten laws, and attempts at codification can only touch their surface.

Yet if people are to discuss poetry at all, they will want to fall back on theory and categorization. Classical and romantic, urban and rural, paleface and redskin, Ego and Id ... In Britain it has been found convenient at varying levels—a telegraphese for journalism and academic use alike—to subsume the period under two poets, Philip Larkin and Ted Hughes. Their contemporaries can then be located at intervals on the line stretching between these two not wholly imaginary points, with Robert Lowell appearing now at one end, then at the other. An ill effect of this rough-and-ready schematism is that it has helped to impel writers into excogitated gimmickry, the one-finger étude, the all-thumbs concrete poem, the four-letter ejaculation, and other practices which at least denote a certain if not particularly enterprising acquaintance with the movements or the twitches of the past.

The dealings of academic critics with contemporary poetry seem to have turned into a virtually autonomous activity. The more elaborate the critical treatment, the more reductive it is of what is being treated —public import dwindles into private ingenuity—or at best the more inconsequential. The oddity is accentuated in that twenty people are able to talk sophisticatedly about 'literature' for every single person who can actually tell good writing from bad. 'When we search out the motives for most of the criticism being written today,' Lionel Abel remarked recently, 'we are unlikely to find love or hatred of particular works or authors.' What are the motives? Perhaps the untiring industry of the human brain, its appetite for newfangledness, for fresh fields to colonize ... Perhaps the circumstance that criticism is something that enables you to get a job—a job that enables you to compose criticism. We recall the remark of a character in Balzac's *La Peau de Chagrin*: 'University chairs are not made for philosophy. Philosophy was made for the chairs.' At all events modern criticism turns a deaf ear on Arnold's insistence that a critic's labours amount to mere dilettantism unless they help him to distinguish between the better and the worse, to develop 'a clearer sense and a deeper enjoy-ment of what is truly excellent'; and, if anything, it has served to alienate the general public further. If being written about like this is what poetry is for, then poetry is not for them.*

But to complain that criticism has come close to killing poetry is to flog a moribund horse: during recent years literary criticism has come even closer to killing literary criticism.

> In this superb contraption here, you see
> The Self-moved Mover as Machinery ...
> Pure Criticism, without thought or fuss;
> Pure Theory formed, with nothing to discuss!
> This rare device embodies in its guts
> No cranks or levers, pistons, cogs or nuts;
> A 'magic eye' looks inward and controls
> Pure Critics musing on their own pure souls.†

Yet we should guard against taking as a prime and wanton cause what is also an effect, even to some extent an effect of poetry. Reflecting on the takeover of poetry by the university, Theodore Weiss makes a wry point: 'Alas, in an increasingly unliterate, if not illiterate, age where else can poetry be preserved?' And of course there are honourable exceptions, in whose hands the critique still serves the text instead of contrariwise. There are honourable exceptions among periodical reviewers of poetry too, some of whom are able to give an intelligent and disinterested account of what they see as its intrinsic strengths and weaknesses. This may be thought a small thing to ask of a reviewer. Not so, for much reviewing of new verse is coterie in spirit, whether hatchet-job or puff, meanly judicious or vacuously benign, offering unmediated verdicts whose real significance can only be deduced by students of 'form', and serenely ignoring the public whom the periodicals themselves profess to address.

No wonder then that serious-minded readers have turned, successfully or not, to the novel for information about life and how it is or was or may be led. In terms of spectator sport, that prodigy of our time, poetry—a prodigy of other times—has sunk in the hierarchy to around the level of marbles or yo-yo. 'The great instrument of moral good is the imagination; and poetry administers to the effect by acting

---

* It was some thirty years ago that one poet appearing in this anthology, Randall Jarrell, himself an elegant and moving writer on literature, quoted another, Elizabeth Bishop, as saying: 'After I go through one of the quarterlies I don't feel like reading a poem for a week, much less like writing one.'

† A. D. Hope, *Dunciad Minor*.

upon the cause...' We have come a long way since those grand old affirmations of poetry's nature and use: the high-flown language of Shelley's *Defence of Poetry* raises an uneasy smile in an age that veers between bluster and stutter—though the essay could still be taught, sensibly, with profit in schools.*

Rather than try to apportion blame for what has happened to poetry's public standing (and possibly more markedly in Britain than elsewhere), it is wiser to note the pathetic waste, the sheer silliness of the situation—and then to insist that poetry is a *unique* form of expression and communication, not to be superseded in its potentialities, in what it so generously offers writer and reader, not merely a superior or inferior variant of some other activity—'not a branch of authorship', if one dare invoke Hazlitt, but 'the stuff of which our life is made'. And then to remind ourselves that, like the reputations of individual artists, art forms are bound to the wheel of fortune, and we have no reason to believe that the wheel has stopped turning. I quote from a letter written by Thomas Mann to an unidentified questioner in 1932, partly because Mann is a character as little Shelleyan as may be, and he is here employing a language so remote from grandiosity as to sound like a bureaucratic minute: 'I regard art as a primal phenomenon that in no conceivable circumstances can be banished from the world ... Self-examination teaches me that artistic representation is a natural and indispensable mode of vital expression. Therefore I cannot believe that even the most utilitarian and mechanized society could ever permit the general type I modestly represent to become extinct ... I am convinced that man will always need the holy and liberating form of play that is called art in order to feel himself as properly human.'

One thing I hope this anthology will do—by virtue of the poems in it and through the juxtaposition of British writing with American and

---

*But, 'A mention of *A Defence of Poetry* to these would suggest only some local Agitprop meeting,' laments A. A. Cleary, a teacher and editor of a poetry magazine, in discussing the encouragement of 'creativity' in schoolchildren who have not been taught the rudiments of the language they are to create in, not to mention live with. There is nothing we can do about this. Verse is a gift to the classroom: it is allowed to take liberties with grammar, it isn't required to fill up the paper, nor (though it did alas in my schooldays) does it have to obey any apparent rules. All the more reason why poetry needs a 'defence'.

Commonwealth—is to shake the notion that British poetry of the period has been discreditably or pitiably provincial or parochial. Those who have voiced the complaint have not invariably been famous cosmopolitans or renowned for their understanding of the wide world. Their internationalism has largely taken the shape of regression to modes (such as surrealism) which reached their modest apex several decades ago, or else of snapping up the extraneous mannerisms of more recent European writers, some of whom have enjoyed the unfair advantages of revolution, proscription, imprisonment and even death. (The curiosity of 'translation' whereby foreign poets come out all looking much the same—except for Cavafy, whose irreducible spirit manages to shine through, and on occasion Brecht—and then 'original' writers are seen to be writing in the same flavourless, anonymous fashion is an interesting one, and a disturbing one for those who regard the translation of poetry, despite all that can be argued against its possibility, as a necessary process.) Provincialism and its opposite—whatever its opposite is—are a question not of techniques or accessories, but of attitudes of mind; and when we are reproachfully referred to 'the mainstream' of European culture or world literature we are entitled to ask where exactly that stream is and what flows in it. However modish on the international poetry circuit, a concrete poem or a 'sound' poem (less ambiguously termed *Lautgedichte*) can be a good deal more parochial—C.O.D.: 'confined to narrow area'—and more trivial than a conventionally metrical sonnet: the effects may be striking, but they do not strike very deep. 'Look in thy heart, and write'—perhaps the advice isn't quite as foolish as we were brought up to believe, if you consider its context, and if you think of the places people choose to look in nowadays.

A related charge is that of gentility, which in 1962 A. Alvarez described with some degree of truth as 'the disease so often found in English culture'. 'Gentility,' said Mr Alvarez at that time, 'is a belief that life is always more or less orderly, people always more or less polite, their emotions and habits more or less decent and more or less controllable; that God, in short, is more or less good.' I doubt that any poet will be found in this volume who believes all of those things simultaneously—though he may believe some of them and wish he could believe others. Civility is an apple off another tree, and not to be confused with gentility; in my early experience gentility would never dream of writing poetry at all, but that was some while ago. Those who subsequently seized on Mr Alvarez's diagnosis for their own purposes have wanted blood all over the streets, 'madhouse and the whole thing there'. Art is not an outbreak of violence—something readily come by elsewhere—or a mere imitation of it, but an ordering of experience, however precarious-seeming, of internal and external events, which enacts and interprets disorder more firmly and poignantly than anything else can do, even while containing it. Howard Nemerov has said, 'There is no thought so secret or so unique, so wicked or shameful or sublime, that the same has not quietly occurred to many others. Poetry is a realm in which such thoughts, such feelings may be tested without imprecating disaster as a consequence in the practical realm; hence its subversive character is highly civilized and civilizing.' To this one would only wish to add the rider that poetry as exorcism or, to use Mr Nemerov's word, 'testing' is in a different category from poetry as a means of solely personal therapy or self-exhibition.

They write most fluently of scars who never felt a wound. 'Violent' verse is not far removed from its seeming and equally common opposite, the bland, disembodiedly sensitive or namby-pamby verse that never puts a foot wrong, or right; both add, supererogatorily, to the stock of available unreality. The poetry of civility, passion and order is the true antithesis of both.

Certainly there is plenty of boring verse around: there always has been. But it may be worth dwelling briefly on the dullness or, more politely, unambitiousness with which our period has been charged. The complaint has not come from the general public, needless to say, but from poetry writers and professional fanciers themselves. Granted, it would be splendid to have on the scene a sublime and unmistakable genius or two, a Shakespeare or a Milton, even a Wordsworth or a Pope: and more splendid still if the complainant himself could be seen as that overmastering genius. Somewhat similarly, the idea of a strong and scintillating national leader is exciting at a time of laborious democratic procedures. It may seem that there is a fairly constant supply of creative genius available, and in an age of egalitarian feeling and institutions this is spread widely and hence rather thinly. The truth more probably is that the arts have their rhythms, not inevitably and certainly not traceably linked to external conditions, and as yet unpredictable and as inexplicable as their laws. The impetus towards excellence persists, despite well-intentioned agencies, and so does the desire for it. And one bright aspect of the period is that, whether or not it can show any towering mountains, its landscape is manifold and variegated. The call for towering mountains resembles the wartime demand for war poets in that it usually comes from those who don't really want poetry at all, let alone towering poetry. If the politico-social analogy is valid, there is reason for hoping that individualism can survive in an egalitarian and hence constrained environment, and even in a society apparently more excited by theory and doctrine than exercised by the actualities which these are reckoned to account for or determine. But enough on this topic—the present is an Oxford Book, not an Old Moore's Almanac.

Teachers or students, critics or civilian readers, we can all discourse more cogently on what we dislike than on what we like. And it is easier for an anthologist to say what he has not done than to explain what he has. The latter, as regards the present anthology, can only be demonstrated at all effectively by its contents, in which I repose more confidence than in these prefatory observations.

It was unfortunate that the great modernists of the early part of this century should have promulgated the theory that 'poetry in our civilization ... must be difficult', for it was bound to find a welcome with those averse to the hard labour entailed in achieving lucidity. It is a tribute to Eliot's poetry and to Pound's that, so long afterwards, obscurity should be regarded in some circles as a wellnigh infallible sign of seriousness and its absence as indicative of shallowness. Someone said to me recently, 'I wouldn't want to trouble myself with a poem I could understand.' This was not, as it turned out, a jokily modest allusion to Groucho Marx's disinclination to join any club that would admit the likes of *him*, though it may have concealed a sour awareness of the embarrassment caused by poetry unamenable to high-level exegesis: try, for example, to give a lecture course on the work of Edward Thomas. Less modestly—though total comprehension is not a claim I would make—I can say that there is no poem included here which I have not understood at least in a rewarding measure.

That not to understand a piece of writing is in some way preferable to understanding it—a mark of superiority in the poem, or in the reader—is a superstition whose perniciousness soon supplants its initial amiable charm. Of course in poetry of any stature there may well be a nimbus-like fringe which defies certainty, and to which readers respond in varying ways, but this is a bonus that has to be earned, by the poet in working for the effects he wants and by the reader in working to follow him. The distinction we need to make is between the difficulty of what is in its nature hard to grasp and the difficulty of what the writer himself has failed to grasp. Our instinct helps us to tell the one sort of difficulty from the other: does the poem draw us on, does it make us *want* to understand? Our instinct should also enable us to recognize the pursuit of the *outré* in various shapes and sizes* by those who (in Samuel Johnson's phrase) 'being able to add nothing to truth, hope for eminence from the heresies of paradox', or more plainly those who, because they cannot think to much effect, assure themselves that thought (sometimes given the dirtier names of 'rationality', 'logic', 'intellectuality') plays no part in poetry. This is a sin against our central faith in the seriousness of art, in literature as an illumination, criticism and enhancement of the rest of life, and in poetry as the finest, most efficient vehicle for the passing on of what wisdom and courage the race has painfully acquired.

Aggrievedly or gamely, much has been said about the 'struggle with words', as if to suggest that the writer is engaged in mortal combat with some alien monster. Struggle there must be—to resist the seductive and wrong word and to embrace the right and liberating one, and while the former is at your throat, the latter is generally several streets away. But language is at least as much an ally as an enemy. One wouldn't get very far without it, or with a merely 'conscript army', as R. S. Thomas has it. It was in talking of the likelihood of poets needing to be difficult 'in our civilization, as it exists at present' that Eliot opined that the poet, if he is to cope with the variety and complexity of that civilization, must become more comprehensive,

---

* Among them the ambition to be 'purely linguistic'—the mind boggles at this concept of purity!—and sidestep the ticklish question of meaning *via* the assumption that 'particular linguistic usages not only shape decisively, but *are* the significant insights of poets.' I quote Robert M. Adams, who also remarks that 'Apart from other considerations, language makes a marvellously comfortable nest for the mind, far downier than anything the rude empirical world can provide.'

allusive and indirect 'in order to force, to dislocate if necessary, language into his meaning'. In fact, and although he very probably had his own literary needs more in mind than the enunciation of categorical directives, Eliot was not himself a notable dislocator of language outside that singular poem, *The Waste Land*. (Of which A. Walton Litz has remarked, 'Few works can have remained *avant-garde* for so long': exactly, and where was the rest of the guard?) In any case, I have not included here those who, having gathered that important poets are to all-in wrestlers near allied, suppose that a solemn and methodical deformation of syntax will procure strong effects for their writing. The thud-thud of unexpectedness conventionalized is no advance on the thud-thud of conventional expectedness—the one bullies where the other lulls or insinuates. The procedure brings to mind the deliberate maiming of beggars in dreadful and occasionally ingenious ways for the betterment of their vocational prospects.

In passing, and since I seem to have laid at Eliot's door practices over which he had no control, it is fair to add that the modernism of which he was the greater part left one precious legacy, of true liberalism: the proposition that, far from poetry being a preserve or reserve, no subject is in itself unsuitable for poetic treatment. That proposition too can be misapplied, in that subjectlessness has been mistaken for one manifestation of freedom of subject; and we have to concede, adapting Eliot's fine epigram on *vers libre*, that no subject is free for the man who wants to do a good job.

The present anthology contains no 'confessional' poetry—Robert Lowell is only to be so described when he is writing at his lowest ebb and, rather than leave John Berryman out altogether, I have selected work by him which may well though not indisputably be judged unrepresentative—since if poetry is a public matter it is not the place for private revelations, and if it is not a public matter it has no place in a published book. Keats spoke of the 'chameleon poet' possessing no identity, no self, the most unpoetical of all God's creatures. A latter-day equivalent of what Wordsworth termed 'gross and violent stimulants' and the contrary of Confucius's 'joy without licentiousness and grief without heart-rending', the cult of confessional poetry, itself an obsession with 'identity', is one of the saddest epidemics of recent years. Here, alas, poetry does appear to have made something happen. It has been said—we have our own brand of romantic grandiosity—that the poet's courage lies in keeping ajar the door that leads into madness: are we to suppose, then, that some high-handed vulgarian has taken it on himself to lock and bar that door? My own sympathies are with the wit who observed that there are tears that do often lie too deep for thoughts.

This last comment could apply to another species of writing, popular (if not for long at a time) among those who may not recognize poetry but always know a good cause when they hear it recited. 'Protest poetry' can at least be said to boast a subject, but it soon declines into a nervous tic, a mechanical reiteration by its practitioners: 'I protest, therefore I am'; and in its public aspect, like many another operation, it is subject to the law of diminishing returns. One sense there is in which words are cheap. Not a few poems in the present book are properly, naturally, unavoidably, concerned with what man has made and continues to make of man. There is a distinction not of degree but of kind, hard to define in theory but quickly spotted in practice, between the telling of truths and the self-regarding exploitation of them, between the classical process Heine epitomized in 'Aus meinen grossen Schmerzen / Mach' ich die kleinen Lieder' and the vampire-like transactions of the full-time bleeding heart.

The poets printed here, I would venture, subscribe to the spirit of Johnson's reminder that words are the daughters of earth while things are the sons of heaven, and this decent sense of priority helps to invest their work with a generic validity and power, to preserve them against the narcissism which (though its manifestations are frequently the reverse of beautiful) is today's version of aestheticism. This selection from them may suggest a mild and harmless predisposition on the editor's part towards verse that 'tells a story' as against 'mood' verse: the former comprehends the latter, after all, and can deliver it from the gratuitousness to which it is vulnerable. And while there was never the faintest intention to supplement Kingsley Amis's *New Oxford Book of Light Verse*, the editor remains unpersuaded that wit is necessarily evasive in some shabby way or emotionally lowering, or that humour is trivial or philistine: these faculties are at the least as necessary today as they ever were.

In their diverse ways these poets are writing out of and about the nature of our species and our time, about real things rather than 'literary' confections—and in my own dealings I must hope I have not interpreted the concepts *real* and *unreal* in an unduly narrow sense (an element of fantasy has found its way in, I now see, though not the sort that is quaintly called 'free'), for the imagination is both discoverer and inventor, moving at ease between the existent and the inexistent, tempering or transmuting both. For reasons hinted at above, the anthology may be considered reactionary. It could with equal justice be reckoned revolutionary—and with equal senselessness, since neither adjective has any certain or central place in this domain. The clever young Ottilie of Goethe's *Elective Affinities* notes in her journal that the surest way of delivering yourself from the world is through art; and so is the surest way of binding yourself to it. If in the end I had to admit to one general principle or guiding preference or profession of faith, then in spirit it would have much in common with Ottilie's aphorism.

1979   D. J. ENRIGHT

STEVIE SMITH

Distractions and the Human Crowd

Ormerod was deeply troubled
When he read in philosophy and religion
Of man's lust after God,
And the knowledge of God,
And the experience of God
In the achievement of solitary communion and the loss of self.
For he said that he had known this knowledge,
And experienced this experience,
Before life and after death;
But that here in temporal life, and in temporal life only, was permitted,
(As in a flaw of divine government, a voluntary recession),
A place where man might impinge upon man,
And be subject to a thousand and one idiotic distractions.
And thus it was that he found himself
Ever at issue with the Schools,
For ever more and more he pursued the distractions,
Knowing them to be ephemeral, under time, peculiar,
And in eternity without place or puff.
Then, ah then, he said, following the tea-parties,
(And the innumerable conferences for social rearrangement),
I knew, and shall know again, the name of God, closer than close;
But now I know a stranger thing,
That never can I study too closely, for never will it come again,—
Distractions and the human crowd.

Magna est Veritas

With my looks I am bound to look simple or fast I would rather look
    simple
So I wear a tall hat on the back of my head that is rather a temple
And I walk rather queerly and comb my long hair
And people say, Don't bother about her.
So in my time I have picked up a good many facts,
Rather more than the people do who wear smart hats

And I do not deceive because I am rather simple too
And although I collect facts I do not always know what they amount
  to.
I regard them as a contribution to almighty Truth, magna est veritas
  et praevalebit,
Agreeing with that Latin writer, Great is Truth and will prevail in
  a bit.

One of Many

You are only one of many
And of small account if any,
You think about yourself too much.
This touched the child with a quick touch
And worked his mind to such a pitch
He threw his fellows in a ditch.
This little child
That was so mild
Is grown too wild.

Murder in the first degree, cried Old Fury,
Recording the verdict of the jury.

Now they are come to the execution tree.
The gallows stand wide. Ah me, ah me.

Christ died for sinners, intoned the Prison Chaplain from his
  miscellany.
Weeping bitterly the little child cries: I die one of many.

The After-thought

Rapunzel Rapunzel let down your hair
It is I your beautiful lover who am here
And when I come up this time I will bring a rope ladder with me
And then we can both escape into the dark wood immediately.

This must be one of those things, as Edgar Allan Poe says somewhere
   in a book,
Just because it is perfectly obvious one is certain to overlook.

I wonder sometimes by the way if Poe isn't a bit introspective,
One can stand about getting rather reflective,
But thinking about the way the mind works, you know,
Makes one inactive, one simply doesn't know which way to go;
Like the centipede in the poem who was corrupted by the toad
And ever after never did anything but lie in the middle of the road,
Or the old gurus of India I've seen, believe it or not,
Standing seventy-five years on their toes until they dropped.
Or Titurel, for that matter, in his odd doom
Crying: I rejoice because by the mercy of the Saviour I continue to
   live in the tomb.

What is that darling? You cannot hear me?
That's odd. I can hear you quite distinctly.

I Remember

It was my bridal night I remember,
An old man of seventy-three
I lay with my young bride in my arms,
A girl with t.b.
It was wartime, and overhead
The Germans were making a particularly heavy raid on Hampstead.
What rendered the confusion worse, perversely
Our bombers had chosen that moment to set out for Germany.
Harry, do they ever collide?
I do not think it has ever happened,
Oh my bride, my bride.

Anger's Freeing Power

I had a dream three walls stood up wherein a raven bird
Against the walls did beat himself and was not this absurd?

For sun and rain beat in that cell that had its fourth wall free
And daily blew the summer shower and the rain came presently

And all the pretty summer time and all the winter too
That foolish bird did beat himself till he was black and blue.

Rouse up, rouse up, my raven bird, fly by the open wall
You make a prison of a place that is not one at all.

I took my raven by the hand, Oh come, I said, my Raven,
And I will take you by the hand and you shall fly to heaven.

But oh he sobbed and oh he sighed and in a fit he lay
Until two fellow ravens came and stood outside to say:

You wretched bird, conceited lump
You well deserve to pine and thump.

See now a wonder, mark it well
My bird rears up in angry spell,

Oh do I then? he says, and careless flies
O'er flattened wall at once to heaven's skies.

And in my dream I watched him go
And I was glad, I loved him so,

Yet when I woke my eyes were wet
To think Love had not freed my pet,

Anger it was that won him hence
As only Anger taught him sense.

Often my tears fall in a shower
Because of Anger's freeing power.

Correspondence between Mr Harrison in Newcastle and Mr Sholto Peach Harrison in Hull

Sholto Peach Harrison you are no son of mine
And do you think I bred you up to cross the River Tyne
And do you think I bred you up (and mother says the same)
And do you think I bred you up to live a life of shame
To live a life of shame my boy as you are thinking to
Down south in Kingston-upon-Hull a traveller in glue?
Come back my bonny boy nor break your father's heart
Come back and marry Lady Susan Smart
She has a mint in Anglo-Persian oil
And Sholto never more need think of toil.

You are an old and evil man my father
I tell you frankly Sholto had much rather
Travel in glue unrecompensed unwed
Than go to church with oily Sue and afterwards to bed.

Private Means is Dead

Private Means is dead
God rest his soul, officers and fellow-rankers said.

Captive Good, attending Captain Ill
Can tell us quite a lot about the Captain, if he will.

Major Portion
Is a disingenuous person
And as for Major Operation well I guess
We all know what his reputation is.

The crux and Colonel
Of the whole matter
(As you may read in the Journal
If it's not tattered)

Lies in the Generals Collapse Debility Panic and Uproar
Who are too old in any case to go to the War.

Satin-Clad

Satin-clad, with many a pearl,
Is this rich and wretched girl.
Does she weep? Her tears are crystal,
And she counts them as they fall.

Be off!

I'm sorry to say my dear wife is a dreamer,
And as she dreams she gets paler and leaner.
'Then be off to your Dream, with his fly-away hat,
I'll stay with the girls who are happy and fat.'

Who is this Who Howls and Mutters?

Who is this who howls and mutters?
It is the Muse, each word she utters
Is thrown against a shuttered door
And very soon she'll speak no more.

Cry louder, Muse, make much more noise
The world is full of rattling toys
I thought she'd say, Why should I then?
I have spoke low to better men
But oh she did not speak at all but went away
And now I search for her by night and day.

Night and day I seek my Muse
Seek the one I did abuse
She had so sweet a face, so sweet a voice
But oh she did not make sufficient noise.

False plea. I did not listen then
That listen now and listen now in vain.
And still the tale of talent murdered
Untimely and untimely buried

Works in my soul. Forgive me, Lord, I cry
Who only makest Muses howl and sigh
Thou, Lord, repent and give her back to me
Weeping uncomforted, Lord have pity.

He did repent. I have her now again
Howling much worse, and oh the door is open.

Man is a Spirit

Man is a spirit. This the poor flesh knows,
Yet serves him well for host when the wind blows,
Why should this guest go wrinkling up his nose?

EARLE BIRNEY

Can. Hist.

Once upon a colony
there was a land that was
almost a real
country called Canada

But people began to
feel
different
and no longer *Acadien*
or French
and rational
but *Canadien*
and *Mensch*
and passional

Also no longer English
but Canad*ian*
and national
(though some were less specific-
ally Canadian
Pacific)

After that it was fashionable
for a time to be Internationable

But now we are all quite
grown up & fir-
mly agreed to assert our right
not to be Amer-
icans   perhaps
though on the other hand
not ever to be
unamerican

(except for the French
who still want to be *Mensch*)

Charité Espérance et Foi
(*a tender tale from early ca-nada*)

Once there were 3 little Indian girls
Champlain adopted them from the Montagnais
to show King Louis & the Cardinal it was possible
to make Christian Ladies out of savages
He baptized them Foi (11) Espérance (12) et Charité (15)
then put them in a fort to learn their French

Little Foi wriggled away & split for the woods
but Espérance & Charité quickly mastered irregular verbs
& sewing   developed bosoms   went on to embroidery
When Champlain saw they had acquired piety & table manners
he dressed them in style & sailed downstream to Tadoussac
en route to the French Court with Espérance et Charité

But a wicked merchant named Nicholas Marsolet of Tadoussac
got Espérance aside & told her she was what he had to have
She said she had a date in France with King & God
Nick snarled he could have her & her sister given back
to the Indians   & grabbed her round her corset
She pulled a knife & got away to Charité

Les deux étudiantes then wrote Nicholas a letter
Hope began it:
    'Monsieur Marsolet, it was an honour & a pleasure to
    meet you, & I look forward to our next rencontre.
    In anticipation I have sharpened my knife so that
    I may on that occasion give myself the added joy
    of cutting out your heart'
& Charity added:
    'It will give me, monsieur, great pleasure
    to help my sister eat it.'
All this sounded more elegant in the original of course
because that was in correct seventeenth-century French

They showed their letter to Champlain
He was impressed   no mistakes in tenses
He told them he was proud they had stood firm
especially against that méchant marchand Marsolet
who ate meat both Fridays & Saturdays   an Anglophile
& sold hooch to their cousin Indians in Tadoussac
However   ˉChamplain added   he didnt think
that Espérance et Charité were ready yet for France

The two young ladies wept   unrolled their broderie
Champlain agreed they were bien civilisées
They went down on their knees   showed him their petticoats
Champlain was kind   admired the sewing   but was firm
It was France   he said   that wasnt ready yet for them
He gave them each a wooden rosary
& sent them back to Québec with Guillaume Couillard

Couillard was a respectable churchwarden & crop inspector
no merchant   he couldnt read & had 10 children of his own
He was the first to use the plough in Canada

but when Champlain got back from France nobody knew
where Hope & Charity had got to
or if they ever found their Faith again

Twenty-third Flight

Lo as I pause in the alien vale of the airport
fearing ahead the official ambush
a voice languorous and strange as these winds of Oahu
calleth my name and I turn to be quoited in orchids
and amazed with a kiss perfumed and soft as the *lei.*
Straight from a travel poster thou steppest,
thy arms like mangoes for smoothness,
o implausible shepherdess for this one ageing sheep,
and leadest me through the righteous paths of the Customs
in a mist of my own wild hopes.
Yea though I walk through the valley of Immigration
I fear no evil, for thou art a vision beside me
and my name is correctly spelled
and I shall dwell in the Hawaiian Village Hotel
where thy kindred prepareth a table before me.
Thou restoreth my baggage, and by limousine leadest me
to where I may lie on coral sands by a stream-lined pool.

Nay but thou stayest not?
Thou anointest not my naked head with oil?
O shepherdess of Flight Number Twenty-three only
thou hastenest away on thy long brown legs to enchant
thy fellow members in Local Five of the Greeters' Union
or that favoured professor of Commerce mayhap
who leadeth thee into higher courses in Hotel Management.
O nubile goddess of the Kaiser Training Program
is it possible that tonight my cup runneth not over
and that I shall sit in the still pastures of the lobby
whilst thou leadest another old ram in garlands past me,
and, bland as papaya, appearest not to remember me?
And that I shall lie by the waters of Waikiki, and want?

EARLE BIRNEY

A Small Faculty Stag for the Visiting Poet

but a large quantity of brandy
     on whisky
     on sherry

At one table's end the Necessary Dean
has broken out cigars
At the other the Oxonian Canon
splotchfaced now
is putting us all down with naughty quotes
from Persius we're too slow to get
—except the Czech professor & the Hungarian
who dig everything
so civilized they're savage with disappointment
in us all & no doubt saying so this moment
safely across my chest in at least 2 languages

somewhere in the smoke the Librarian
is heard toasting the cummunwealth
& feck the Yenks
The Padre winces & gradually
like Yahweh in the Zohar withdraws his presence
leaving behind that vacuum of Evil
which is us

The Physics Department's chief cultural exhibit
also a very anthropologetical Native Son
have just asked me unanswerable questions
simultaneously from across the centrepiece
I am the dead eye of this verbal typhoon
I am the fraudulent word-doctor
stripped to dumbness by their tribal ritual
I am neither civilized nor savage but also Necessary

    grinning
    & stoned
    & desolate

Christchurch, N.Z.

I have just flown 1100 miles from Australia
& landed in a Victorian bedroom
They send up cindered muttonchops for lunch
There is an elderly reporter in my room with pince-nez
He wants to know why I have sideburns
& if I dont think being patronized by the Canada Council
isnt dangerous for my art or dont I feel I need to suffer?
In stone outside my window Capt. Scott
is nobly freezing to death near the South Pole
Suddenly I know the reporter is right
Sideburns have been sapping my strength

Museum of Man

The trustful curator has left me alone
in the closed wing of the aboriginal section
What's here? 3000 spears from Arnhemland waiting
for a computer to calculate their principle of balance
—but what's in those wooden drawers?   i peek
sheeezz!   shrunken heads   from new guinea
& dozens upon dozens of twelve-inch penis sheaths
I'm going to lock doors   plant spears at windows
& try on everything for size.

Sinalóa

Si señor, is halligators here, your guidebook say it,
si, jaguar in the montañas, maybe helephants, quién sabe?
You like, dose palmas in the sunset? Certamente very nice,
it happen each night in the guía tourista.
But who de hell eat jaguar, halligator, you heat em?
Mira my fren, wat dis town need is muy big breakwater—
    I like take hax to dem jeezly palmas.

So you want buy machete? Por favor I give you
sousand machetes you give me one grand bulldozer, hey?
Wat dis country is lack, señor, is real good goosin,
is need pinehapple shove hup her bottom
(sure, sure, is bella all dose water-ayacints)
is need drains for sugarcane in dem pitoresco swamps—
    and shoot all dem anarquista egrets.

Hokay, you like bugambilla, ow you say, flower-hung cliffs?
Is ow old, de Fort? Is Colhuan, muy viejo, before Moses, no?
Is for you, señor, take em away, send us helevator for w'eat.
It like me to see all dem fine boxcar stuff full rice,
sugar, flax, rollin down to dose palmstudded ports
were Cortés and all dat crap (you heat history?)—
    and bugger de pink flamingos.

Amigo, we make you present all dem two-wheel hoxcart,
you send em Québec, were my brudder was learn to be padre—
we take ditchdiggers, tractors, Massey-Arris yes?
Sinalóa want ten sousand mile irrigation canals,
absolutamente. Is fun all dat organ-cactus fence?
Is for de birds, señor; is more better barbwire, verdad?—
    and chingar dose cute little burros.

Sin argumento, my fren, is a beautiful music,
all dem birds. Pero, wy you no like to ear combos,
refrigerator trucks? Is wonderful on straight new ighway,
jampack wit melons, peppers, bananas, tomatoes, si, si....
Chirrimoyas? Mangos? You like! Is for Indios, solamente,
is bruise, no can ship, is no bueno, believe me, señor—
    and defecar on dose goddam guidebook.

Hot Springs

Here's a hotel where even the stairs
cascade with elixir
Moctezuma washed in these springs
        and not just to keep clean   *no señor*
        it was recommended for gout
        it was in the days of Diaz
        when *caballeros* had gout

13

Now

> IT REMEDIES
> THE CONSEQUENCES
> OF BUSINESS STRAIN

or to put it straight on the line

> IT ACTIVATES THE GLANDULAR SEXUAL SYSTEM
> BOTH MALE AND FEMALE

wheeeee!
Here come the blacksuited old bankers
plump small generals
retired   except from their uniforms
even   watch the step *señor*
a leading firecracker millionaire

And FEMALE?
These downycheeked *chiquitas*
sliding their little pomegranate bottoms
out from the Italian sports cars
surely have come only to render
supplementary thermal assistance

By the cantina across from the carpark
the dusty goatherds are sipping *pulque*
in the open while   with their fiery old eyes
they casually shoot every general
and strip the laughing ladies

Poet-tree

i fear that i shall never make
a poem slippier than a snake
or oozing with as fine a juice
as runs in girls or even spruce
no i wont make not now nor later
pnomes as luverlee as pertaters
trees is made by fauns or satyrs
but only taters make pertaters

& trees is grown by sun from sod
& so are the sods who need a god
but poettrees lack any clue
they just need me   & maybe you

A. D. HOPE

Tiger

'At noon the paper tigers roar'—Miroslav Holub

The paper tigers roar at noon;
The sun is hot, the sun is high.
They roar in chorus, not in tune,
Their plaintive, savage hunting cry.

O, when you hear them, stop your ears
And clench your lids and bite your tongue.
The harmless paper tiger bears
Strong fascination for the young.

His forest is the busy street;
His dens the forum and the mart;
He drinks no blood, he tastes no meat:
He riddles and corrupts the heart.

But when the dusk begins to creep
From tree to tree, from door to door,
The jungle tiger wakes from sleep
And utters his authentic roar.

It bursts the night and shakes the stars
Till one breaks blazing from the sky;
Then listen! If to meet it soars
Your heart's reverberating cry,

My child, then put aside your fear:
Unbar the door and walk outside!
The real tiger waits you there;
His golden eyes shall be your guide.

And, should he spare you in his wrath,
The world and all the worlds are yours;
And should he leap the jungle path
And clasp you with his bloody jaws,

Then say, as his divine embrace
Destroys the mortal parts of you:
I too am of that royal race
Who do what we are born to do.

Paradise Saved
(another version of the Fall)

Adam, indignant, would not eat with Eve,
They say, and she was driven from his side.
Watching the gates close on her tears, his pride
Upheld him, though he could not help but grieve

And climbed the wall, because his loneliness
Pined for her lonely figure in the dust:
Lo, there were two! God who is more than just
Sent her a helpmeet in that wilderness.

Day after day he watched them in the waste
Grow old, breaking the harsh unfriendly ground,
Bearing their children, till at last they died;
While Adam, whose fellow God had not replaced,
Lived on immortal, young, with virtue crowned,
Sterile and impotent and justified.

Prometheus Unbound

Still fettered, still unconquered, still in pain,
Bold in his hope and steadfast in his right,
The Friend of Man on the Caucasian height
Saw one vast flash to northward blast the plain.
As Hermes, swooping down, struck off the chain
And raised him, smiling, in that dazzling light,
'Does the old tyrant, then, repent his spite,'
He asked, 'or has Zeus ceased at last to reign?'

'His wisdom is not mocked,' the god replied,
'Nor alters nor repeals the great decree.
These are his words: "Go, set the Titan free;
And let his torment be to wander wide
The ashes of mankind from sea to sea,
Judging that theft of fire from which they died."'

The Female Principle
(*A reply to Blake*)

Father dead and mother dead,
Now I come into my joy:
They begot me in their bed
Meaning me to be a boy.

But the graceless, wilful seed,
Sowed at midnight, half in jest,
Would not have its course decreed,
Travelled east instead of west.

Father groaned and mother wept,
Such a romping girl was I;
Raging from their arms I leapt,
Broke their hearts and saw them die.

Glorying in that act of birth,
Though their tears pursue me still,
I am served in heaven and earth;
Sun and moon obey my will.

Splendid in my rage, I go
Shaking out my burning hair,
Spreading terror to and fro,
Searching, searching everywhere;

Searching for the one embrace,
Seeking for that man alone
Who dare meet me face to face,
Bed me and beget my son.

E questo il nido in che la mia fenice?

Were I the palm tree which your love returning
Chose for its roost of fronds and bitter spices,
Gladly would I embrace you with those burning
Branches from which renewed the phoenix rises,
Though from my ashes on the desolate plain
No palm should spring again.

But were I not that palm, and were the peasant
To fell and faggot me for winter fuel,
Still in the seasoned timber would be present
Such passion, such desire for that renewal,
That in my glowing embers he might see
The burning bird and tree.

The House of God

Morning service! parson preaches;
People all confess their sins;
God's domesticated creatures
Twine and rub against his shins;

Tails erect and whiskers pricking,
Sleeking down their Sunday fur,
Though demure, alive and kicking,
All in unison they purr:

'Lord we praise Thee; hear us Master!
Feed and comfort, stroke and bless!
And not too severely cast a
Glance upon our trespasses:

'Yesterday we were not able
To resist that piece of fish
Left upon the kitchen table
While You went to fetch the dish;

'Twice this week a scrap with Rover;
Once, at least, we missed a rat;
And we *do* regret, Jehovah,
Having kittens in Your hat!

'Sexual noises in the garden,
Smelly patches in the hall—
Hear us, Lord, absolve and pardon;
We are human after all!'

Home at last from work in Heaven,
This is all the rest God gets;
Gladly for one day in seven
He relaxes with His pets.

Looking down He smiles and ponders,
Thinks of something extra nice:
From His beard, O joy, O wonders!
Falls a shower of little mice.

The Bed

The doctor loves the patient,
The patient loves his bed;
A fine place to be born in,
The best place to be dead.

The doctor loves the patient
Because he means to die;
The patient loves the patient bed
That shares his agony.

The bed adores the doctor,
His cool and skilful touch
Soon brings another patient
Who loves her just as much.

On Shakespeare Critics
from *Dunciad Minor*: Book V

A Double Boiler fixed on fiery wheels,
Hisses hysteric or ecstatic squeals;
He takes a play, *The Tempest*, from his poke,
Kisses the boards and drops it in the smoke.
The smoke redoubles and the cauldron roars;
At length he turns a cock and out there pours
The play—Ah, no! it cannot be the play
To myth and symbolism boiled away;
Where are the plot, the actors and the stage?
These are irrelevant, explains the sage;
Damn action and discourse: The play's no more
Than drifts of an extended metaphor.
Did simple Shakespeare think: 'The play's the thing'?
What Shakespeare thought is hustled from the ring.
He's shouted down: 'Fallacious by intent';
Critics repudiate what the author meant.
Is *Lear* the story of a King? Ah, no,
A tract on clothing and what lurks below.

Well, but the audience came to see men act
And not to hear a philosophic tract?
Wrong once again, my friend: we won't admit
That many-headed monster of the pit,
Who think *The Tempest* tells a tale perhaps
And not a long-drawn metaphor, poor chaps;
In three short hours how could *they* hope to judge
What takes a critic twenty years of drudge?
But who would write a play with this in view?
That only proves that Shakespeare scorned them too.
A sovereign critic is a mighty god;
Author and audience vanish at his nod;
He takes the poet's place, re-weaves the spell,
And is its only audience as well.

NORMAN MacCAIG

Fetching Cows

The black one, last as usual, swings her head
And coils a black tongue round a grass-tuft. I
Watch her soft weight come down, her split feet spread.

In front, the others swing and slouch; they roll
Their great Greek eyes and breathe out milky gusts
From muzzles black and shiny as wet coal.

The collie trots, bored, at my heels, then plops
Into the ditch. The sea makes a tired sound
That's always stopping though it never stops.

A haycart squats prickeared against the sky.
Hay breath and milk breath. Far out in the West
The wrecked sun founders though its colours fly.

The collie's bored. There's nothing to control...
The black cow is two native carriers
Bringing its belly home, slung from a pole.

Movements

Lark drives invisible pitons in the air
And hauls itself up the face of space.
Mouse stops being comma and clockworks on the floor.
Cats spill from walls. Swans undulate through clouds.
Eel drills through darkness its malignant face.

Fox, smouldering through the heather bushes, bursts
A bomb of grouse. A speck of air grows thick
And is a hornet. When a gannet dives
It's a white anchor falling. And when it lands
Umbrella heron becomes walking-stick.

I think these movements and become them, here,
In this room's stillness, none of them about,
And relish them all—until I think of where,
Thrashed by a crook, the cursive adder writes
Quick V's and Q's in the dust and rubs them out.

Sheep Dipping

The sea goes flick-flack or the light does. When
John chucks the ewe in, she splays up two wings
That beat once and are water once again.

Pushing her nose, she trots slow-motion through
The glassy green. The others beat and plunge—
If she must do it, what else is there to do?

They leap from ledges, all legs in the air
All furbelows and bulged eyes in the green
Turned suds, turned soda with the plumping there.

They haul themselves ashore. With outraged cries
They waterfall uphill, spread out and stand
Dribbling salt water into flowers' eyes.

Flooded Mind

When the water fell
the trees rose up again
and fish stopped being birds
among the branches.

The trees were never the same again, though,
and the birds
often regarded him
with a very fishy eye
as he walked the policies of himself,
his own keeper.

Also, he was afraid to go fishing
in case he landed a fish
with feathers that would sing
in his net.

No wonder his eyes were
noticeboards saying
Private. Keep out.

Orgy

Thinking of painters, musicians, poets,
who visited the world outside them and the world
inside them and brought back
their sweet discoveries, only to be devoured
by those they brought them to,
I remembered
a wood near Queensferry, where
a banquet of honeydew, that sweet exudation,
was spread on a million airy leaf-tables
in an avenue of lime trees.

Under the tables,
on the broad path below,
a million bees crawled and fell about,
blind drunk.

And a million ants
bit into their soft bellies
for the intoxicating liquor stored
in these tiny tuns—having discovered
that the innkeeper was the inn.

In My Mind

I go back ways to hurl rooftops
into that furze-blazing sunset.

I stare at water
frilling a stone, flexing a muscle.

Down sidestreets I sniff
cats in passages, old soup and

in one hot room
the fierce smell of hyacinths.

From the tops of spires
I lasso two counties in an eye-blink

and break my ears with a jukebox
in a frowsy cellar.

I am an honorary citizen
of these landscapes and a City Father

of this city. I walk
through its walls and burn

as traffic lights. It is all
lines on my hand.

But I turn away
from that terrible cul-de-sac.

I turn away from
the smiling house there

and the room in it
with green blinds drawn

and a bed with a bed lamp shedding
its kind light down

on a dead hand
and a book fallen from it.

Old Maps and New

There are spaces
where infringements are possible.
There are notices that say:
Trespassers will be welcome.

Pity leaks through the roof
of the Labour Exchange.
In the Leader's pocket,
wrapped in the plans for the great offensive,
are sweets for the children
and a crumpled letter.

There are spaces still to be filled
before the map is completed—
though these days it's only
in the explored territories
that men write, sadly,
Here live monsters.

Ringed Plover by a Water's Edge

They sprint eight feet and—
stop. Like that. They
sprintayard (like that) and
stop.

They have no acceleration
and no brakes.
Top speed's their only one.

They're alive—put life
through a burning-glass, they're
its focus—but they share
the world of delicate clockwork.

In spasmodic
Indian file
they parallel the parallel ripples.

When they stop
they, suddenly, are
gravel.

Close-ups of Summer

That creepycrawly traversing the stone
six inches from my nose makes me a caveman
fanned by pterodactyls and roared at
by dinosaurs.

A butterfly dangles by, delicate
as a carrot leaf. If only it could write
its flowery memoirs. If only it could paint
the rich halls it has visited.

The weather doodles a faint cloud
on the blue
then pensively washes it out,
making the blue boastful.

There's something whirring
in the cat's mouth. It opens it
and a beetle flies out. The cat
is Amazement, in fur.

Hens sloven. But the cock
struts by—one can almost see
the tiny set of bagpipes
he's sure he's playing.

The sun's the same—pipemajoring
across space, where the invisible judges
sit, wrapped in their knowledge,
taking terrible notes.

Cock before Dawn

Those dabbing hens I ferociously love
sag on their perches, half deflated.
I'll have none of it. I'm regimental. A plumbline
goes from my head to my toes. I burnish
the dark with my breast.

Lucifer's my blood brother. When I spread my wings
I'm crystal battlements and thunderbolts. I tread the earth
by pretending not to.

The West and the East are measured from me ...
It's time I crowed. The sun will be waiting.

Gone are the Days

Impossible to call a lamb a lambkin
or say eftsoons or spell you ladye.
My shining armour bleeds when it's scratched;
I blow the nose that's part of my visor.

When I go pricking o'er the plain
I say *Eightpence please* to the sad conductress.
The towering landscape you live in has printed
on its portcullis *Bed and breakfast*.

I don't regret it. There are wildernesses
enough in Rose Street or the Grassmarket
where dragons' breaths are methylated
and social workers trap the unwary.

So don't expect me, lady with no e,
to look at a lamb and feel lambkin
or give me a down look because I bought
my greaves and cuisses at Marks and Spencers.

Pishtushery's out. But oh, how my heart swells
to see you perched, perjink, on a bar stool.
And though epics are shrunk to epigrams, let me
buy a love potion, a gin, a double.

The Drowned

Somebody said wrecks
come ashore, looking for the drowned
crews, as if they felt guilt, or love, or loneliness.

Timbers for boats, bones for men.

Their friends shut their minds, their
recollections, themselves
to the dogfish love, the ten inch wide
appetite of crabs.

... The tide washes in. And somebody
sings a song. And his friend, picked clean
to the delicate timber of bones,
drifts in the song, complete
as an archangel.

ELIZABETH BISHOP

Seascape

This celestial seascape, with white herons got up as angels,
flying as high as they want and as far as they want sidewise
in tiers and tiers of immaculate reflections;
the whole region, from the highest heron
down to the weightless mangrove island
with bright green leaves edged neatly with bird-droppings
like illumination in silver,
and down to the suggestively Gothic arches of the mangrove roots
and the beautiful pea-green back-pasture
where occasionally a fish jumps, like a wild-flower
in an ornamental spray of spray;
this cartoon by Raphael for a tapestry for a Pope:
it does look like heaven.
But a skeletal lighthouse standing there
in black and white clerical dress,
who lives on his nerves, thinks he knows better.
He thinks that hell rages below his iron feet,
that that is why the shallow water is so warm,
and he knows that heaven is not like this.
Heaven is not like flying or swimming,
but has something to do with blackness and a strong glare
and when it gets dark he will remember something
strongly worded to say on the subject.

Large Bad Picture

Remembering the Strait of Belle Isle or
some northerly harbour of Labrador,
before he became a schoolteacher
a great-uncle painted a big picture.

Receding for miles on either side
into a flushed, still sky
are overhanging pale blue cliffs
hundreds of feet high,

their bases fretted by little arches,
the entrances to caves
running in along the level of a bay
masked by perfect waves.

On the middle of that quiet floor
sits a fleet of small black ships,
square-rigged, sails furled, motionless,
their spars like burnt match-sticks.

And high above them, over the tall cliffs'
semi-translucent ranks,
are scribbled hundreds of fine black birds
hanging in n's in banks.

One can hear their crying, crying,
the only sound there is
except for occasional sighing
as a large aquatic animal breathes.

In the pink light
the small red sun goes rolling, rolling,
round and round and round at the same height
in perpetual sunset, comprehensive, consoling,

while the ships consider it.
Apparently they have reached their destination.
It would be hard to say what brought them there,
commerce or contemplation.

The Shampoo

The still explosions on the rocks,
the lichens, grow
by spreading, grey, concentric shocks.
They have arranged
to meet the rings around the moon, although
within our memories they have not changed.

And since the heavens will attend
as long on us,
you've been, dear friend,
precipitate and pragmatical;
and look what happens. For Time is
nothing if not amenable.

The shooting stars in your black hair
in bright formation
are flocking where,
so straight, so soon?
—Come, let me wash it in this big tin basin,
battered and shiny like the moon.

Arrival at Santos

Here is a coast; here is a harbour;
here, after a meagre diet of horizon, is some scenery:
impractically shaped and—who knows?—self-pitying mountains,
sad and harsh beneath their frivolous greenery,

with a little church on top of one. And warehouses,
some of them painted a feeble pink, or blue,
and some tall, uncertain palms. Oh, tourist,
is this how this country is going to answer you

and your immodest demands for a different world,
and a better life, and complete comprehension
of both at last, and immediately,
after eighteen days of suspension?

Finish your breakfast. The tender is coming,
a strange and ancient craft, flying a strange and brilliant rag.
So that's the flag. I never saw it before.
I somehow never thought of there *being* a flag,

but of course there was, all along. And coins, I presume,
and paper money; they remain to be seen.
And gingerly now we climb down the ladder backward,
myself and a fellow passenger named Miss Breen,

descending into the midst of twenty-six freighters
waiting to be loaded with green coffee beans.
Please, boy, do be more careful with that boat hook!
Watch out! Oh! It has caught Miss Breen's

skirt! There! Miss Breen is about seventy,
a retired police lieutenant, six feet tall,
with beautiful bright blue eyes and a kind expression.
Her home, when she is at home, is in Glens Fall

s, New York. There. We are settled.
The customs officials will speak English, we hope,
and leave us our bourbon and cigarettes.
Ports are necessities, like postage stamps, or soap,

but they seldom seem to care what impression they make,
or, like this, only attempt, since it does not matter,
the unassertive colours of soap, or postage stamps—
wasting away like the former, slipping the way the latter

do when we mail the letters we wrote on the boat,
either because the glue here is very inferior
or because of the heat. We leave Santos at once;
we are driving to the interior.

A Summer's Dream

To the sagging wharf
few ships could come.
The population numbered
two giants, an idiot, a dwarf,

a gentle storekeeper
asleep behind his counter,
and our kind landlady—
the dwarf was her dressmaker.

The idiot could be beguiled
by picking blackberries,
but then threw them away.
The shrunken seamstress smiled.

By the sea, lying
blue as a mackerel,
our boarding house was streaked
as though it had been crying.

Extraordinary geraniums
crowded the front windows,
the floors glittered with
assorted linoleums.

Every night we listened
for a horned owl.
In the horned lamp flame,
the wallpaper glistened.

The giant with the stammer
was the landlady's son,
grumbling on the stairs
over an old grammar.

He was morose,
but she was cheerful.
The bedroom was cold,
the feather bed close.

We were wakened in the dark by
the somnambulist brook
nearing the sea,
still dreaming audibly.

12 O'Clock News

gooseneck lamp

As you all know, tonight is the night of the full
moon, half the world over. But here the moon
seems to hang motionless in the sky. It gives very
little light; it could be dead. Visibility is poor.
Nevertheless, we shall try to give you some idea
of the lay of the land and the present situation.

The escarpment that rises abruptly from the central plain is in heavy shadow, but the elaborate terracing of its southern glacis gleams faintly in the dim light, like fish scales. What endless labour those small, peculiarly shaped terraces represent! And yet, on them the welfare of this tiny principality depends.

typewriter

A slight landslide occurred in the northwest about an hour ago. The exposed soil appears to be of poor quality: almost white, calcareous, and shaly. There are believed to have been no casualties.

pile of mss.

Almost due north, our aerial reconnaissance reports the discovery of a large rectangular 'field', hitherto unknown to us, obviously man-made. It is dark-speckled. An airstrip? A cemetery?

typed sheet

In this small, backward country, one of the most backward left in the world today, communications are crude and 'industrialization' and its products almost nonexistent. Strange to say, however, signboards are on a truly gigantic scale.

envelopes

We have also received reports of a mysterious, oddly shaped, black structure, at an undisclosed distance to the east. Its presence was revealed only because its highly polished surface catches such feeble moonlight as prevails. The natural resources of the country being far from completely known to us, there is the possibility that this may be, or may contain, some powerful and terrifying 'secret weapon'. On the other hand, given what we *do* know, or have learned from our anthropologists and sociologists about this people, it may well be nothing more than a *numen*, or a great altar recently erected to one of their gods, to which, in their present historical state of superstition and helplessness, they attribute magical powers, and may even regard as a

ink-bottle

'saviour', one last hope of rescue from their grave difficulties.

_At last! One of the elusive natives has been spotted! He appears to be—rather, to have been —a unicyclist-courier, who may have met his end by falling from the height of the escarpment because of the deceptive illumination. Alive, he would have been small, but undoubtedly proud and erect, with the thick, bristling black hair typical of the indigenes.

typewriter eraser

From our superior vantage point, we can clearly see a sort of dugout, possibly a shell crater, a 'nest' of soldiers. They lie heaped together, wearing the camouflage 'battle dress' intended for 'winter warfare'. They are in hideously contorted positions, all dead. We can make out at least eight bodies. These uniforms were designed to be used in guerrilla warfare on the country's one snow-covered mountain peak. The fact that these poor soldiers are wearing them *here*, on the plain, gives further proof, if proof were necessary, either of the childishness and hopeless impracticality of this inscrutable people, our opponents, or of the sad corruption of their leaders.

ashtray

Manners

for a Child of 1918

My grandfather said to me
as we sat on the wagon seat,
'Be sure to remember to always
speak to everyone you meet.'

We met a stranger on foot.
My grandfather's whip tapped his hat.
'Good day, sir. Good day. A fine day.'
And I said it and bowed where I sat.

Then we overtook a boy we knew
with his big pet crow on his shoulder.
'Always offer everyone a ride;
don't forget that when you get older,'

my grandfather said. So Willy
climbed up with us, but the crow
gave a 'Caw!' and flew off. I was worried.
How would he know where to go?

But he flew a little way at a time
from fence post to fence post, ahead;
and when Willy whistled he answered.
'A fine bird,' my grandfather said,

'and he's well brought up. See, he answers
nicely when he's spoken to.
Man or beast, that's good manners.
Be sure that you both always do.'

When automobiles went by,
the dust hid the people's faces,
but we shouted 'Good day! Good day!
Fine day!' at the top of our voices.

When we came to Hustler Hill,
he said that the mare was tired,
so we all got down and walked,
as our good manners required.

ROY FULLER

The Unremarkable Year

The great thrushes have not appeared this year,
No more the sickness of excessive
Evacuation. Taking one year
With another the debits and credits seem to cancel out.

When I recall the family
That fell like a camouflaged platoon
On the garden in 'sixty-eight
(Or was it 'sixty-nine?) I can't help feeling regret.

But there is much to be said for a summer
Without alarms. The plum crop is modest,
The monarch has remained unchanged,
Small differences only in one's teeth and hair and verse-forms.

There'll be no memories like the visit
Of the orchestra of *gamelans*—
Enhanced by the naked mamelons
Of the dancers—influence that goes on reverberating.

So that the year of painting the shed,
Of missing strange calls, deep dappled breasts,
Is also that of harmonies
That have made one's life and art for evermore off-key.

Edmond Halley

'Dr Halley never eat any Thing
but Fish, for he had no Teeth'—so after
Royal Society meetings dinner
was invariably 'Fish and Pudding'.
As on a silly marriage, he embarked
at sixty-five on a programme of moon
watching planned to last a whole sarotic
period (223
lunations, near enough eighteen years)
and saw to the end his voyeurism through.

In the eyepieces of his telescopes
the cross hairs were dried cobwebs split in half—
to fairy means opened a fairy world.
Despite his long life his greatest triumph
was delayed till after his demise.

In 1758, Christ's season,
(as 55 years before he'd foretold)
the old comet reappeared in the skies,
announcing not the birth of a god but
the temporary triumph of reason.

Observe on a roof in New College Lane
his Oxford observatory, hard by
my son's undergraduate rooms of times
when I little recked that I, too, should be
an Oxford professor, not far now from
the fish and pudding stage. Comet-like ways
of destiny! Quite disproved by Halley,
the notion of human life written out
by the night's constellations returns to
grizzled craniums, in uncertain days.

Outside the Supermarket

Grasping with opposite hand the side of his pram
As though an idle sceptre or marshal's baton,
A look of serious surveillance on his face,
This infant for an instant restores to me
                    The sense of mankind's worth.

No matter that soon he'll be in floods of tears:
Who can blame his frustration at a recalcitrant world?
Thus wept Isaiah over Jerusalem.
Long years must pass before like Caligula
                    He weeps for a single neck.

Autobiography of a Lungworm

My normal dwelling is the lungs of swine,
    My normal shape a worm,
But other dwellings, other shapes, are mine
    Within my natural term.
Dimly I see my life, of all, the sign,
    Of better lives the germ.

The pig, though I am inoffensive, coughs,
   Finding me irritant:
My eggs go with the contents of the troughs
   From mouth to excrement—
The pig thus thinks, perhaps, he forever doffs
   His niggling resident.

The eggs lie unconsidered in the dung
   Upon the farmyard floor,
Far from the scarlet and sustaining lung:
   But happily a poor
And humble denizen provides a rung
   To make ascension sure.

The earthworm eats the eggs; inside the warm
   Cylinder larvae hatch:
For years, if necessary, in this form
   I wait the lucky match
That will return me to my cherished norm,
   My ugly pelt dispatch.

Strangely, it is the pig himself becomes
   The god inside the car:
His greed devours the earthworms; so the slums
   Of his intestines are
The setting for the act when clay succumbs
   And force steers for its star.

The larvae burrow through the bowel wall
   And, having to the dregs
Drained ignominy, gain the lung's great hall.
   They change. Once more, like pegs,
Lungworms are anchored to the rise and fall
   —And start to lay their eggs.

What does this mean? The individual,
   Nature, mutation, strife?
I feel, though I am simple, still the whole
   Is complex; and that life—
A huge, doomed throbbing—has a wiry soul
   That must escape the knife.

The Family Cat

This cat was bought upon the day
That marked the Japanese defeat;
He was anonymous and gay,
But timorous and not discreet.

Although three years have gone, he shows
Fresh sides of his uneven mind:
To us—fond, lenient—he grows
Still more eccentric and defined.

He is a grey, white-chested cat,
And barred with black along the grey;
Not large, and the reverse of fat,
His profile good from either way.

The poet buys especial fish,
Which is made ready by his wife;
The poet's son holds out the dish:
They thus maintain the creature's life.

It's not his anniversary
Alone that's his significance:
In any case mortality
May not be thought of in his presence.

For brief as are our lives, more brief
Exist. Our stroking hides the bones,
Which none the less cry out in grief
Beneath the mocking, loving tones.

Consolations of Art

J.M.W. Turner on Switzerland:
'The Country on the whole surpasses Wales.'
—As parsimonious with praise as cash.

It was this little down-to-brass-tacks man
Who saw that nature, history and time
Were mostly fields for Cataclysm's advent;

And on his 'waking eye' (he wrote in verse)
'Rushed the still ruins of dejected Rome.'
The exciting revolution also brings

A constant sense of parallel disasters—
As well I know, who followed '17
Like artists who came after '89.

No doubt the dying age, not dying fast;
The new society murdered in its youth;
The need for stoic individuals

Recall the line of empty cities, force
Poets to see in all phenomena
(Even in landscape) culture's coming doom.

A sky of Turner's, said the critics, is
'A heap of marble mountains.'
The painter himself·observed about a salad

(Conversing with his neighbour at a dinner):
'A nice cool green that lettuce, isn't it?
The beetroot pretty red though not quite strong enough.

Add mustard and you've got an oil of mine!'
Despairing of the State, Euripides
Became a quietist. Thus creators end.

Reading in the Night

In the Stravinsky book by Lillian Libman:
The old idea that this very hour
(Because the sun lies farthest off from man)

Is the worst hour of the twenty-four.
Initially surprised we still depend
On that outmoded god, that dying fire,

One soon is reconciled—for, after all,
The star had grandeur and is ours alone.
Besides, far back it gave us life, although

We now may look askance at the donation.
The ambiguities of day return.
Light enough to discover with a pang

A spider drowned, like scribble, in a bucket.
Yet seeing that emblematic, as if art
Had vanquished superstition, even death;

As if one didn't know the final plight—
For it to be beyond our human powers
Even to orchestrate another's fugue.

The Other Side

'You've had your operation, Mrs Brown.
Wake up!' The cry undoubtedly recurs
(It seems to me, who's also lying there,

Scarcely more wide awake than Mrs Brown)
In some congested docking-station for
The dead. The utter strangers strewn about,

The sexes intermingled sexlessly;
The far-off burning of an ancient pain
In my prone, sheeted figure; busy, white

Androgynous attendants; and the lack
Of memory of things before, confirm
After-life's ludicrous reality.

From the Joke Shop

'Why doesn't somebody buy *me* false ears?'
I can't help remarking as I pack the same,
Plus a few boils and scars, in Christmas paper.

Returning from a stroll some hours later,
I see my ears are big and red enough.
Even a scar may be discerned. Life-long

Ambition to amuse fulfilled, it seems,
Without adventitious aid. Although some boils,
God-given, might more surely make for laughs.

Shop Talk

'We have the mauve or the cerise,
And of course the peach.'

'I think that striped is gorgeous.'

'Can these be repaired again?'
'I'm afraid it's your welt that's gone.'

'Four packets of Player's, please.'
'These ones?' 'Those ones.'

'Have you got the I, Claudius?'

'Is it real cream in them buns?'

Poor voices, calling each to each,
In a strange but transparent idiom
(So I think, the ageing bard, all-knowing).

'Hi, dad, you're forgetting your stamps!' So I am.
Another world is also going.

R. S. THOMAS

Aside

Take heart, Prytherch.
Over you the planets stand,
And have seen more ills than yours.
This canker was in the bone
Before man bent to his image
In the pool's glass. Violence has been
And will be again. Between better
And worse is no bad place

For a labourer, whose lot is to seem
Stationary in traffic so fast.
Turn aside, I said; do not turn back.
There is no forward and no back
In the fields, only the year's two
Solstices, and patience between.

Lore

Job Davies, eighty-five
Winters old, and still alive
After the slow poison
And treachery of the seasons.

Miserable? Kick my arse!
It needs more than the rain's hearse,
Wind-drawn, to pull me off
The great perch of my laugh.

What's living but courage?
Paunch full of hot porridge,
Nerves strengthened with tea,
Peat-black, dawn found me

Mowing where the grass grew,
Bearded with golden dew.
Rhythm of the long scythe
Kept this tall frame lithe.

What to do? Stay green.
Never mind the machine,
Whose fuel is human souls.
Live large, man, and dream small.

The One Furrow

When I was young, I went to school
With pencil and foot-rule
Sponge and slate,
And sat on a tall stool
At learning's gate.

When I was older, the gate swung wide;
Clever and keen-eyed
In I pressed,
But found in the mind's pride
No peace, no rest.

Then who was it taught me back to go
To cattle and barrow,
Field and plough;
To keep to the one furrow,
As I do now?

A Welshman to Any Tourist

We've nothing vast to offer you, no deserts
Except the waste of thought
Forming from mind erosion;
No canyons where the pterodactyl's wing
Casts a cold shadow.
The hills are fine, of course,

Bearded with water to suggest age
And pocked with caverns,
One being Arthur's dormitory;
He and his knights are the bright ore
That seams our history,
But shame has kept them late in bed.

The Woman

So beautiful—God himself quailed
at her approach: the long body curved
like the horizon. Why had he made
her so? How would it be, she said,
leaning towards him, if, instead of
quarrelling over it, we divided it
between us? You can have all the credit
for its invention, if you will leave the ordering
of it to me. He looked into her
eyes and saw far down the bones
of the generations that would navigate
by those great stars, but the pull of it
was too much. Yes, he thought, give me their minds'
tribute, and what they do with their bodies
is not my concern. He put his hand in his side
and drew out the thorn for the letting
of the ordained blood and touched her with
it. Go, he said. They shall come to you for ever
with their desire, and you shall bleed for them in return.

The Hand

It was a hand. God looked at it
and looked away. There was a coldness
about his heart, as though the hand
clasped it. As at the end
of a dark tunnel, he saw cities
the hand would build, engines

that it would raze them with. His sight
dimmed. Tempted to undo the joints
of the fingers, he picked it up.
But the hand wrestled with him. 'Tell
me your name,' it cried, 'and I will write it
in bright gold. Are there not deeds
to be done, children to make, poems
to be written? The world
is without meaning, awaiting
my coming.' But God, feeling the nails
in his side, the unnerving warmth
of the contact, fought on in
silence. This was the long war with himself
always foreseen, the question not
to be answered. What is the hand
for? The immaculate conception
preceding the delivery
of the first tool? 'I let you go,'
he said, 'but without blessing.
Messenger to the mixed things
of your making, tell them I am.'

At It

I think he sits at that strange table
of Eddington's, that is not a table
at all, but nodes and molecules
pushing against molecules
and nodes; and he writes there
in invisible handwriting, the instructions
the genes follow. I imagine his
face that is more the face
of a clock, and the time told by it
is now, though Greece is referred
to and Egypt and empires
not yet begun.

And I would have
things to say to this God
at the judgement, storming at him
as Job stormed, with the eloquence
of the abused heart. But there will be
no judgement other than the verdict
of his calculations, that abstruse
geometry that proceeds eternally
in the silence beyond right and wrong.

Poetry for Supper

'Listen, now, verse should be as natural
As the small tuber that feeds on muck
And grows slowly from obtuse soil
To the white flower of immortal beauty.'

'Natural, hell! What was it Chaucer
Said once about the long toil
That goes like blood to the poem's making?
Leave it to nature and the verse sprawls,
Limp as bindweed, if it break at all
Life's iron crust. Man, you must sweat
And rhyme your guts taut, if you'd build
Your verse a ladder.'
                            'You speak as though
No sunlight ever surprised the mind
Groping on its cloudy path.'

'Sunlight's a thing that needs a window
Before it enter a dark room.
Windows don't happen.'
                            So two old poets,
Hunched at their beer in the low haze
Of an inn parlour, while the talk ran
Noisily by them, glib with prose.

Pisces

Who said to the trout,
You shall die on Good Friday
To be food for a man
And his pretty lady?

It was I, said God,
Who formed the roses
In the delicate flesh
And the tooth that bruises.

Postscript

As life improved, their poems
Grew sadder and sadder. Was there oil
For the machine? It was
The vinegar in the poets' cup.

The tins marched to the music
Of the conveyor belt. A billion
Mouths opened. Production,
Production, the wheels

Whistled. Among the forests
Of metal the one human
Sound was the lament of
The poets for deciduous language.

After Jericho

There is an aggression of fact
to be resisted successfully
only in verse, that fights language
with its own tools. Smile, poet,

among the ruins of a vocabulary
you blew your trumpet against.
It was a conscript army; your words,
every one of them, are volunteers.

JOHN BERRYMAN

A Professor's Song

(... rabid or dog-dull.) Let me tell you how
The Eighteenth Century couplet ended. Now
Tell me. Troll me the sources of that Song—
Assigned last week—by Blake. Come, come along,
Gentlemen. (Fidget and huddle, do. Squint soon.)
I want to end these fellows all by noon.

'That deep romantic chasm'—an early use;
The word is from the French, by our abuse
Fished out a bit. (Red all your eyes. O when?)
'A poet is a man speaking to men':
But I am then a poet, am I not?—
Ha ha. The radiator, please. Well, what?

Alive now—no—Blake would have written prose,
But movement following movement crisply flows,
So much the better, better the much so,
As burbleth Mozart. Twelve. The class can go.
Until I meet you, then, in Upper Hell
Convulsed, foaming immortal blood: farewell.

King David Dances

Aware to the dry throat of the wide hell in the world,
O trampling empires, and mine one of them,
and mine one gross desire against His sight,
slaughter devising there,

50

some good behind, ambiguous ahead,
revolted sons, a pierced son, bound to bear,
mid hypocrites amongst idolaters,
mockt in abysm by one shallow wife,
with the ponder both of priesthood & of State
heavy upon me, yea,
all the black same I dance my blue head off!

Certainty Before Lunch

Ninety per cent of the mass of the Universe
(90%!) may be gone in collapsars,
pulseless, lightless, forever, if they exist.
My friends the probability man & I

& his wife the lawyer are taking a country walk
in the flowerless April snow in exactly two hours
and maybe won't be back. Finite & unbounded
the massive spirals absolutely fly

distinctly apart, by math *and* observation,
current math, this morning's telescopes
& inference. My wife is six months gone
so won't be coming. That mass must be somewhere!

or not? just barely possibly *may not*
BE anywhere? My Lord, I'm glad we don't
on x or y depend for Your being there.
I know You are there. The sweat is, I am here.

from *Eleven Addresses to the Lord*

1

Master of beauty, craftsman of the snowflake,
inimitable contriver,
endower of Earth so gorgeous & different from the boring Moon,
thank you for such as it is my gift.

I have made up a morning prayer to you
containing with precision everything that most matters.
'According to Thy will' the thing begins.
It took me off & on two days. It does not aim at eloquence.

You have come to my rescue again & again
in my impassable, sometimes despairing years.
You have allowed my brilliant friends to destroy themselves
and I am still here, severely damaged, but functioning.

Unknowable, as I am unknown to my guinea pigs:
how can I 'love' you?
I only as far as gratitude & awe
confidently & absolutely go.

I have no idea whether we live again.
It doesn't seem likely
from either the scientific or the philosophical point of view
but certainly all things are possible to you,

and I believe as fixedly in the Resurrection-appearances to Peter
   and to Paul
as I believe I sit in this blue chair.
Only that may have been a special case
to establish their initiatory faith.

Whatever your end may be, accept my amazement.
May I stand until death forever at attention
for any your least instruction or enlightenment.
I even feel sure you will assist me again, Master of insight & beauty.

2

Holy, as I suppose I dare to call you
without pretending to know anything about you
but infinite capacity everywhere & always
& in particular certain goodness to me.

Yours is the crumpling, to my sister-in-law terrifying thunder,
yours the candelabra buds sticky in Spring,
Christ's mercy,
the gloomy wisdom of godless Freud:

yours the lost souls in ill-attended wards,
those agonized thro' the world
at this instant of time, all evil men,
Belsen, Omaha Beach,—

incomprehensible to man your ways.
May be the Devil after all exists.
'I don't try to reconcile anything' said the poet at eighty,
'This is a damned strange world.'

Man is ruining the pleasant earth & man.
What at last, my Lord, will you allow?
Postpone till after my children's deaths your doom
if it be thy ineffable, inevitable will.

I say 'Thy kingdom come', it means nothing to me.
Hast Thou prepared astonishments for man?
One sudden Coming? Many so believe.
So not, without knowing anything, do I.

3

Sole watchman of the flying stars, guard me
against my flicker of impulse lust: teach me
to see them as sisters & daughters. Sustain
my grand endeavours: husbandship & crafting.

Forsake me not when my wild hours come;
grant me sleep nightly, grace soften my dreams;
achieve in me patience till the thing be done,
a careful view of my achievement come.

Make me from time to time the gift of the shoulder.
When all hurt nerves whine shut away the whisky.
Empty my heart toward Thee.
Let me pace without fear the common path of death.

Cross am I sometimes with my little daughter:
fill her eyes with tears. Forgive me, Lord.
Unite my various soul,
sole watchman of the wide & single stars.

4

If I say Thy name, art Thou there? It may be so.
Thou art not absent-minded, as I am.
I am so much so I had to give up driving.
You attend, I feel, to the matters of man.

Across the ages certain blessings swarm,
horrors accumulate, the best men fail:
Socrates, Lincoln, Christ mysterious.
Who can search Thee out?

except Isaiah & Pascal, who saw.
I dare not ask that vision, though a piece of it
at last in crisis was vouchsafèd me.
I altered then for good, to become yours.

Caretaker! take care, for we run in straits.
Daily, by night, we walk naked to storm,
some threat of wholesale loss, to ruinous fear.
Gift us with long cloaks & adrenalin.

Who haunt the avenues of Angkor Wat
recalling all that prayer, that glory dispersed,
haunt me at the corner of Fifth & Hennepin.
Shield & fresh fountain! Manifester! Even mine.

5

Holy, & holy. The damned are said to say
'We never thought we would come into this place.'
I'm fairly clear, my Friend, there's no such place
ordained for inappropriate & evil man.

Surely they fall dull, & forget. We too,
the more or less just, I feel fall asleep
dreamless forever while the worlds hurl out.
Rest may be your ultimate gift.

Rest or transfiguration! come & come
whenever Thou wilt. My daughter & my son
fend will without me, when my work is done
in Your opinion.

Strengthen my widow, let her dream on me
thro' tranquil hours less & down to less.
Abrupt elsewhere her heart, I sharply hope.
I leave her in wise Hands.

6

Under new management, Your Majesty:
Thine. I have solo'd mine since childhood, since
my father's blow-it-all when I was twelve
blew out my most bright candle faith, and look at me.

I served at Mass six dawns a week from five,
adoring Father Boniface & you,
memorizing the Latin he explained.
Mostly we worked alone. One or two women.

Then my poor father frantic. Confusions & afflictions
followed my days. Wives left me.
Bankrupt I closed my doors. You pierced the roof
twice & again. Finally you opened my eyes.

My double nature fused in that point of time
three weeks ago day before yesterday.
Now, brooding thro' a history of the early Church,
I identify with everybody, even the heresiarchs.

10

Fearful I peer upon the mountain path
where once Your shadow passed, Limner of the clouds
up their phantastic guesses. I am afraid,
I never until now confessed.

I fell back in love with you, Father, for two reasons:
You were good to me, & a delicious author,
rational and passionate. Come on me again,
as twice you came to Azarias & Misael.

President of the brethren, our mild assemblies
inspire, & bother the priest not to be dull;
keep us week-long in order; love my children,
my mother far & ill, far brother, my spouse.

Oil all my turbulence as at Thy dictation
I sweat out my wayward works.
Father Hopkins said the only true literary critic is Christ.
Let me lie down exhausted, content with that.

RANDALL JARRELL

A Lullaby

For wars his life and half a world away
The soldier sells his family and days.
He learns to fight for freedom and the State;
He sleeps with seven men within six feet.

He picks up matches and he cleans out plates;
Is lied to like a child, cursed like a beast.
They crop his head, his dog tags ring like sheep
As his stiff limbs shift wearily to sleep.

Recalled in dreams or letters, else forgot,
His life is smothered like a grave, with dirt;
And his dull torment mottles like a fly's
The lying amber of the histories.

The Truth

When I was four my father went to Scotland.
They *said* he went to Scotland.

When I woke up I think I thought that I was dreaming—
I was so little then that I thought dreams
Are in the room with you, like the cinema.
That's why you don't dream when it's still light—
They pull the shades down when it is, so you can sleep.
I thought that then, but that's not right.
Really it's in your head.

And it was light then—light at *night*.
I heard Stalky bark outside.
But really it was Mother crying—
She coughed so hard she cried.
She kept shaking Sister,
She shook her and shook her.
I thought Sister had had her nightmare.
But he wasn't barking, he had died.
There was dirt all over Sister.
It was all streaks, like mud. I cried.
She didn't, but she was older.
                                    I thought she didn't
Because she was older, I thought Stalky had just gone.
I got *everything* wrong.
I didn't get one single thing right.
It seems to me that I'd have thought
It didn't happen, like a dream,
Except that it was light. At night.

They burnt our house down, they burnt down London.
Next day my mother cried all day, and after that
She said to me when she would come to see me:
'Your father has gone away to Scotland.
He will be back after the war.'

The war then was different from the war now.
The war now is *nothing*.

I used to live in London till they burnt it.
What was it like? It was just like here.
No, that's the truth.
My mother would come here, some, but she would cry.
She said to Miss Elise, 'He's not himself';
She said, 'Don't you love me any more at all?'
I was *my*self.
Finally she wouldn't come at all.
She never said one thing my father said, or Sister.
Sometimes she did.
Sometimes she was the same, but that was when I dreamed it.
I could tell I was dreaming, she was just the same.

That Christmas she bought me a toy dog.

I asked her what was its name, and when she didn't know
I asked her over, and when she didn't know
I said, 'You're not my mother, you're not my mother.
She *hasn't* gone to Scotland, she is dead!'
And she said, 'Yes, he's dead, he's dead!'
And cried and cried; she *was* my mother,
She put her arms around me and we cried.

A Front

Fog over the base: the beams ranging
From the five towers pull home from the night
The crews cold in fur, the bombers banging
Like lost trucks down the levels of the ice.
A glow drifts in like mist (how many tons of it?),
Bounces to a roll, turns suddenly to steel
And tyres and turrets, huge in the trembling light.
The next is high, and pulls up with a wail,
Comes round again—no use. And no use for the rest
In drifting circles out along the range;
Holding no longer, changed to a kinder course,
The flights drone southward through the steady rain.
The base is closed.... But one voice keeps on calling,
The lowering pattern of the engines grows;
The roar gropes downward in its shaky orbit
For the lives the season quenches. Here below
They beg, order, are not heard; and hear the darker
Voice rising: *Can't you hear me? Over. Over—*
All the air quivers, and the east sky glows.

A Camp in the Prussian Forest

I walk beside the prisoners to the road.
Load on puffed load,
Their corpses, stacked like sodden wood,
Lie barred or galled with blood

By the charred warehouse. No one comes today
In the old way
To knock the fillings from their teeth;
The dark, coned, common wreath

Is plaited for their grave—a kind of grief.
The living leaf
Clings to the planted profitable
Pine if it is able;

The boughs sigh, mile on green, calm, breathing mile,
From this dead file
The planners ruled for them.... One year
They sent a million here:

Here men were drunk like water, burnt like wood.
The fat of good
And evil, the breast's star of hope
Were rendered into soap.

I paint the star I sawed from yellow pine—
And plant the sign
In soil that does not yet refuse
Its usual Jews

Their first asylum. But the white, dwarfed star—
This dead white star—
Hides nothing, pays for nothing; smoke
Fouls it, a yellow joke,

The needles of the wreath are chalked with ash,
A filmy trash
Litters the black woods with the death
Of men; and one last breath

Curls from the monstrous chimney.... I laugh aloud
Again and again;
The star laughs from its rotting shroud
Of flesh. O star of men!

Protocols

(Birkenau, Odessa; the children speak alternately)

We went there on the train. *They had big barges that they towed,*
We stood up, there were so many I was squashed.
There was a smoke-stack, then they made me wash.
It was a factory, I think. *My mother held me up*
And I could see the ship that made the smoke.

When I was tired my mother carried me.
She said, 'Don't be afraid.' But I was only tired.
Where we went there is no more Odessa.
They had water in a pipe—like rain, but hot;
The water there is deeper than the world

And I was tired and fell in in my sleep
And the water drank me. That is what I think.
And I said to my mother, 'Now I'm washed and dried,'
My mother hugged me, and it smelled like hay
And that is how you die. And that is how you die.

The Woman at the Washington Zoo

The saris go by me from the embassies.

Cloth from the moon. Cloth from another planet.
They look back at the leopard like the leopard.

And I....
                    this print of mine, that has kept its colour
Alive through so many cleanings; this dull null
Navy I wear to work, and wear from work, and so
To my bed, so to my grave, with no
Complaints, no comment: neither from my chief,
The Deputy Chief Assistant, nor his chief—
Only I complain.... this serviceable
Body that no sunlight dyes, no hand suffuses
But, dome-shadowed, withering among columns,
Wavy beneath fountains—small, far-off, shining

In the eyes of animals, these beings trapped
As I am trapped but not, themselves, the trap,
Ageing, but without knowledge of their age,
Kept safe here, knowing not of death, for death—
Oh, bars of my own body, open, open!

The world goes by my cage and never sees me.
And there come not to me, as come to these,
The wild beasts, sparrows pecking the llamas' grain,
Pigeons settling on the bears' bread, buzzards
Tearing the meat the flies have clouded....
                              Vulture,
When you come for the white rat that the foxes left,
Take off the red helmet of your head, the black
Wings that have shadowed me, and step to me as man:
The wild brother at whose feet the white wolves fawn,
To whose hand of power the great lioness
Stalks, purring....
                    You know what I was,
You see what I am: change me, change me!

In Nature There Is Neither Right
nor Left nor Wrong

Men are what they do, women are what they are.
These erect breasts, like marble coming up for air
Among the cataracts of my breathtaking hair,
Are goods in my bazaar, a door ajar
To the first paradise of whores and mothers.

Men buy their way back into me from the upright
Right-handed puzzle that men fit together
From their deeds, the pieces. Women shoot from
Or dive back into its interstices
As squirrels inhabit a geometry.

We women sell ourselves for sleep, for flesh,
to those wide-awake, successful spirits, men—
Who, lying each midnight with the sinister
Beings, their dark companions, women,
Suck childhood, beasthood, from a mother's breasts.

A fat bald rich man comes home at twilight
And lectures me about my parking tickets; gowned in gold
Lamé, I look at him and think: 'You're old,
I'm old.' Husband, I sleep with you every night
And like it; but each morning when I wake
I've dreamed of my first love, the subtle serpent.

A Sick Child

The postman comes when I am still in bed.
'Postman, what do you have for me today?'
I say to him. (But really I'm in bed.)
Then he says—what shall I have him say?

'This letter says that you are president
Of—this word here; it's a republic.'
Tell them I can't answer right away.
'It's your duty.' No, I'd rather just be sick.

Then he tells me there are letters saying everything
That I can think of that I want for them to say.
I say, 'Well, thank you very much. Good-bye.'
He is ashamed, and turns and walks away.

If I can think of it, it isn't what I want.
I want ... I want a ship from some near star
To land in the yard, and beings to come out
And think to me: 'So this is where you are!

Come.' Except that they won't do,
I thought of them.... And yet somewhere there must be
Something that's different from everything.
All that I've never thought of—think of me!

The Lonely Man

A cat sits on the pavement by the house.
It lets itself be touched, then slides away.
A girl goes by in a hood; the winter noon's
Long shadows lengthen. The cat is grey,
It sits there. It sits there all day, every day.

A collie bounds into my arms: he is a dog
And, therefore, finds nothing human alien.
He lives at the preacher's with a pair of cats.
The soft half-Persian sidles to me;
Indoors, the old white one watches blindly.

How cold it is! Some snow slides from a roof
When a squirrel jumps off it to a squirrel-proof
Feeding-station; and, a lot and two yards down,
A fat spaniel snuffles out to me
And sobers me with his untrusting frown.

He worries about his yard: past it, it's my affair
If I halt Earth in her track—his duty's done.
And the cat and the collie worry about the old one:
They come, when she's out too, so uncertainly....
It's my block; I know them, just as they know me.

As for the others, those who wake up every day
And feed these, keep the houses, ride away
To work—I don't know them, they don't know me.
Are we friends or enemies? Why, who can say?
We nod to each other sometimes, in humanity,

Or search one another's faces with a yearning
Remnant of faith that's almost animal....
The grey cat that just sits there: surely it is learning
To be a man; will find, soon, *some especial
Opening in a good firm for a former cat.*

RANDALL JARRELL

The Author to the Reader

I've read that Luther said (it's come to me
So often that I've made it into metre):
And even if the world should end tomorrow
I still would plant my little apple-tree.
Here, reader, is my little apple-tree.

C. H. SISSON

Family Fortunes

1

I was born in Bristol, and it is possible
To live harshly in that city

Quiet voices possess it, but the boy
Torn from the womb, cowers

Under a ceiling of cloud. Tramcars
Crash by or enter the mind

A barred room bore him, the backyard
Smooth as a snake-skin, yielded nothing

In the fringes of the town parsley and honeysuckle
Drenched the hedges.

2

My mother was born in West Kington
Where ford and bridge cross the river together

John Worlock farmed there, my grandfather
Within sight of the square church-tower

The rounded cart-horses shone like metal
My mother remembered their fine ribbons

She lies in the north now where the hills
Are pale green, and I

64

Whose hand never steadied a plough
Wish I had finished my long journey.

3

South of the march parts my father
Lies also, and the fell town

That cradles him now sheltered also
His first unconsciousness

He walked from farm to farm with a kit of tools
From clock to clock, and at the end

Only they spoke to him, he
Having tuned his youth to their hammers.

4

I had two sisters, one I cannot speak of
For she died a child, and the sky was blue that day

The other lived to meet blindness
Groping upon the stairs, not admitting she could not see

Felled at last under a surgeon's hammer
Then left to rot, surgically

And I have a brother who, being alive
Does not need to be put in a poem.

Marcus Aurelius

I do not want to pour out my heart any more
Like a nightingale bursting or a tap dripping:
Father no more verses on me, Marcus Aurelius
I will be an emperor and think like you.

Quiet, dignified, stretched out under a clothes line
The garden of my soul is open for inspection
 As the gardener left it, chaque cheveu à sa place
And if you do not believe me you can comb through my papers
    yourself.

Of course you may not agree with: No hurt because the lips are tight.
The psychologists have been too much for you, but that rascal Freud
Did nothing but devise his own superficial entanglements
For his readers to trip over, while he smiled.

Old devil of Vienna, moving among the porcelain,
You were the beetle under the ruins of an empire
And where the Habsburgs had protruded their lips
You pinched your nostrils.

If I were a plain man I would do the same,
Dexterous, money-making, conforming to another pattern
Than the one I seek which will cover me entirely:
I hope to be an emperor under my own mausoleum.

Over the Wall: Berlin, May 1975

1

He will go over and tell the king
Or whoever is top dog in that country
How there is feasting here, the wastes are empty
The nine governors sleeping

Not a prophetic sleep, with the lids opening
Upon passion, dreaming of conflict
But the eyes turned inwards so that the whites
Gaze upon the world, and the heart ticks steadily
To the combustion of a strange engine
Not in the heart, more like a bee
Buzzing in the neighbourhood. Over the wall,
Knives drawn, teeth drawn back,
Swallowing the rattle they make in case the night
Should interpret their wishes.
Here in the west, far west, slumber
While death collects his paces.

I am not warlike but, once the frontiers are falling
Each man must put on his belt; it has been done before
And the whimpering must stop, Death being the kingdom
Of this world.

2

I have seen the doomed city, it was not my own
Love has no city like this, with barred hatreds
All bitterness, all shames. I do not think there is any
Feast to be eaten or long shawls
Trailed in the dust before the fanatic mob
Only quiet people live here, eating their sandwiches
Under the lilac while the boats go by,
Interminable imitation of reality
Which is not to be had, and should the frost fall
Should the eagle turn its head
The city of too many desperate adventures
I have seen them all, or so it seems, the Uhlans ...
And now from the steppes
It is as if the Dalmatian horsemen came back,
Yet they do not stir, or make themselves visible ...
One street I remember
There is no majesty in its lost endeavours
Speak to me no more, I have heard only
The marching men.
Sleep comes to those who deserve
Funerals under the chipped archways.

3

I do not think this is the end of the story
There are battalions enough behind the wall.
The tall policeman bent over me like the priest
Of an evil religion, as if I were the elements
And he the emissary who was empowered to transform me.
That was not the same
Dream-ridden solitude I had known before
Where a flame climbed the walls there was no one by.

4

I know only aspen, beech, oak
But here in these wastes the turtle
Sang among the sands, sitting upon a pine-tree
No man has meditated this regress
Yet the afternoon sun falls upon faces
Less tame than tigers.

C. H. SISSON

The Queen of Lydia

Candaules, King of Lydia,
Whose mouth was bigger than his prick

Boasted about the Queen his wife:
'You ought to see her in her bath;

She is a smasher.' Gyges said
He thought it inappropriate.

He was a soldier and he knew
The elements of discipline.

He also knew you did not trust
A master with an outsized mouth.

The King insisted, and arranged
Gyges should stand behind the door

While she came in and got undressed.
And this he did. Candaules lay

Discreetly in his double bed,
His nose above the counterpane.

He liked the Queen to take her time
And put her folded garments on

A bench some distance from the bed,
Then strut about the room a bit.

All this she did; and Gyges watched.
Was his mind on his duty then?

He shook as he stood by the door.
As the Queen turned her lovely back

He made a noise and then went out.
Alas, he was not quick enough.

The Queen said nothing; she was sly
And thought instead and went to sleep.

Next day she sent for Gyges and
He trembled as behind the door.

She gave him this alternative:
'One of you two goes to the pot.

Either you kill the shameless king
And lie beside me in his bed

And also govern Lydia
Or I will have him murder you.'

The choice was easy: no one dies
Rather than sleep beside a girl.

And the Queen's motive? She believed
(The Lydians are barbarians)

To be seen naked was a shame
Which only death could expiate

Or marriage, as in Gyges' case.
So you see how barbarians are.

A and B

A
I was in the lane and saw the car pass.
The white face of the girl showed through the windscreen,
Beside her a youth with a tight grip on the wheel.
B
There was a blue Anglia; I remember.
A
I caught the girl's eyes as she passed;
They were in deepest contentment.
She communicated in perfect freedom to me
The candour with which she would undress when they reached the
    wood.
It was a point that had been troubling the boy.

B

And what has their pleasure to do with us?

A

You think a philosopher should stick to his port.
That is not my opinion.
What is enacted in these hills
Is a sacrifice as any propounded
Under the shadow of the Giant of Cerne
And sacrifice is not for the actors.

B

What nonsense is this about a sacrifice?
This is what two people did, and that is all.

A

What they did in a flurry of consciousness,
Their hands upon one another's sides,
Was trivial enough. But what were their intentions?
Some hope perhaps of giving or taking pleasure.

B

I should think they might have been partially successful.

A

I met an old man on a tall horse
He had ridden for thirty years. It was his intention
When he had seen the last of it, to bury it
Out in that field beside his dead mare.
Do you think he had planned that harmony?
Did not a spirit seize him by the throat
And tell him what to do: there, under the old church
Rising there on that mound above the groin?

B

I am afraid, A, you are not a philosopher.
You are merely an inconsiderate fool who loves his country
At the very moment when love has become vain.

A

See there where a party of picnickers
Trace their way over the springy turf
And the world proceeds without understanding.
Perhaps all will be well.

At First

Nothing that is said or done
Can equal in the end
The first apprehension of love.
And so it is at last.
Speak, God, to the encumbered
Servant I am. It will be news
If you tell me I am saved.

GAVIN EWART

The Dell

My mother took us, when we went walking
    across Hyde Park, to the rural dell
where wild rabbits occasioned excited talking
    and a kind of rustic enchantment fell,
    a woodland spell,

over our London whose traffic, roaring,
    was distanced there; but never odd
did it seem to us that our spirit's soaring
    was at the command of a country god;
    and brock and tod

might too be hiding in that green hollow—
    this was our simple, childish thought.
Given the premise, conclusions follow.
    That was the magic we found (and sought),
    as children ought.

The great black rock that towered there only
    seemed unusual, out of place
we never thought it; barbaric, lonely,
    hiding a dreamlike Freudian face,
    removed from Grace,

or primitive; such thoughts came later,
    with knowledge. A darkly standing stone
didn't disturb us, our joy was greater;
    though in a railed, forbidden zone
    it stood alone.

Years, years after, in summer twilight,
    I stood there, before the dell, with you
and the stone gleamed black with a lamplit highlight,
    and then and there, at once I knew
    yes, what was true.

That you, as rare as a four-leaf clover,
    wouldn't hurry now, as once, so gay;
that, like my childhood, your love was over,
    the dell an excuse for one more delay
    on our homeward way.

The Lovesleep

In an exciting world of love-bites, nipple-nipping,
unbuttoning and unzipping,
kisses that are
the highest kind of communication,
the lovers experience their timeless elation;

perhaps they reach those peaks where, like a bomb exploding,
the angels sing, encoding
ecstasies that
our language can never really deal with—
its nouns and its adjectives that no one can feel with;

but when the woman lies in the man's arms—soft, sleeping,
in perfect trust, and keeping
faith, you might say,
that is the truest peace and disarming—
no one can sleep in the arms of an enemy, however charming.

Fiction: A Message

'My dear fellow!' said the great poet, putting his arm affably round
  Ponsonby's neck,
'I respect your feelings for Gertrude. I realize they have something
  to do with sec
or secs or whatever they call it. Of course in my little backwater I
  haven't moved with the times—
just listen to the bells of St Josef—how I love those chimes!'

Down below, the Austrian lake reflected his agonized incomprehension
  sleepily in the sun.
'I'm at the end of my tether!' cried Ponsonby. 'But you—your race
  is nearly run—
I look to you for a message. I know that behind her spectacles she
  has the most beautiful eyes,
I've heard her playing Chopin at midnight with rapt, adoring cries!'

'These things are sent to try us' said Anzeiger. 'You'll find something
  in Apollonius of Rhodes,
or one of the Desert Fathers, that proves fairly conclusively that
  women are toads.'
'I've told myself so, yet I often have the most incomprehensible
  puzzling dreams.
I dream of the Kaiserhof, of milk churns, of chocolate creams.

Sometimes I run into a dark wood of feathery soft perfumed aromatic
  trees
or I'm sinking in unimaginable sweetness like honey, right up to my
  knees,
or I see Gertrude waving from a cottage with a very attractive
  rose-circled door.
I'm wearing my Norfolk jacket and, I'm ashamed to say, nothing
  more!'

'That sounds like the Flesh' pondered Anzeiger, fingering gently
    Ponsonby's fair curls.
'We know well that St Anthony was tempted in dreams by demons and
    dancing girls.
Though these apparitions, old fellow, seem so irrational, so disturbing,
    so unaccountably odd,
I think we can safely assume, in your case, they don't come from God.

Though, of course, He has been known to work in some really very
    mysterious ways.'
'But what shall I do?' cried Ponsonby. 'Offer it up. Just pray and
    give praise.
We'll take the pony and trap and go down on Sunday, dear boy, to
    Linz.
The Lord will lend a kindly ear to your account of your sins.'

They turned and walked towards the house, arm in arm. The sun had
    nearly set.
As they approached the pretty garden, by the last dark sentinel pine
    trees they met
Gertrude in a light summer dress, confidently smiling, friendly and
    demure.
Ponsonby smiled back. He was above her. Of that he was now sure.

On the Tercentenary of Milton's Death

E. Jarvis-Thribb (17) and Keith's Mum
don't reckon you;
even students of English get lost
in your syntax,
the long sentences and the Greek idioms
('he knew to build')
confuse the lovers of what's simple,
the multitudinous
classical allusions just fill them with boredom.
Eliot's hypothesis
was that your magniloquence led on to Wordsworth
and Coleridge, poets
who could write (or talk) the hind leg off a donkey.

You didn't have much use for humour,
wit vanished early
from your verse (in any sense) and rhyme
you thought barbarous;
perhaps in your day nothing much was funny,
as now in Ulster,
and how could you have the needed detachment?
But like a rocket
you took off for outer space and the SF demons,
you really did go
into overdrive, no short-haul aircraft,
medium range bomber
or helicopter, but a giant blockbuster.

So for this kind of verse, which has a genuine grandeur,
you are the best one—
Wordsworth's dim mountains are only molehills,
I think, compared.
You truly invented your own mighty language—
like Ulysses' bow,
nobody else could handle it; *it* bent *them*.
Of course you took sides
and suffered for it; if pride was your fault, still
you had cause for that.
The young undergraduate of Christ's College
combing his long blond hair
with an ivory comb? As well as arrogance, beauty.

Pastoral

Dominic Francis Xavier Brotherton-Chancery
had an egg for breakfast every morning
and revelled in obsolete forms. For example
he called an eclogue an eglog (like the Elizabethans).
He went everywhere on a bicycle. He knew very well
that ordinary people had never heard of an eclogue.
How he despised them! When his rough friend
made savage fun of Gerard Manley Hopkins,
jokingly speaking of 'The Burglar's First Communion'
and hinting at the lust concealed in a work called 'Hairy Ploughman',

although he giggled Dominic was shocked—
such a lack of Faith! But what he loved in his friend
was exactly the shaggy goat-footed Philistine roughness,
it made *him* seem at least twice as cultivated.
His coarse moustache was an animal temptation.
His coltish clumsiness—oh, Dominic adored!
They were both sheepheards. His mother was a nymphe.
The sheepheardesses lived in a different valley.
He literally wanted (as Gus guffawed)
no part of them! Lithe on his bicycle
he rode contented through a summer idyll.

An Exeter Riddle

Sitters on the mead-bench,   quaffing among questions,
I saw a thing—   tell me its totality.
A boy sped by,   his feet did not grind gravel,
high was his head,   incautious in the company
of the might of mountains   and a rock-rent liquid.
His hands moved little,   his legs seemed listless,
yet he woke the wind   and exacerbated echoes,
wending not to war   in a charging chariot,
unhelped by horses   whirling like the wind.
Test-tube technology   covered him completely.
Seen for a second,   he was gone ghostly
as though he had never been.   Vouchsafe me this vision!

From V.C. (*a Gentleman of Verona*)

Give me the Daulian bird and Locrian Arsinoë.
I want to arrange a protest in high places.
I just want to say to a few fat-nippled goddesses: It isn't fair.

It's your door that I'm complaining about.
It's far too neutral. It admits revolting lovers,
fast talkers and political nitwits. I hate it.

It never speaks but if it did I know it
would have an American accent, smacking
its lips and saying, glutinously: 'That girl's a cocksucker.'

If I had my way it would be closed for ever
against those pretentious people whose main crime
is that they aren't me. It should only open, youwise, mewards.

Doors are disgusting. They'll let in anything—
secret police, creditors, puritan censors,
men with eviction orders. They're great painted layabouts.

But that I know it can keep out competition,
I'd have it off its hinges. Don't talk about oiling!
It's a Public Enemy—to me, you, and Venus a complacent traitor.

They flee from me that sometime did me seek

At this moment in time
the chicks that went for me
in a big way
are opting out;
as of now, it's an all-change situation.

The scenario was once,
for me, 100% better.
Kissing her was viable
in a nude or semi-nude situation.
It was *How's about it, baby?*,
her embraces were relevant
and life-enhancing.

I was not hallucinating.
But with regard to that one
my permissiveness
has landed me in a forsaking situation.
The affair is no longer on-going.

She can, as of now, explore new parameters—
How's about it? indeed!
I feel emotionally underprivileged.
What a bitch!
(and that's meaningful!).

Prayer

Lord I am not entirely selfish
Lord I am not entirely helpish
O Lord to me be slightly lavish
O Lord be in a minor way lovish

Lord I am not completely bad-mannered
Lord I am not a crusader, mad-bannered
O Lord to me be quite well disposed
O Lord to me be calm and composed

Lord I am not a dog downed and to-heeled
Lord I am not thick about what has been revealed
O Lord you have it in your power to hurt me
O Lord in your odd way please do not desert me

CHARLES CAUSLEY

At the British War Cemetery, Bayeux

I walked where in their talking graves
And shirts of earth five thousand lay,
When history with ten feasts of fire
Had eaten the red air away.

I am Christ's boy, I cried, I bear
In iron hands the bread, the fishes.
I hang with honey and with rose
This tidy wreck of all your wishes.

On your geometry of sleep
The chestnut and the fir-tree fly,
And lavender and marguerite
Forge with their flowers an English sky.

Turn now towards the belling town
Your jigsaws of impossible bone,
And rising read your rank of snow
Accurate as death upon the stone.

About your easy heads my prayers
I said with syllables of clay.
What gift, I asked, shall I bring now
Before I weep and walk away?

Take, they replied, the oak and laurel.
Take our fortune of tears and live
Like a spendthrift lover. All we ask
Is the one gift you cannot give.

For an Ex-Far East Prisoner of War

I am that man with helmet made of thorn
Who wandered naked in the desert place,
Wept, with the sweating sky, that I was born
And wore disaster in my winter face.

I am that man who asked no hate, nor pity.
I am that man, five-wounded, on the tree.
I am that man, walking his native city,
Hears his dead comrade cry, *Remember me!*

I am that man whose brow with blood was wet,
Returned, as Lazarus, from the dead to live.
I am that man, long-counselled to forget,
Facing a fearful victory, to forgive:

And seizing these two words, with the sharp sun
Beat them, like sword and ploughshare, into one.

CHARLES CAUSLEY

Loss of an Oil Tanker

Over our heads the missiles ran
Through skies more desolate than the sea.
In jungles, where man hides from man,
Leaves fell, in springtime, from the tree.

A cracked ship on the Seven Stones lies
Dying in resurrection weather.
With squalid hands we hold our prize:
A drowned fish and a sea-bird's feather.

Infant Song

Don't you love my baby, mam,
Lying in his little pram,

Polished all with water clean,
The finest baby ever seen?

Daughter, daughter, if I could
I'd love your baby as I should,

But why the suit of signal red,
The horns that grow out of his head,

Why does he burn with brimstone heat,
Have cloven hooves instead of feet,

Fishing hooks upon each hand,
The keenest tail that's in the land,

Pointed ears and teeth so stark
And eyes that flicker in the dark?

Don't you love my baby, mam?

Dearest, I do not think I can.
I do not, do not think I can.

Ten Types of Hospital Visitor

1

The first enters wearing the neon armour
Of virtue.
Ceaselessly firing all-purpose smiles
At everyone present
She destroys hope
In the breasts of the sick,
Who realize instantly
That they are incapable of surmounting
Her ferocious goodwill.

Such courage she displays
In the face of human disaster!

Fortunately, she does not stay long.
After a speedy trip round the ward
In the manner of a nineteen-thirties destroyer
Showing the flag in the Mediterranean,
She returns home for a week
—With luck, longer—
Scorched by the heat of her own worthiness.

2

The second appears, a melancholy splurge
Of theological colours;
Taps heavily about like a healthy vulture
Distributing deep-frozen hope.

The patients gaze at him cautiously.
Most of them, as yet uncertain of the realities
Of heaven, hell-fire, or eternal emptiness,
Play for safety
By accepting his attentions
With just-concealed apathy,
Except one old man, who cries
With newly sharpened hatred,

'Shove off! Shove off!
'Shove ... shove ... shove ... shove
Off!
Just you
Shove!'

3

The third skilfully deflates his weakly smiling victim
By telling him
How the lobelias are doing,
How many kittens the cat had,
How the slate came off the scullery roof,
And how no one has visited the patient for a fortnight
Because everybody
Had colds and feared to bring the jumpy germ
Into hospital.
The patient's eyes
Ice over. He is uninterested
In lobelias, the cat, the slate, the germ.
Flat on his back, drip-fed, his face
The shade of a newly dug-up Pharaoh,
Wearing his skeleton outside his skin,
Yet his wits as bright as a lighted candle,
He is concerned only with the here, the now,
And requires to speak
Of nothing but his present predicament.

It is not permitted.

4

The fourth attempts to cheer
His aged mother with light jokes
Menacing as shell-splinters.
'They'll soon have you jumping round
Like a gazelle,' he says.
'Playing in the football team.'
Quite undeterred by the sight of kilos
Of plaster, chains, lifting-gear,
A pair of lethally designed crutches,
'You'll be leap-frogging soon,' he says.
'Swimming ten lengths of the baths.'

At these unlikely prophecies
The old lady stares fearfully
At her sick, sick offspring
Thinking he has lost his reason—

Which, alas, seems to be the case.

5

The fifth, a giant from the fields
With suit smelling of milk and hay,
Shifts uneasily from one bullock foot
To the other, as though to avoid
Settling permanently in the antiseptic landscape.
Occasionally he looses a scared glance
Sideways, as though fearful of what intimacy
He may blunder on, or that the walls
Might suddenly close in on him.

He carries flowers, held lightly in fingers
The size and shape of plantains,
Tenderly kisses his wife's cheek
—The brush of a child's lips—
Then balances, motionless, for thirty minutes
On the thin chair.

At the end of visiting time
He emerges breathless,
Blinking with relief, into the safe light.

He does not appear to notice
The dusk.

6

The sixth visitor says little,
Breathes reassurance,
Smiles securely.
Carries no black passport of grapes
And visa of chocolate. Has a clutch
Of clean washing.

Unobtrusively stows it
In the locker; searches out more.
Talks quietly to the Sister
Out of sight, out of earshot, of the patient.
Arrives punctually as a tide.
Does not stay the whole hour.

Even when she has gone
The patient seems to sense her there:
An upholding
Presence.

7

The seventh visitor
Smells of bar-room after-shave.
Often finds his friend
Sound asleep: whether real or feigned
Is never determined.

He does not mind; prowls the ward
In search of second-class, lost-face patients
With no visitors
And who are pretending to doze
Or read paperbacks.

He probes relentlessly the nature
Of each complaint, and is swift with such
Dilutions of confidence as,
'Ah! You'll be worse
Before you're better.'

Five minutes before the bell punctuates
Visiting time, his friend opens an alarm-clock eye.
The visitor checks his watch.
Market day. The Duck and Pheasant will be still open.

Courage must be refuelled.

8

The eighth visitor looks infinitely
More decayed, ill and infirm than any patient.
His face is an expensive grey.

He peers about with antediluvian eyes
As though from the other end
Of time.
He appears to have risen from the grave
To make this appearance.
There is a whiff of white flowers about him;
The crumpled look of a slightly used shroud.
Slowly he passes the patient
A bag of bullet-proof
Home-made biscuits,
A strong, death-dealing cake—
'To have with your tea,'
Or a bowl of fruit so weighty
It threatens to break
His glass fingers.

The patient, encouraged beyond measure,
Thanks him with enthusiasm, not for
The oranges, the biscuits, the cake,
But for the healing sight
Of someone patently worse
Than himself. He rounds the crisis-corner;
Begins a recovery.

9

The ninth visitor is life.

10

The tenth visitor
Is not usually named.

ROBERT CONQUEST

Guided Missiles Experimental Range

Soft sounds and odours brim up through the night
A wealth below the level of the eye;
Out of a black, an almost violet sky
Abundance flowers into points of light.

Till from the south-west, as their low scream mars
And halts this warm hypnosis of the dark,
Three black automata cut swift and stark,
Shaped clearly by the backward flow of stars.

Stronger than lives, by empty purpose blinded,
The only thought their circuits can endure is
The target-hunting rigour of their flight;

And by that loveless haste I am reminded
Of Aeschylus' description of the Furies:
'O barren daughters of the fruitful night.'

Lake Success

Fall in Long Island:
Deep in the dying fires of beech and sumach
Under a motionless air holding vapour
Invisible but enough to filter the sun
From a rage of light to a source of clarity,
In these buildings there is talk of peace.

In the Security Council and the six Committees,
In the air-conditioned ambience and too-ideal lighting,
A notoriously maladministered state is smug about mandates,
The sponsor of an aggressor utters pacific phrases,
A state ruled by a foreign marshal condemns colonial oppression,
A middle-easterner makes a statesmanlike speech in very elegant
  French.

These little men, vain and silly, tough and intelligent, cunning and
    mean,
Good and patient, selfish and loud, cultured and weak,
Are here distinguished by a different standard of value:
One represents twenty-five thousand tanks,
One speaks with the voice of a whole potential continent,
One has successfully resisted the will of a powerful neighbour,
One of the most impressive is merely an empty voice.

Miles away to the west, high in the air which is
A pale single fluid, the summits of great buildings
Glitter like masked and very distant snow;
In the foreground, outside the vacant lawns,
Amazingly vivid leaves are slowly falling;
And in here, in a sense at the heart of the human world,
These tangibles are merely memory,
And paper and words are immediately real. And yet,
In this web of power and propaganda, sufficient
Devotion and intelligence are assembled
To ensure at least a painstaking effort to see
That the chances of peace may not (and that bombs may not)
Fall in Long Island.

747 (*London–Chicago*)

After the horrors of Heathrow
A calmness settles in.
A window seat, an ambient glow,
A tonic-weakened gin.

The pale grey wings, the pale-blue sky;
The tiny sun's sharp shine,
The engines' drone, or rather sigh;
A single calm design.

Those great wings flex to altering air.
Ten thousand feet below
We watch the endless miles of glare,
Like slightly lumpy dough.

Below that white all's grey and grim,
The wrong side of the sky.
Reality's down in that dim
Old formicary? Why?

What though through years, the same old way,
That world spins on its hub?
The mayfly's simple summer day
Beats lifetimes as a grub!

A geologic fault, this flight:
Those debts, that former wife,
Make some moraine down out of sight,
Old debris of a life.

(Only one figure, far and clear
Looks upward from that trough:
A face still visible from here
—The girl who saw him off.)

The huge machine's apart, alone.
The yielding hours go by.
We form a culture of our own
Inhabiting the sky.

Too short? Yet every art replies,
Preferring for its praise
To Egypt's smouldering centuries
The brief Athenian blaze . . .

That flame-point sun, a blue-set jewel,
Blazed blurredly as it went.
Our arguments run out of fuel.
We dip for our descent.

We drift down from pure white and blue
To what awaits us there
In customs shed and passport queue
—The horrors of O'Hare.

To be a Pilgrim

We got away—for just two nights.
She'd booked us in at some hotel
Over in the Isle of Wight's
Western corner. Friends spoke well

Of it. The name just slipped me by
And only half-way up the drive
A revelation came, a cry,
'Farringford—Tennyson's old dive!'

Beautiful! Unchanged in mood.
The swimming pool discreetly far.
The kitchens (for quite decent food)
Hidden by firs. Thank God, a bar.

Beneath the boughs, the green-gold leaves
Of this most grand of whatsit trees
He wrote—that is, if one believes
Old Robert Graves—of drunk Chinese.

And Garibaldi came!—A plaque
Below a tall and swaying pine;
(And in the modern Visitors' Book
Just you and me and Phil. E. Stein).

The track he pushed his wife up, on
The downs' low edge, to see the sea.
—Could a Swiss or Paraguayan
Dream of writing poetry?

But now how piercingly my charmer
Yells! Above her furious gasps
I hear among the furze the murmur
Of innumerable wasps.

'You see, there's been no winter snow.
We gets them thick in such a year.'
Did *he* get stung much? Well, if so,
His closest to the sure-thrust spear.

Our room. I gaze at sheaf and stack
While she's proceeding to anoint
The sting with sal ammoniac;
'This really is a pleasant joint!'

A notice opposite the bar:
The Tennyson and TV Room
—His cloak, his stick, some books. And—ah!—
Grandstand bright through Gothic gloom.

Those books though—classic, pastoral—
That taught his verse its solemn stride.
My head still ringing with the call
Of Hesiod, we go outside.

'Hera! Pylos' teeming great
Herds!' Unmoved the Jerseys munch.
'Kore! Maiden! If ...' Too late.
The old words fail. It's time for lunch.

And then, why don't we drive across
To seek through scents of salt and rose
The chine-hid church where Swinburne was
—Baptized? buried?—One of those.

Appalachian Convalescence

Eastward, etched in purple by a sun
Invisible behind us, the Great Smokies
Loom clear through a transcendent unconcern.

In this valley nothing strong, no love,
No despair, no stabbing memory even,
Has had me. And yet, such a negative

Is false as saying that we do not see
The almost fallen sun behind this hillside
While we stare east through its fecundity.

All passion spent? No passions even start.
Yet here tranquillity's an active radiance,
The slow pulse strong from the unbroken heart.

So fade along the westering Tennessee
Light of all conscious feeling! Let the night-time
Confirm, as once it clawed, a mind made free.

Excerpt from a Report to the Galactic Council

... on the third planet too, life is found.

LXI

(These sections are presented in this form under the regulation
Which requires a local language and an attempt at least
To employ its fullest method: so that the Council's evaluation
Of the species may be in accord with the nature of the beast.)

The race is one of those which use (in this case orally) discrete
Invariant symbols, recombination of whose elements
Can in no sort of circumstances be complete
Or even sound as descriptions of real events.

The 'poem' (at which this, in the biped dialect 'English', is an attempt)
Is an integration of symbols which may be defined
As a semantic composition fusing what is thought and dreamt,
And working in senses and thalamus as well as what is called mind.

Moreover it liberates their symbolism from over-definition,
In that unwonted flexibility is released by the act
Of no longer holding the symbols' split for rigid fission
Nor the symbol itself as object, but as artefact.

Observation of real events includes the observer, 'heart' and all;
(The common measurable features are obtained by omitting this part).
But there is also a common aspect in the emotional
Shared by other members of the species: this is conveyed by 'art'.

The poem combines all these, so that the whole scene
Can penetrate the biped's organism at every level.

With the aid of the empathy conditioner and the translation machine
We believe that the Council will find the method intelligible.

A further note on this race is that, like those of Deneb III,
Its reproductive method is the sexual, which has led
(Relevant at this point) to ability to conceive otherness, mystery,
Illumining life, thought, and especially poem, from the bed.

Before the body of the report it would be well to enter the caveat
That 'verse' is better than the race's thought as a whole.
In general practice they reify abstractions; at
The price of wars, etc., fail to keep symbols under control.

LXII

We can now proceed to the detailed evidence. An O.P.
Was established on the nearby satellite, from which
Descent was effected to the surface, in spite of the higher g;
Normal secrecy precautions worked without a hitch.

Accompanying records show ...

Generalities

Late April. Taking stock
Of love, a long year's hoard:
What can define that luck?
For love's a general word
Diluting brilliant essence
With seepage of other minds
And dead experience.
Who froze a fire that blinds?

—In winter poems he tried
For strictness, for the rough
Undecorated ode;
Now he'd be pleased enough
If sentiment were stated
Vaguely among these blooms
With his heart completed
And his words in his arms.

ROBERT LOWELL

The Dead in Europe

After the planes unloaded, we fell down
Buried together, unmarried men and women;
Not crown of thorns, not iron, not Lombard crown,
Not grilled and spindle spires pointing to heaven
Could save us. Raise us, Mother, we fell down
Here hugger-mugger in the jellied fire:
Our sacred earth in our day was our curse.

Our Mother, shall we rise on Mary's day
In Maryland, wherever corpses married
Under the rubble, bundled together? Pray
For us whom the blockbusters marred and buried;
When Satan scatters us on Rising-day,
O Mother, snatch our bodies from the fire:
Our sacred earth in our day was our curse.

Mother, my bones are trembling and I hear
The earth's reverberations and the trumpet
Bleating into my shambles. Shall I bear,
(O Mary!) unmarried man and powder-puppet,
Witness to the Devil? Mary, hear,
O Mary, marry earth, sea, air and fire;
Our sacred earth in our day is our curse.

A Mad Negro Soldier Confined at Munich

'We're all Americans, except the Doc,
a Kraut DP, who kneels and bathes my eye.
The boys who floored me, two black maniacs try
to pat my hands. Rounds, rounds! Why punch the clock?

In Munich the zoo's rubble fumes with cats;
hoydens with air-guns prowl the Koenigsplatz,
and pink the pigeons on the mustard spire.
Who but my girl-friend set the town on fire?

Cat-houses talk cold turkey to my guards;
I found my *fräulein* stitching outing shirts
in the black forest of the coloured wards—
lieutenants squawked like chickens in her skirts.

Her German language made my arteries harden—
I've no annuity from the pay we blew.
I chartered an aluminum canoe,
I had her six times in the English Garden.

Oh mama, mama, like a trolley-pole
sparking at contact, her electric shock—
the power-house! ... The doctor calls our roll—
no knives, no forks. We file before the clock,

and fancy minnows, slaves of habit, shoot
like starlight through their air-conditioned bowl.
It's time for feeding. Each subnormal boot-
black heart is pulsing to its ant-egg dole.'

Skunk Hour

Nautilus Island's hermit
heiress still lives through winter in her Spartan cottage;
her sheep still graze above the sea.
Her son's a bishop. Her farmer
is first selectman in our village,
she's in her dotage.

Thirsting for
the hierarchic privacy
of Queen Victoria's century,
she buys up all
the eyesores facing her shore,
and lets them fall.

the season's ill—
we've lost our summer millionaire,
who seemed to leap from an L. L. Bean
catalogue. His nine-knot yawl
was auctioned off to lobstermen.
A red fox stain covers Blue Hill.

And now our fairy
decorator brightens his shop for fall,
his fishnet's filled with orange cork,
orange, his cobbler's bench and awl,
there is no money in his work,
he'd rather marry.

One dark night,
my Tudor Ford climbed the hill's skull,
I watched for love-cars. Lights turned down,
they lay together, hull to hull,
where the graveyard shelves on the town....
My mind's not right.

A car radio bleats,
'Love, O careless Love ...' I hear
my ill-spirit sob in each blood cell,
as if my hand were at its throat....
I myself am hell,
nobody's here—

only skunks, that search
in the moonlight for a bite to eat.
They march on their soles up Main Street:
white stripes, moonstruck eyes' red fire
under the chalk-dry and spar spire
of the Trinitarian Church.

I stand on top
of our back steps and breathe the rich air—
a mother skunk with her column of kittens swills the garbage pail.
She jabs her wedge-head in a cup
of sour cream, drops her ostrich tail,
and will not scare.

ROBERT LOWELL

Waking Early Sunday Morning

O to break loose, like the chinook
salmon jumping and falling back,
nosing up to the impossible
stone and bone-crushing waterfall—
raw-jawed, weak-fleshed there, stopped by ten
steps of the roaring ladder, and then
to clear the top on the last try,
alive enough to spawn and die.

Stop, back off. The salmon breaks
water, and now my body wakes
to feel the unpolluted joy
and criminal leisure of a boy—
no rainbow smashing a dry fly
in the white run is free as I,
here squatting like a dragon on
time's hoard before the day's begun!

Vermin run for their unstopped holes;
in some dark nook a fieldmouse rolls
a marble, hours on end, then stops;
the termite in the woodwork sleeps—
listen, the creatures of the night
obsessive, casual, sure of foot,
go on grinding, while the sun's
daily remorseful blackout dawns.

Fierce, fireless mind, running downhill.
Look up and see the harbour fill:
business as usual in eclipse
goes down to the sea in ships—
wake of refuse, dacron rope,
bound for Bermuda or Good Hope,
all bright before the morning watch
the wine-dark hulls of yawl and ketch.

I watch a glass of water wet
with a fine fuzz of icy sweat,

silvery colours touched with sky,
serene in their neutrality—
yet if I shift, or change my mood,
I see some object made of wood,
background behind it of brown grain,
to darken it, but not to stain.

O that the spirit could remain
tinged but untarnished by its strain!
Better dressed and stacking birch,
or lost with the Faithful at Church—
anywhere, but somewhere else!
And now the new electric bells,
clearly chiming, 'Faith of our fathers',
and now the congregation gathers.

O Bible chopped and crucified
in hymns we hear but do not read,
none of the milder subtleties
of grace or art will sweeten these
stiff quatrains shovelled out four-square—
they sing of peace, and preach despair;
yet they gave darkness some control,
and left a loophole for the soul.

No, put old clothes on, and explore
the corners of the woodshed for
its dregs and dreck: tools with no handle,
ten candle-ends not worth a candle,
old lumber banished from the Temple,
damned by Paul's precept and example,
cast from the kingdom, banned in Israel,
the wordless sign, the tinkling cymbal.

When will we see Him face to face?
Each day, He shines through darker glass—
In this small town where everything
is known, I see His vanishing
emblems, His white spire and flag-
pole sticking out above the fog,
like old white china doorknobs, sad,
slight, useless things to calm the mad.

Hammering military splendour,
top-heavy Goliath in full armour—
little redemption in the mass
liquidations of their brass,
elephant and phalanx moving
with the times and still improving,
when that kingdom hit the crash:
a million foreskins stacked like trash ...

Sing softer! But what if a new
diminuendo brings no true
tenderness, only restlessness,
excess, the hunger for success,
sanity of self-deception
fixed and kicked by reckless caution,
while we listen to the bells—
anywhere, but somewhere else!

O to break loose. All life's grandeur
is something with a girl in summer ...
elated as the President
girdled by his establishment
this Sunday morning, free to chaff
his own thoughts with his bear-cuffed staff,
swimming nude, unbuttoned, sick
of his ghost-written rhetoric!

No weekends for the gods now. Wars
flicker, earth licks its open sores,
fresh breakage, fresh promotions, chance
assassinations, no advance.
Only man thinning out his kind
sounds through the Sabbath noon, the blind
swipe of the pruner and his knife
busy about the tree of life ...

Pity the planet, all joy gone
from this sweet volcanic cone;
peace to our children when they fall
in small war on the heels of small

war—until the end of time
to police the earth, a ghost
orbiting forever lost
in our monotonous sublime.

Ford Madox Ford

Taking Ford's dictation on Samuel Butler
in longhand: 'A novelist has one novel, his own.'
He swallowed his words, I garbled each seventh word—
'You have no ear,' he said, 'for civilized prose,
Shakespeare's best writing: *No king, be his cause never so spotless,
will try it out with all unspotted soldiers.*'
I brought him my loaded and overloaded lines.
He said: 'You live a butterfly's existence,
flitting, flying, botching inspiration.
Conrad spent a day finding the *mot juste*; then killed it.'
Ford doubted I could live and be an artist.
'Most of them are born to fill the graveyards.'
Ford wrote my father, 'If he fails as a writer, at least
he'll be head of Harvard or your English Ambassador.'

Identification in Belfast (*I.R.A. Bombing*)

The British Army now carries two rifles,
one with rubber rabbit-pellets for children,
the other's of course for the Provisionals....
'When they first showed me the boy, I thought oh good,
it's not him because he is a blond—
I imagine his hair was singed dark by the bomb.
He had nothing on him to identify him,
except this box of joke trick matches;
he liked to have them on him, even at mass.
The police were unhurried and wonderful,
they let me go on trying to strike a match ...
I just wouldn't stop—you cling to anything—
I couldn't believe I couldn't light one match—
only joke-matches.... Then I knew he was Richard.'

ROBERT LOWELL

The Holy Innocents

Listen, the hay-bells tinkle as the cart
Wavers on rubber tyres along the tar
And cindered ice below the burlap mill
And ale-wife run. The oxen drool and start
In wonder at the fenders of a car,
And blunder hugely up St Peter's hill.
These are the undefiled by woman—their
Sorrow is not the sorrow of this world:
King Herod shrieking vengeance at the curled
Up knees of Jesus choking in the air,

A king of speechless clods and infants. Still
The world out-Herods Herod; and the year,
The nineteen-hundred forty-fifth of grace,
Lumbers with losses up the clinkered hill
Of our purgation; and the oxen near
The worn foundations of their resting-place,
The holy manger where their bed is corn
And holly torn for Christmas. If they die,
As Jesus, in the harness, who will mourn?
Lamb of the shepherds, Child, how still you lie.

JOHN HEATH-STUBBS

Preliminary Poem

'The hour gets later, the times get worse, let us therefore keep awake'—
I set this down as one who shall outlive heartbreak,
A contumacious poet in an unjust, barbarous age:
Hope, the butterfly, but seldom brushes my page
With her mazarine wing. May I hope Faith is there,
Only a little disguised in her gorgon-mask, Despair?
As for the third, flaming-hearted sister Compassion,
She will intercede for her prodigal brother Passion;
Or else, quiver-bearing, succinct, with buskined knee,
Pursue the wild game through thickets of irony.

Virgin Martyrs

Catherine, describing a perfect circle
 Upon your wheel of fire,
Cecily, improvising three-part inventions
 On the Neronian lyre,

Lucy, squeezing your bright blue eyes out,
 Agatha, with a penknife
Slicing your pretty half-formed titties,
 The might-have-been founts of life,

Ursula, massacred eleven thousand times
 By the anonymous Huns,
Teasing and stripped Eulalia, with
 A snow-drift about your loins,

Intrepid Margaret, whom even the Dragon
 Found indigestible—
Heavenly Alices of a sadistic
 Wonderland; incorruptible

Lolitas, up in the dock in front of
 A worried Governor,
Declining a minimal pinch of incense
 To poor old Jupiter

(Who came in a shower of chinking guineas
 To Danäe, in his time,
Outbellowing the bulls of Bashan and Hereford—
 But now was past his prime):

I praise, I celebrate, I invoke your refusal,
 In intricate dances who move,
Garlanded with blood-red lilies, for ever
 And ever and ever, in love.

Not being Oedipus

Not being Oedipus he did not question the Sphinx
Nor allow it to question him. He thought it expedient
To make friends and try to influence it.
In this he entirely succeeded,

And continued his journey to Thebes. The abominable thing
Now tame as a kitten (though he was not unaware
That its destructive claws were merely sheathed)
Lolloped along beside him—

To the consternation of the Reception Committee.
It posed a nice problem: he had certainly overcome
But not destroyed the creature—was he or was he not
Entitled to the hand of the Princess

Dowager Jocasta? Not being Oedipus
He saw it as a problem too. For frankly he was not
By natural instinct at all attracted to her.
The question was soon solved—

Solved itself, you might say; for while they argued
The hungry Sphinx, which had not been fed all day,
Sneaked off unobserved, penetrated the royal apartments,
And softly consumed the lady.

So he ascended the important throne of Cadmus,
Beginning a distinguished and uneventful reign.
Celibate, he had nothing to fear from ambitious sons;
Although he was lonely at nights,

With only the Sphinx, curled up upon his eiderdown.
Its body exuded a sort of unearthly warmth
(Though in fact cold-blooded) but its capacity
For affection was strictly limited.

Granted, after his death it was inconsolable,
And froze into its own stone effigy
Upon his tomb. But this was self-love, really—
It felt it had failed in its mission.

While Thebes, by common consent of the people, adopted
His extremely liberal and reasonable constitution,
Which should have enshrined his name—but not being Oedipus,
It vanished from history, as from legend.

The Unpredicted

The goddess Fortune be praised (on her toothed wheel
I have been mincemeat these several years)
Last night, for a whole night, the unpredictable
Lay in my arms, in a tender and unquiet rest—
(I perceived the irrelevance of my former tears)—
Lay, and at dawn departed. I rose and walked the streets,
Where a whitsuntide wind blew fresh, and blackbirds
Incontestably sang, and the people were beautiful.

Send for Lord Timothy

The Squire is in his library. He is rather worried.
Lady Constance has been found stabbed in the locked Blue Room,
    clutching in her hand
A fragment of an Egyptian papyrus. His degenerate half-brother
Is on his way back from New South Wales.
And what was the butler, Glubb,
Doing in the neolithic stone-circle
Up there on the hill, known to the local rustics
From time immemorial as the Nine Lillywhite Boys?
The Vicar is curiously learned
In Renaissance toxicology. A greenish Hottentot,
Armed with a knobkerrie, is concealed in the laurel bushes.

Mother Mary Tiresias is in her parlour.
She is rather worried. Sister Mary Josephus
Has been found suffocated in the scriptorium,
Clutching in her hand a somewhat unspeakable
Central American fetish. Why was the little novice,
Sister Agnes, suddenly struck speechless
Walking in the herbarium? The chaplain, Fr O'Goose,

Is almost too profoundly read
In the darker aspects of fourth-century neo-Platonism.
An Eskimo, armed with a harpoon
Is lurking in the organ loft.

The Warden of St Phenol's is in his study.
He is rather worried. Professor Ostracoderm
Has been found strangled on one of the Gothic turrets,
Clutching in his hand a patchouli-scented
Lady's chiffon handkerchief.
The brilliant undergraduate they unjustly sent down
Has transmitted an obscure message in Greek elegiacs
All the way from Tashkent. Whom was the Domestic Bursar
Planning to meet in that evil smelling
Riverside tavern? Why was the Senior Fellow,
Old Doctor Mousebracket, locked in among the incunabula?
An aboriginal Filipino pygmy,
Armed with a blow-pipe and poisoned darts, is hiding behind
The statue of Pallas Athene.

A dark cloud of suspicion broods over all. But even now
Lord Timothy Pratincole (the chinless wonder
With a brain like Leonardo's) or Chief Inspector Palefox
(Although a policeman, patently a gentleman,
And with a First in Greats) or that eccentric scholar,
Monsignor Monstrance, alights from the chuffing train,
Has booked a room at the local hostelry
(*The Dragon of Wantley*) and is chatting up Mine Host,
Entirely democratically, noting down
Local rumours and folk-lore.

Now read on. The murderer will be unmasked,
The cloud of guilt dispersed, the church clock stuck at three,
And the year always
Nineteen twenty or thirty something,
Honey for tea, and nothing
Will ever really happen again.

Carol for Advent

Let love come under your roof:
  Oh house him, vagrant;
Happy the eaves where he builds a space—
  That light-winged migrant.
Italian airs shall echo and hang
  Under each rafter;
He'll touch into silver foil
  Your peeling plaster,
Set geraniums round your door,
  On hearth lay tinder;
So spread your nets to detain him here—
  Don't let him wander.

Love has no manners, and pays no rent,
  Full of evasions,
Is rude to your influential friends,
  And sneaks the rations;
Sulkily packs his bag and is gone
  At your reproof,
Leaving the plaster peeling still,
  A leaking roof.
Likely, he'll not be back any more
  For tea, nor dinner—
Love is, by nature, impossible—
  Learn your dishonour:

Love, Love is a king uncrowned;
  In their dumb motion
All the republican stars lament
  His abdication.
Once he taught them solfeggios,
  Danced in their choirs,
Till intellectual pride untuned
  The shining spheres.
If he'd be glad of a share of your board,
  Or a place by the fire,
Draw back the bolts, and give up to Love
  Your easiest chair.

The Gifts

Three kings stood before the manger—
And one with a black face—
Holding boxes. Out of the first box,
In bright armour, the spirit of gold
Jumped, a fiery gnome:
'I come from the black mine. I have cheated and corrupted,
A slave to tyrants. Lord, have mercy—
A sign of royalty, a medium of exchange,
I glitter and play in your service.'

Out of the second box streamed forth
In smoke, the spirit of frankincense:
'Before a thousand idolatrous shrines
I've danced my swirling and indefinite dance.
Christ, have mercy—Now at your altar
I burn and sweat myself away in prayer.'

With a rustle of leaves, out of the third box
The spirit of myrrh: 'A bitter herb of the earth,
One of the tares watered by Adam's tears
And mingled with his bread. Lord have mercy—
Making the taste of death
Medicinal, preservative.'

To a Poet a Thousand Years Hence

I who am dead a thousand years
And wrote this crabbed post-classic screed
Transmit it to you—though with doubts
That you possess the skill to read,

Who, with your pink, mutated eyes,
Crouched in the radioactive swamp,
Beneath a leaking shelter, scan
These lines beside a flickering lamp;

Or in some plastic paradise
Of pointless gadgets, if you dwell,
And finding all your wants supplied
Do not suspect it may be Hell.

But does our art of words survive—
Do bards within that swamp rehearse
Tales of the twentieth century,
Nostalgic, in rude epic verse?

Or do computers churn it out—
In lieu of songs of War and Love,
Neat slogans by the State endorsed
And prayers to *Them*, who sit above?

How shall we conquer?—all our pride
Fades like a summer sunset's glow:
Who will read me when I am gone—
For who reads Elroy Flecker now?

Unless, dear poet, you were born,
Like me, a deal behind your time,
There is no reason you should read,
And much less understand, this rhyme.

D. J. ENRIGHT

The Verb 'To Think'

The verb 'to think'
Is represented by the same sign as
'To yearn for', 'to be sad',
'To be unable to forget'

In many cases
'To love' is rendered as 'to like'
(Thus, a man is said to 'like' his wife)

The symbol for 'feeling' also signifies
'A certificate of merit'.
It is meritorious to feel,
Though 'to love' is more often 'to like'

For love comes in two forms alone:
That of a mother for her child
And carnal

The verb 'to do' is homophonous with
The verb 'to pick someone's pocket'.
This, we should note, is not
(As it is in some languages) slang

Slang would be to say that you 'love'
Someone or something when more properly
You 'like'

The verb 'to be'
Seems not to exist.
Yet you cannot say that the verb 'to be'
Does not seem 'to be'

'To be sad' does not imply 'to be',
It implies 'to think'.
'To think' is 'to yearn for', 'to be without',
And to be a man of feeling is to be certified.
'To like' is more common than 'to love'
And 'to be' is most uncommon—

Unwise it is, in the long watches,
When the leaves litter the misty streets,
To be reading a Japanese lexicon
And to be unable to forget.

In Cemeteries

This world a vale of soul-making—
To what intent the finished wares?

Is the ore enforced and fired through
Harsh mills, only to fall aside?

Who is this soulmaster? What say
Do souls have in their made futures?

We mourn the untried young, unmade
In small coffins. What of grown graves?

At times in cemeteries, you hear
Their voices, sad and even-toned,

Almost see the made souls, in their
Curious glory. If you are old.

Poet Wondering What He Is Up To

—A sort of extra hunger,
Less easy to assuage than some
—Or else an extra ear

Listening for a telephone,
Which might or might not ring
In a distant room

—Or else a fear of ghosts
And fear lest ghosts might not appear,
Double superstition, double fear

—To miss and miss and miss,
And then to have, and still to know
That you must miss and miss anew

—It almost sounds like love,
Love in an early stage,
The thing you're talking of

—(but Beauty—no,
Problems of Leisure—no,
Maturity—hardly so)

—And this? Just metaphors
Describing metaphors describing—what?
The eccentric circle of your years.

R-and-R Centre:
An Incident from the Vietnam War

We built a palace for them, made of bedrooms.
We even tracked down playmates for them
(No easy job since prostitutes went out
When self-rule came). We dug a pool,
Constructed shops, and a hut for movies
With benches outside for the girls to wait on.
Serene House was what we called it.
We did our bit in that war.

Air America brought them from the battlefield.
We lifted the girls from the suburbs by buses:
Chinese, Indian, Malay, Eurasian,
Healthy and well-fed and full of play.

There were cameras in plenty, tape-recorders
And binoculars for the soldiers to buy
For the girls; for the girls to sell back
To the shops; for the shops to sell to the soldiers.

Serene House was near the varsity. The G.I.s
Strayed across the campus with Nikons and blank faces:
It was feared they might assault the female students.
They seemed scared of their own cameras.
They looked at nobody; nobody looked at them.
                    That violence down the road—
It was good for business, and we did our bit.
Otherwise it was a vulgar subject.

Once I found a G.I. in the corridor,
Young and dazed, gazing at the notice-boards.
The Misses Menon, Lee, Fernandez, Poh and Noor
Should report for a tutorial at 3 p.m.
Bringing their copies of The Revenger's Tragedy...
If Mr Sharma fails to pass his essay up this week
He will find himself in serious trouble...
The Literary Society seeks help in cutting sandwiches...

He was still there thirty minutes later,
A stunned calf. I asked if I could help.
He shrank away: 'Is it not allowed to stand here?'
The corridor was dingy, walls streaked with bat shit,
Somewhere a typewriter clacked like small arms.
'Is there ... would there be a ... library?'
One of the best in fact in South-East Asia.—
I offered to show him. He trembled
With a furtive pleasure. His only licence
Was to kill, to copulate and purchase cameras.

What sort of books would he like to see?
Outside in the quad he was jumpy,
As if unused to the open. He glanced behind,
Then whispered. Yes, there was something...
Did I think...

What could he be after? The Natural History
Of the Poontang, with Plates, by some defrocked
Medico called Aristotle? How to Get to Sweden
By Kontiki through the Indian Ocean?

'Would they have anything...' A quick look
Round— '... by Cardinal Newman, do you think?'
I left him in the stacks, the *Apologia* in his hands,
He didn't notice when I went away.

Inside Serene House, in the meantime,
Girls galore (such lengths we went to!)
Lolled on the benches, played with binoculars,
Clicked their empty cameras, and groused.

The soldiers were happy to quit Vietnam;
Five days with us, and they were glad to go back,
Rest and recreation, they said, was too much for them.
We weren't surprised when the Americans didn't win.

Anecdote from William IV Street

Entering the publisher's warehouse, a foreign young lady
Asks for Volume XXIV of The Complete Works of Freud.

(This being the Index, at last, which directs the reader
To a wealth of unconscious wants he might else overlook.)

'I also desire,' says she, extending an elegant arm,
'An image of Jesus Christ approximately this high.'

Guest

Is the kitchen tap still dripping?
You should always chain the door at nights.
Soon the roof will need repairing.
What's happening these days at the office?
Too much coffee agitates the nerves.
Now don't forget to spray the roses.
Do see the doctor about those twinges.

But tell me where you are! How is it there?
Are you in pain or bliss? And what is bliss?
Are you lonely? Do we live for ever?
How do you pass the time, if time there is?
Does God exist? Is God loving?
Why must his ways be so mysterious?
Is there a purpose in our living?

*

Why won't you speak of things that matter?
You used to be so wise, so serious.

Now all our talk is roofs and roses
Like neighbours chatting at the corner.

Here wisdom is as common as the air,
Great matters are the ground I tread.
Tell me, what weather are you having?
Are the planes still noisy overhead?
Ask my old mates how work is going—

Don't be angry, dear. This hasn't changed:
Those things we lack are what we covet.
I am the guest, the one to be indulged.

Midstream

Half-way across the racing river
The big man groans: 'So heavy though so small—
You bring my life in danger.'

'There is no wonder,' says the child
Behind his shoulder. 'See, you bear the world
And all its sins as well.'

The other halts. 'What credit do I gain
By this? How long my fame?
Wiser to drop you where I stand.'

'Go on you must,' the child replies.
One thing at least he knows for certain.
'I was not born to drown.'

The other sighs: the world shall have its ride
Then, here's no place to bandy words.
He bends his strength against the flood.

History of World Languages

They spoke the loveliest of languages.
Their tongues entwined in Persian, ran
And fused. Words kissed, a phrase embraced,
Verbs conjugated sweetly. Verse began.
So Eve and Adam lapped each other up
The livelong day, the lyric night.

Of all known tongues most suasive
Was the Snake's. His oratory was Arabic,
Whose simile and rhetoric seduced her
('Sovran of creatures, universal dame').
So potent its appeal—
The apple asked for eating,
To eat it she was game.

Now Gabriel turned up, the scholars say,
Shouting in Turkish. Harsh and menacing,
But late. And sounds like swords were swung.
Fault was underlined, and crime defined.
The gate slammed with the clangour of his tongue.

Eden was gone. A lot of other things
Were won. Or done. Or suffered.
Thorns and thistles, dust and dearth.
The words were all before them, which to choose.
Their tongues now turned to English,
With its colonies of twangs.
And they were down to earth.

HOWARD NEMEROV

To the Rulers

We read and hear about you every day,
What you decide we need, or want, or may
Be made to stand still for ... Now let us pray.

Approaching the year One Thousand of Your Lord,
Men fixed that date for the ending of the world;
Truth and round numbers naturally in accord.

One of society's earlier ego trips,
That hinted only this to your Lordships:
A calendar implies apocalypse.

That passed. And all the reborn sceptics smiled
Over such fancies as could have beguiled
No one who was not but a simple child.

Now, as we near the next millennium,
Reality's caught up with Kingdom Come—
Why wait two dozen years to round the sum?

O Conscript Fathers, sponsors of the draft,
Prospective survivors on the little raft
That when the world sinks will be what is left,

I hear you praying, as your fingers trill
Unnervingly at night beside the pill,
The button, the hot line to the Other Will,

Your prayer, that used to be Caligula's too,
If they all only had one neck ... It's so
Unnecessary and out of date. We do.

September, the First Day of School

1

My child and I hold hands on the way to school,
And when I leave him at the first-grade door
He cries a little but is brave; he does
Let go. My selfish tears remind me how
I cried before that door a life ago.
I may have had a hard time letting go.

Each fall the children must endure together
What every child also endures alone:
Learning the alphabet, the integers,
Three dozen bits and pieces of a stuff
So arbitrary, so peremptory
That worlds invisible and visible

Bow down before it, as in Joseph's dream
The sheaves bowed down and then the stars bowed down
Before the dreaming of a little boy.
That dream got him such hatred of his brothers
As cost the greater part of life to mend,
And yet great kindness came of it in the end.

2

A school is where they grind the grain of thought,
And grind the children who must mind the thought.
It may be those two grindings are but one,
As from the alphabet come Shakespeare's Plays,
As from the integers comes Euler's Law,
As from the whole, inseparably, the lives,

The shrunken lives that have not been set free
By law or by poetic phantasy.
But may they be. My child has disappeared
Behind the schoolroom door. And should I live
To see his coming forth, a life away,
I know my hope, but do not know its form

Nor hope to know it. May the fathers he finds
Among his teachers have a care of him
More than his father could. How that will look
I do not know, I do not need to know.
Even our tears belong to ritual.
But may great kindness come of it in the end.

A Picture

Of people running down the street
Among the cars, a good many people.
You could see that something was up,
Because people in American towns
Don't ordinarily run, they walk,
And not in the street. The camera caught
A pretty girl tilted off-balance
And with her mouth in O amazed;
A man in a fat white shirt, his tie
Streaming behind him, as one flat foot
Went slap on the asphalt—you could see
He was out of breath, but dutifully
Running along with all the others,
Maybe at midday, on Main Street somewhere.

The running faces did not record
Hatred or anger or great enthusiasm
For what they were doing (hunting down
A Negro, according to the caption),
But seemed rather solemn, intent,
With the serious patience of animals
Driven through a gate by some
Urgency out of the camera's range,
On an occasion too serious
For private feeling. The breathless faces
Expressed a religion of running,
A form of ritual exaltation
Devoted to obedience, and
Obedient, it might be, to the Negro,

Who was not caught by the camera
When it took the people in the street
Among the cars, toward some object,
Seriously running.

The Backward Look

As once in heaven Dante looked back down
From happiness and highest certainty
To see afar the little threshing floor
That makes us be so fierce, so we look now
And with what difference from this stony place,
Our sterile satellite with nothing to do,
Not even water in the so-called seas.

No matter the miracles that brought us here,
Consider the end. Even the immense power
Of being bored we brought with us from home
As we brought all things else, even the golf
Balls and the air. What are we doing here,
Foreshadowing the first motels in space?
'They found a desert and they left the Flag.'

From earth we prayed to heaven; being now
In heaven, we reverse the former prayer:
Earth of the cemeteries and cloudy seas,
Our small blue agate in the big black bag,
Earth mother of us, where we make our death,
Earth that the old man knocked on with his staff
Beseeching, 'Leve moder, let me in,'

Hold us your voyagers safe in the hand
Of mathematics, grant us safe return
To where the food is, and the fertile dung,
To generation, death, decay; to war,
Gossip and beer, and bed whether warm or cold,
As from the heaven of technology
We take our dust and rocks and start back down.

Extract from Memoirs

Surely one of my finest days, I'd just
Invented the wheel, and in the afternoon
I stuck a bit of charcoal under the bark
And running it along a wall described
The cycloid curve. When darkness came, I sang
My hymn to the great original wheels of heaven,
And sank into a sleep peopled with gods.

When I communicated my results
To the celestial academies, sending them
Models along with my descriptions, and
Their emissaries came to ask of me
'What are the implications of the "wheel"
For human values?' I was very lofty—
'I made the damn thing go around,' I said,
'You fellows go and figure what it's for.'

The Death of God

The celebrants came chanting 'God is dead!'
And all as one the nations bowed the head
Thanksgiving; knowing not how shrewdly the rod
Would bite the back in the kingdom of dead God.

Money

an introductory lecture

This morning we shall spend a few minutes
Upon the study of symbolism, which is basic
To the nature of money. I show you this nickel.
Icons and cryptograms are written all over
The nickel: one side shows a hunchbacked bison
Bending his head and curling his tail to accommodate
The circular nature of money. Over him arches
UNITED STATES OF AMERICA, and, squinched in

Between that and his rump, E PLURIBUS UNUM,
A Roman reminiscence that appears to mean
An indeterminately large number of things
All of which are the same. Under the bison
A straight line giving him a ground to stand on
Reads FIVE CENTS. And on the other side of our nickel
There is the profile of a man with long hair
And a couple of feathers in the hair; we know
Somehow that he is an American Indian, and
He wears the number nineteen-thirty-six.
Right in front of his eyes the word LIBERTY, bent
To conform with the curve of the rim, appears
To be falling out of the sky Y first; the Indian
Keeps his eyes downcast and does not notice this;
To notice it, indeed, would be shortsighted of him.
So much for the iconography of one of our nickels,
Which is now becoming a rarity and something of
A collectors' item: for as a matter of fact
There is almost nothing you can buy with a nickel,
The representative American Indian was destroyed
A hundred years or so ago, and his descendants'
Relations with liberty are maintained with reservations,
Or primitive concentration camps; while the bison,
Except for a few examples kept in cages,
Is now extinct. Something like that, I think,
Is what Keats must have meant in his celebrated
Ode on a Grecian Urn.
                              Notice, in conclusion,
A number of circumstances sometimes overlooked
Even by experts: (*a*) Indian and bison,
Confined to obverse and reverse of the coin,
Can never see each other; (*b*) they are looking
In opposite directions, the bison past
The Indian's feathers, the Indian past
The bison's tail; (*c*) they are upside down
To one another; (*d*) the bison has a human face
Somewhat resembling that of Jupiter Ammon.
I hope that our studies today will have shown you
Something of the import of symbolism
With respect to the understanding of what is symbolized.

On Being Asked for a Peace Poem

Here is Joe Blow the poet
Sitting before the console of the giant instrument
That mediates his spirit to the world.
He flexes his fingers nervously,
He ripples off a few scale passages
(Shall I compare thee to a summer's day?)
And resolutely readies himself to begin
His poem about the War in Vietnam.

This poem, he figures, is
A sacred obligation: all by himself,
Applying the immense leverage of art,
He is about to stop this senseless war.
So Homer stopped that dreadful thing at Troy
By giving the troops the Iliad to read instead;
So Wordsworth stopped the Revolution when
He felt that Robespierre had gone too far;
So Yevtushenko was invited in the *Times*
To keep the Arabs out of Israel
By smiting once again his mighty lyre.
Joe smiles. He sees the Nobel Prize
Already, and the reading of his poem
Before the General Assembly, followed by
His lecture to the Security Council
About the Creative Process; probably
Some bright producer would put it on TV.
Poetry might suddenly be the in thing.

Only trouble was, he didn't have
A good first line, though he thought that for so great
A theme it would be right to start with O,
Something he would not normally have done,

O

And follow on by making some demands
Of a strenuous sort upon the Muse
Polyhymnia of Sacred Song, that Lady
With the fierce gaze and implacable small smile.

On Certain Wits

*who amused themselves over the simplicity of
Barnett Newman's paintings shown at Bennington
College in May of 1958*

When Moses in Horeb struck the rock,
And water came forth out of the rock,
Some of the people were annoyed with Moses
And said he should have used a fancier stick.

And when Elijah on Mount Carmel brought the rain,
Where the prophets of Baal could not bring rain,
Some of the people said that the rituals of the prophets of Baal
Were aesthetically significant, while Elijah's were very plain.

GEORGE MACKAY BROWN

Old Fisherman with Guitar

A formal exercise for withered fingers.
   The head is bent,
     The eyes half closed, the tune
Lingers
     And beats, a gentle wing the west had thrown
    Against his breakwater wall with salt savage lament.

So fierce and sweet the song on the plucked string,
   Know now for truth
     Those hands have cut from the net
The strong
     Crab-eaten corpse of Jock washed from a boat
    One old winter, and gathered the mouth of Thora to his mouth.

Trout Fisher

Semphill, his hat stuck full of hooks
   Sits drinking ale
      Among the English fishing visitors,
   Probes in detail
         Their faults in casting, reeling, selection of flies.
'Never', he urges, 'do what it says in the books.'
      Then they, obscurely wise,
     Abandon by the loch their dripping oars
And hang their throttled tarnish on the scale.

'Forgive me, every speckled trout,'
   Says Semphill then,
     'And every swan and eider on these waters.
   Certain strange men
      Taking advantage of my poverty
Have wheedled all my subtle loch-craft out
     So that their butchery
    Seem fine technique in the ear of wives and daughters.
And I betray the loch for a white coin.'

Beachcomber

   Monday I found a boot—
   Rust and salt leather.
   I gave it back to the sea, to dance in.

   Tuesday a spar of timber worth thirty bob.
   Next winter
   It will be a chair, a coffin, a bed.

   Wednesday a half can of Swedish spirits.
   I tilted my head.
   The shore was cold with mermaids and angels.

   Thursday I got nothing, seaweed,
   A whale bone,
   Wet feet and a loud cough.

Friday I held a seaman's skull,
Sand spilling from it
The way time is told on kirkyard stones.

Saturday a barrel of sodden oranges.
A Spanish ship
Was wrecked last month at The Kame.

Sunday, for fear of the elders,
I sit on my bum.
What's heaven? A sea chest with a thousand gold coins.

Tea Poems

Chinaman

Water, first creature of the gods.
It dances in many masks.

> For a young child, milk.
> For a peasant, honey and mud.
> For lovers and poets, wine.
> For the man on his way to the block, many well-directed
> spits.
> For an enemy, mixings of blood.
> For the Dragon-god, ichor.
> For a dead friend, a measure of eye-salt.

A courteous man is entertaining strangers
Among his goldfish and willows.
The musician sits in the pavilion door
(His flute is swathed in silk).
An urn is brought to the table by girls.
This is the water of offered friendship.
Notice the agreeable angle of pouring,
The pure ascending columns of vapour,
The precise arrangement of finger and bowl and lip.
Birds make all about those sippers and smilers ceremonies of
very sweet sound.

Smugglers

Midnight. Measured musical cold sea circles.
The yawl struck suddenly!
Oars wrapped the boat in a tangled web.
The boy cried out—Smith gagged him with tarry fingers.
It was no rock, not the fearful face of Hoy.
The boat spun back from pliant timbers.
A maze of voices above us then.
Our skipper growled, 'Where's your light?'
(A lantern was to hang in the cross-trees
For half-an-hour after midnight.
In 'The Arctic Whaler' that had been harped on well.)
'You comm too litt,' a Dutchman said,
The words like a fankle of rusted wire.
'Now we're here,' said Smith,
'And it's only twenty past twelve, lower down
Twelve kegs rum, tobacco as much as you've got,
A poke of snuff for the laird. Have you rolls of silk?'
He drew out silver, rang it in his fist like a bell.
Now we could see green-black curves of hull
And cropped heads hung over the side,
Even the mouth that was torturing the language.
'Fif box tea, bess China.'
With fearful patience our skipper told on his fingers
The smuggler's litany:
Silk, rum, tobacco. The florins chimed in his fist.
'Rum. Tobacco. Silk. That was the understanding.'
Smith swore to God not he nor any Orkneyman
Would risk rope or irons for women's swill.
He pleaded. He praised. He threatened.
Again the stony voice from the star-web above. 'Tea.
Noding but China tea. For silver. Fif box.'

Afternoon Tea

Drank Mrs Leask, sticking out her pinkie.
Drank Mrs Spence, having poured in a tinkle-tinkle of
　　　　　　　　whisky (I've such a bad cold!).
Drank Mrs Halcrow, kissing her cup like a lover.
Drank Mrs Traill, and her Pekinese filthied the floor
　　　　　　　　with bits of biscuit and chocolate.

Drank Mrs Clouston, through rocky jaws.
Drank Mrs Heddle, her mouth dodging a sliver of lemon.
Drank Bella the tea wife, who then read engagements,
     letters, trips and love in
     every circling clay hollow.

The Desertion of the Women and Seals

Howie gave sentence of slaughter
  To the fifty seals on the skerry.
    For a month now the inland lasses,
  Bella, Jemima, Mary
And Hundaskaill's cold beautiful daughter
     —It was said, because of his hard grudging
      fist—
    Denied their kisses.
      A month he watched the drift of seals in the
      west.

A clean gale out of the sunset
  Would cancel scent and sound
    But make those creatures vivid upon the floods.
  'Maybe,' thought Howie, 'a pound
Or thirty shillings, for powder and shot' ...
      He would change the flock to bag and
      slipper and brooch—
    Entrancing gauds—
      And gather the spendthrift girls back to his
      couch.

That sunset, shrug after shrug,
  The seals abandoned the shore.
    Across the sacrificial rock
  Drifted a delicate smirr,
Tresses of haar, a fleece of fog.
      It scarfed in one cold weave the selkie-flight.
    Then, rook by rook,
      Round Howie's impotence drew in the night.

Carpenter

'Workman, what will you make on the bench today?'
I was going to hammer a crib for Mary.

I went into a multitude of green shadows, early.
I came to the marked tree at last.

I struck the root with my axe.
It groaned in the dust.

Mary came over the fields to call me to dinner—
One glance among trembling branches.

The woodman humped it into the village,
A length of gnarls and knots. A bad bargain.

Could it yield, perhaps,
A wheel for the spinning of coarse yarn?

(It looked ancient enough, that tree, to have carried the seed
Of Adam's Fall.)

I could drag out of the darkness of it, I suppose,
A board
Or wash-tub or shelf or churn, for the village women
—Never a crib for Mary's boy.

I let it lie
Among the adzes and squares, in a dazzle of sawdust, all
    morning.

I lopped, later, boughs and branches and bark.

Then a centurion came
And ordered, in the governor's name, a gallows.

That's all it's good for indeed, a tree of death.

Mary stood in the door, curling cold hands like leaves
Round the fruit in her womb.

'Hurry,' she said. 'Let the saw sing.
Soon it will be time for the cradle to rock my boy.'

The Keeper of the Midnight Gate

What are all the hillmen wanting
Around the alehouse door,
The old one carrying a new lamb?
Drink, likely, and women.
Too cold for them up on the hill
With stars snapping their silver fingers.
They've left a boy
To keep the door of the fold, I hope.

What are you? Come closer, maskers.
Melchior. Caspar. Balthazzar.
No names like that hereabout.
O thank you, sir!
Pass on, Daffodil-face, Ebony-face, Nut-face.
Go in peace
With your foreign stinks and the one clang in your sack.

No bite or blanket in that inn, Lady
Unless you're loaded.
Pass on, man. There might be a corner. I know she's done in.
His furnace mouth
Keeps the ox warm.
The publican's fire is the bleeze of gold in his till.

Yes, colonel, the following village women
As far as I know
Have been brought to bed this past week
Or are ripe to the bursting
Or may be in their sweet pains tonight—
Rachel, Tamar, Deborah,
Ruth, Esther,
Sara, Jemima, Judith.
Yes, sir—
Hooves and swords.

An angel, are you?
Mister, let me tell you
The magistrates
Want no comic-singers in this town this winter.
What are the shadows
There, at the fire's edge, with guitars?
I did not think
Angels stank and had holes in their sleeves.
All right, go through, vagrants.
Say, if you're challenged
You came in by another road.

Worms are feasting
Round the fire at the heart of the earth tonight,
Redbreast.
You can have this crumb from my sandwich.
This cold night
You'd be better in the silver cage of a merchant.

RICHARD WILBUR

Advice to a Prophet

When you come, as you soon must, to the streets of our city,
Mad-eyed from stating the obvious,
Not proclaiming our fall but begging us
In God's name to have self-pity,

Spare us all word of the weapons, their force and range,
The long numbers that rocket the mind;
Our slow, unreckoning hearts will be left behind,
Unable to fear what is too strange.

Nor shall you scare us with talk of the death of the race.
How should we dream of this place without us?—
The sun mere fire, the leaves untroubled about us,
A stone look on the stone's face?

Speak of the world's own change. Though we cannot conceive
Of an undreamt thing, we know to our cost
How the dreamt cloud crumbles, the vines are blackened by frost,
How the view alters. We could believe,

If you told us so, that the white-tailed deer will slip
Into perfect shade, grown perfectly shy,
The lark avoid the reaches of our eye,
The jack-pine lose its knuckled grip

On the cold ledge, and every torrent burn
As Xanthus once, its gliding trout
Stunned in a twinkling. What should we be without
The dolphin's arc, the dove's return,

These things in which we have seen ourselves and spoken?
Ask us, prophet, how we shall call
Our natures forth when that live tongue is all
Dispelled, that glass obscured or broken

In which we have said the rose of our love and the clean
Horse of our courage, in which beheld
The singing locust of the soul unshelled,
And all we mean or wish to mean.

Ask us, ask us whether with the worldless rose
Our hearts shall fail us; come demanding
Whether there shall be lofty or long standing
When the bronze annals of the oak-tree close.

Loves of the Puppets

Meeting when all the world was in the bud,
Drawn each to each by instinct's wooden face,
These lovers, heedful of the mystic blood,
Fell glassy-eyed into a hot embrace.

April, unready to be so intense,
Marked time while these outstripped the gentle weather,
Yielded their natures to insensate sense,
And flew apart the more they came together.

Where did they fly? Why, each through such a storm
As may be conjured in a globe of glass
Drove on the colder as the flesh grew warm,
In breathless haste to be at lust's impasse,

To cross the little bridge and sink to rest
In visions of the snow-occluded house
Where languishes, unfound by any quest,
The perfect, small, asphyxiated spouse.

That blizzard ended, and their eyes grew clear,
And there they lay exhausted yet unsated;
Why did their features run with tear on tear,
Until their looks were individuated?

One peace implies another, and they cried
For want of love as if their souls would crack,
Till, in despair of being satisfied,
They vowed at least to share each other's lack.

Then maladroitly they embraced once more,
And hollow rang to hollow with a sound
That tuned the brooks more sweetly than before,
And made the birds explode for miles around.

Shame

It is a cramped little state with no foreign policy,
Save to be thought inoffensive. The grammar of the language
Has never been fathomed, owing to the national habit
Of allowing each sentence to trail off in confusion.
Those who have visited Scusi, the capital city,
Report that the railway-route from Schuldig passes
Through country best described as unrelieved.

Sheep are the national product. The faint inscription
Over the city gates may perhaps be rendered,
'I'm afraid you won't find much of interest here.'
Census-reports which give the population
As zero are, of course, not to be trusted,
Save as reflecting the natives' flustered insistence
That they do not count, as well as their modest horror
Of letting one's sex be known in so many words.
The uniform grey of the nondescript buildings, the absence
Of churches or comfort-stations, have given observers
An odd impression of ostentatious meanness,
And it must be said of the citizens (muttering by
In their ratty sheepskins, shying at cracks in the sidewalk)
That they lack the peace of mind of the truly humble.
The tenor of life is careful, even in the stiff
Unsmiling carelessness of the border-guards
And *douaniers*, who admit, whenever they can,
Not merely the usual carloads of deodorant
But gypsies, g-strings, hashish, and contraband pigments.
Their complete negligence is reserved, however,
For the hoped-for invasion, at which time the happy people
(Sniggering, ruddily naked, and shamelessly drunk)
Will stun the foe by their overwhelming submission,
Corrupt the generals, infiltrate the staff,
Usurp the throne, proclaim themselves to be sun-gods,
And bring about the collapse of the whole empire.

The Undead

Even as children they were late sleepers,
Preferring their dreams, even when quick with monsters,
To the world with all its breakable toys,
Its compacts with the dying;

From the stretched arms of withered trees
They turned, fearing contagion of the mortal,
And even under the plums of summer
Drifted like winter moons.

Secret, unfriendly, pale, possessed
Of the one wish, the thirst for mere survival,
They came, as all extremists do
In time, to a sort of grandeur:

Now, to their Balkan battlements
Above the vulgar town of their first lives,
They rise at the moon's rising. Strange
That their utter self-concern

Should, in the end, have left them selfless:
Mirrors fail to perceive them as they float
Through the great hall and up the staircase;
Nor are the cobwebs broken.

Into the pallid night emerging,
Wrapped in their flapping capes, routinely maddened
By a wolf's cry, they stand for a moment
Stoking the mind's eye

With lewd thoughts of the pressed flowers
And bric-à-brac of rooms with something to lose,—
Of love-dismembered dolls, and children
Buried in quilted sleep.

Then they are off in a negative frenzy,
Their black shapes cropped into sudden bats
That swarm, burst, and are gone. Thinking
Of a thrush cold in the leaves

Who has sung his few summers truly,
Or an old scholar resting his eyes at last,
We cannot be much impressed with vampires,
Colourful though they are;

Nevertheless, their pain is real,
And requires our pity. Think how sad it must be
To thirst always for a scorned elixir,
The salt quotidian blood

Which, if mistrusted, has no savour;
To prey on life forever and not possess it,
As rock-hollows, tide after tide,
Glassily strand the sea.

John Chapman

Beside the Brokenstraw or Licking Creek,
Wherever on the virginal frontier
New men with rutting wagons came to seek
Fresh paradises for the axe to clear,

John Chapman fostered in a girdled glade
Or river-flat new apples for their need,
Till half the farmsteads of the west displayed
White blossom sprung of his authentic seed.

Trusting in God, mistrusting artifice,
He would not graft or bud the stock he sold.
And what, through nature's mercy, came of this?
No sanguine crops of vegetable gold

As in Phaeacia or Hesperides,
Nor those amended fruit of harsher climes
That bowed the McIntosh or Rambo trees,
Ben Davis, Chandler, Jonathan, or Grimes,

But the old *malus malus*, double-dyed,
Eurasia's wilding since the bitter fall,
Sparse upon branches as perplexed as pride,
An apple gnarled, acidulous, and small.

Out of your grave, John Chapman, in Fort Wayne,
May you arise, and flower, and come true.
We meanwhile, being of a spotted strain
And born into a wilder land than you,

Expecting less of natural tree or man
And dubious of working out the brute,
Affix such hopeful scions as we can
To the rude, forked, and ever savage root.

For the Student Strikers

Go talk with those who are rumoured to be unlike you,
And whom, it is said, you are so unlike.
Stand on the stoops of their houses and tell them why
You are out on strike.

It is not yet time for the rock, the bullet, the blunt
Slogan that fuddles the mind toward force.
Let the new sound in our streets be the patient sound
Of your discourse.

Doors will be shut in your faces, I do not doubt.
Yet here or there, it may be, there will start,
Much as the lights blink on in a block at evening,
Changes of heart.

They are your houses; the people are not unlike you;
Talk with them, then, and let it be done
Even for the grey wife of your nightmare sheriff
And the guardsman's son.

The Writer

In her room at the prow of the house—
Where light breaks, and the windows are tossed with linden,
My daughter is writing a story.

I pause in the stairwell, hearing
From her shut door a commotion of typewriter-keys
Like a chain hauled over a gunwale.

Young as she is, the stuff
Of her life is a great cargo, and some of it heavy:
I wish her a lucky passage.

But now it is she who pauses,
As if to reject my thought and its easy figure.
A stillness greatens, in which

The whole house seems to be thinking,
And then she is at it again with a bunched clamour
Of strokes, and again is silent.

I remember the dazed starling
Which was trapped in that very room, two years ago;
How we stole in, lifted a sash

And retreated, not to affright it;
And how for a helpless hour, through the crack of the door,
We watched the sleek, wild, dark

And iridescent creature
Batter against the brilliance, drop like a glove
To the hard floor, or the desk-top,

And wait then, humped and bloody,
For the wits to try it again; and how our spirits
Rose when, suddenly sure,

It lifted off from a chair-back,
Beating a smooth course for the right window
And clearing the sill of the world.

It is always a matter, my darling,
Of life or death, as I had forgotten. I wish
What I wished you before, but harder.

Pangloss's Song
A Comic-Opera Lyric

1

Dear boy, you will not hear me speak
    With sorrow or with rancour
Of what has paled my rosy cheek
    And blasted it with canker;
'Twas Love, great Love, that did the deed
    Through Nature's gentle laws,
And how should ill effects proceed
    From so divine a cause?

Sweet honey comes from bees that sting,
　　As you are well aware;
To one adept in reasoning,
Whatever pains disease may bring
Are but the tangy seasoning
　　To Love's delicious fare.

2

Columbus and his men, they say,
　　Conveyed the virus hither
Whereby my features rot away
　　And vital powers wither;
Yet had they not traversed the seas
　　And come infected back
Why, think of all the luxuries
　　That modern life would lack!

All bitter things conduce to sweet,
　　As this example shows;
Without the little spirochaete
We'd have no chocolate to eat,
Nor would tobacco's fragrance greet
　　The European nose.

3

Each nation guards its native land
　　With cannon and with sentry,
Inspectors look for contraband
　　At every port of entry,
Yet nothing can prevent the spread
　　Of Love's divine disease:
It rounds the world from bed to bed
　　As pretty as you please.

Men worship Venus everywhere,
　　As plainly may be seen;
The decorations which I bear
Are nobler than the Croix de Guerre,
And gained in service of our fair
　　And universal Queen.

To the Etruscan Poets

Dream fluently, still brothers, who when young
Took with your mothers' milk the mother tongue,

In which pure matrix, joining world and mind,
You strove to leave some line of verse behind

Like a fresh track across a field of snow,
Not reckoning that all could melt and go.

KINGSLEY AMIS

The Last War

The first country to die was normal in the evening,
Ate a good but plain dinner, chatted with some friends
Over a glass, and went to bed soon after ten;
And in the morning was found disfigured and dead.
     That was a lucky one.

At breakfast the others heard about it, and kept
Their eyes on their plates. Who was guilty? No one knew,
But by lunch-time three more would never eat again.
The rest appealed for frankness, quietly cocked their guns,
     Declared 'This can't go on.'

They were right. Only the strongest turned up for tea:
The old ones with the big estates hadn't survived
The slobbering blindfold violence of the afternoon.
One killer or many? Was it a gang, or all-against-all?
     Somebody must have known.

But each of them sat there watching the others, until
Night came and found them anxious to get it over.
Then the lights went out. A few might have lived, even then;
Innocent, they thought (at first) it still mattered what
     You had or hadn't done.

They were wrong. One had been lenient with his servants;
Another ran an island brothel, but rarely left it;
The third owned a museum, the fourth a remarkable gun;
The name of a fifth was quite unknown, but in the end
     What was the difference? None.

Homicide, pacifist, crusader, tyrant, adventurer, boor
Staggered about moaning, shooting into the dark.
Next day, to tidy up as usual, the sun came in
When they and their ammunition were all finished,
     And found himself alone.

Upset, he looked them over, to separate, if he could,
The assassins from the victims, but every face
Had taken on the flat anonymity of pain;
And soon they'll all smell alike, he thought, and felt sick,
     And went to bed at noon.

Alternatives

It starts: a white girl in a dark house
Alone with the piano, playing a short song;
Lilies and silk stand quiet, silent the street,
The oil-lamp void of flame. Her long dress
Is rigid at the hem when her arms move
To hush, not urge, the current of the notes.

Below in a red light stoops the murderer,
Black in the cellar among straw and glass.
Dust cracks under his feet, his finger scrapes
The limed wall, then the bottom stair's edge,
And soon the wooden door creaks and yawns;
He shuffles towards the music. It ends.

Let bewilderment tie his hands, I cry,
Some flower in the wallpaper bind his brain,
So that the girl's room never fills with him
And the song never ends, I never hear
The jangling as her body falls awry
And the black lid shuts on her clenched hands.

But something says: Neither or both for you;
The house always empty, or this end.
Or would you rather she smiled as she played,
Hearing a step she knows, and sitting still,
Waited for the hands to move, not round
Her throat, but to her eager breasts?

Beowulf

So, bored with dragons, he lay down to sleep,
Locking for good his massive hoard of words
(Discuss and illustrate), forgetting now
The hope of heathens, muddled thoughts on fate.

Councils would have to get along without him:
The peerless prince had taken his last bribe
(*Lif is loene*); useless now the byrnie
Hard and hand-locked, fit for a baseball catcher.

Only with Grendel was he man-to-man;
Grendel's dam was his only sort of woman
(Weak conjugation). After they were gone
How could he stand the bench-din, the yelp-word?

Someone has told us this man was a hero.
Must we then reproduce his paradigms,
Trace out his rambling regress to his forbears
(An instance of Old English harking-back)?

The Silent Room

In his low-ceilinged oaken room
The corpse finds pastimes of the tomb
    Cramped into scratching nose
    And counting fingers, toes.

Fed up with cackling folderols,
He longs for books, a wireless, dolls,
   Anything that might keep
   His dusty eyes from sleep.

For sleep would bring too-accurate
Dreams of the heavenly garden-fête
   Where the immortals walk,
   Pledged to immortal talk.

Dazed by respect or laughter, he
Would reel from saw to repartee,
   Ecstatic for the first
   Five thousand hours, at worst.

Verbal set-pieces yet would blaze,
And rocket-patterns yet amaze
   For twice as long, to draw
   His eye, not now his awe;

Then to one glow the varied fire
Would sink, the breezy bangs expire
   In mutters, and the bare
   Sticks char in the bright air.

The walkers on the endless lawn
Talk but to hide an endless yawn,
   Stale in the mouth of each
   An old, unwanted speech.

Foreseeing then a second sleep
(Of unknown dreams), the corpse must keep
   Permanently awake,
   And wait for an earthquake.

Earthquakes are few, brief their effect.
But wood soon rots: he can expect
   A far less rare relief
   From boredom, and less brief;

At last, maddened but merry, he
Finds never-tiring company:
   Slug, with foul rhymes to tell;
   Worm, with small-talk from hell.

Nothing to Fear

All fixed: early arrival at the flat
Lent by a friend, whose note says *Lucky sod*;
Drinks on the tray; the cover-story pat
And quite uncheckable; her husband off
Somewhere with all the kids till six o'clock
(Which ought to be quite long enough);
And all worth while: face really beautiful,
Good legs and hips, and as for breasts—my God.
What about guilt, compunction and such stuff?
I've had my fill of all that cock;
It'll wear off, as usual.

Yes, all fixed. Then why this slight trembling,
Dry mouth, quick pulse-rate, sweaty hands,
As though she were the first? No, not impatience,
Nor fear of failure, thank you, Jack.
Beauty, they tell me, is a dangerous thing,
Whose touch will burn, but I'm asbestos, see?
All worth while—it's a dead coincidence
That sitting here, a bag of glands
Tuned up to concert pitch, I seem to sense
A different style of caller at my back,
As cold as ice, but just as set on me.

Langwell

'Now then, what are you up to, Dai?'
'Having a little bonfire, pet.'
   Bowed down under a sack,
With steps deliberate and sly,
His deacon's face full of regret,
   Evans went out the back.

Where no bugger could overlook
He dumped into a blackened bin
   Sheaves of photogravure,
Now and then an ill-printed book,
Letters in female hands: the thin
   Detritus of amour.

Paraffin-heightened flames made ash
Of *Lorraine Burnet in 3-D*
   And *I'm counting the days*
And *the head girl took off her sash*
And *Naturist* and *can we be*
   Together for always?

He piped an eye—only the smoke—
Then left that cooling hecatomb
   And dashed up to his den,
Where the real hot stuff was. A bloke
Can't give any old tripe house-room:
   Style's something else again.

Shitty

Look thy last on all things shitty
   While thou'rt at it: soccer stars,
Soccer crowds, bedizened bushheads
   Jerking over their guitars.

German tourists, plastic roses,
   Face of Mao and face of Ché,
Women wearing curtains, blankets,
   Beckett at the ICA,

High-rise blocks and action paintings,
   Sculptures made from wire and lead:
Each of them a sight more lovely
   Than the screens around your bed.

Reborn

'Hell' said the Devil, as it might have been,
'Is eternal banishment from God
   And from the whole of his creation.
Your sentence starts now. This is your cell.'

'Even mortal prisoners' I said
'On shorter terms, are allowed more than this
   Featureless box, which excludes me
From man's creation too. Is that entailed?'

The Devil, or whoever it was, said
'I am not a barbarian. This I grant:
   A house literally nowhere,
Solitary confinement, but with things.

'You are denied visitors and pets
And all extrinsic aids, like news or drink;
   But art, man's sole true creation,
I allow in whatever form you choose.'

'I see the house is finite' I said
'And also confined; so books are my choice.'
   'Agreed' he said. 'You will know them
All by heart in a million years or so.'

Returned after some such interval,
'How do you find eternity?' asked
   The Devil, or a similar being.
'Oh, that. All right' I said, and shut my book.

'Take this—most instructive, and about you,
Oddly enough, in more than one role:
   Paradise Lost. Of course you know it.'
'And so must you these days. Every word.'

'Not quite. I spent some millennia
Learning how to annul memory—that
   Much-advertised but precarious
Sole weapon of yours—just as I wish,

'And so am free of you and eternity,
And can do more than either of you,
   Who cannot annul a sparrow's footprint
Once it is a fact. May I read on?'

'To hell with you. No books and no house:
Nothing. No things. Just you in the dark.'
   'Not a barbarian? Continue,
While I every moment am reborn.'

DONALD DAVIE

A Christening

What we do best is breed:
August Bank Holiday, whole
Populations explode

Across the wolds and in a slot
Of small cars pullulate
By couples. Millington Meadows

Flower with campstools. At
Beverley the font
Has a cover carved like a goblet.

The new baby is fed.
I stumble back to bed.
I hear the owls for a long time

Hunting. Or are they never
In the winter grey of before dawn,
Those pure long quavers,

Cries of love? I put my arms around you.
Small mice freeze among tussocks.
The baby wails in the next room.

Upstairs Mrs Ramsden
Dies, and the house
Is full of the cries of the newborn.

In red and smoky wood
A follower of Wren
Carved it at Beverley:

The generous womb that drops
Into the sanctified water immediate fruit.
What we do best is breed.

The Priory of St Saviour, Glendalough

A carving on the jamb of an embrasure,
'Two birds affronted with a human head
Between their beaks', is said to be
'Uncertain in its significance but
A widely known design.' I'm not surprised.

For the guidebook cheats: the green road it advises
In fact misled; and a ring of trees
Screened in the end the level knoll on which
St Saviour's, like a ruin on a raft,
Surged through the silence.

I burst through brambles, apprehensively
Crossed an enormous meadow. I was there.
Could holy ground be such a foreign place?
I climbed the wall, and shivered. There flew out
Two birds affronted by my human face.

Barnsley and District

Judy Sugden! Judy, I made you caper
With rage when I said that the British Fascist
Sheet your father sold was a jolly good paper

And you had agreed and I said, Yes, it holds
Vinegar, and everyone laughed and imagined
The feel of the fish and chips warm in its folds.

That was at Hood Green. Under our feet there shone
The modest view, its slagheaps amethyst
In distance and white walls the sunlight flashed on.

If your father's friends had succeeded, or if I
Had canvassed harder for the Peace Pledge Union,
A world of difference might have leapt to the eye

In a scene like this which shows in fact no change.
That must have been the summer of '39.
I go back sometimes, and find nothing strange –

Short-circuiting of politics engages
The Grammar School masters still. Their bright sixth-formers sport
Nuclear Disarmament badges.

And though at Stainborough no bird's-nesting boy
Nor trespasser from the town in a Sunday suit
Nor father twirling a stick can now enjoy

Meeting old Captain Wentworth, who in grey
And ancient tweeds, gun under arm, keen-eyed
And unemployable, would give a gruff Good-day,

His rhododendrons and his laurel hedge
And tussocked acres are no more unkempt
Now that the Hall is a Teachers' Training College.

The parish primary school where a mistress once
Had every little Dissenter stand on the bench
With hands on head, to make him out a dunce;

Black backs of flourmills, wafer-rusted railings
Where I ran and ran from colliers' boys in jerseys,
Wearing a blouse to show my finer feelings—

These still stand. And Bethel and Zion Baptist,
Sootblack on pavements foul with miners' spittle
And late-night spew and violence, persist.

George Arliss was on at the Star, and Janet Gaynor
Billed at the Alhambra, but the warmth
Was no more real then, nor the manners plainer.

And politics has no landscape. The Silesian
Seam crops out in prospects felt as deeply
As any of these, with as much or as little reason.

To a Teacher of French

Sir, you were a credit to whatever
Ungrateful slate-blue skies west of the Severn
Hounded you out to us. With white, cropped head,
Small and composed, and clean as a Descartes
From as it might be Dowlais, 'Fiery' Evans
We knew you as. You drilled and tightly lipped
Le futur parfait dans le passé like
The Welsh Guards in St James's, your pretence
Of smouldering rage an able sergeant-major's.

We jumped to it all right whenever each
Taut smiling question fixed us. Then it came:
Crash! The ferrule smashed down on the first
Desk of the file. You whispered: *Quelle bêtise!*
Ecoutez, s'il vous plaît, de quelle bêtise
On est capable!
           Yet you never spoke
To us of poetry; it was purely language,
The lovely logic of its tenses and
Its accidence that, mutilated, moved you
To rage or outrage that I think was not
At all times simulated. It would never
Do in our days, dominie, to lose
Or seem to lose your temper. And besides
Grammarians are a dying kind, the day
Of histrionic pedagogy's over.

You never taught me Ronsard, no one did,
But you gave me his language. He addressed
The man who taught him Greek as *Toi qui dores*
(His name was Jean Dorat) *la France de l'or*.
I couldn't turn a phrase like that on 'Evans';
And yet you gild or burnish something as,
At fifty in the humidity of Touraine,
Time and again I profit by your angers.

A Meeting of Cultures

Iced with a vanilla
Of dead white stone, the Palace
Of Culture is a joke

Or better, a vast villa
In some unimaginable suburb
Of Perm or Minsk.

Ears wave and waggle
Over the poignant Vistula,
Horns of a papery stone,

Not a wedding-cake but its doily!
The Palace of Culture sacks
The centre, the dead centre

Of Europe's centre, Warsaw.
The old town,
Rebuilt, is a clockwork toy.

I walked abroad in it,
Charmed and waylaid
By a nursery joy:

Hänsel's and Gretel's city!
Their house of gingerbread
That lately in

Horrific forest glooms
Of Germany
Bared its ferocity

Anew, resumes its gilt
For rocking-horse rooms
In Polish rococo.

Diseased imaginations
Extant in Warsaw's stone
Her air makes sanative.

How could a D.S.O.
Of the desert battles live,
If it were otherwise,

In his wooden cabin
In a country wood
In the heart of Warsaw

As the colonel did, who for
The sake of England took
Pains to be welcoming?

More jokes then. And the wasps humming
Into his lady's jam
That we ate with a spoon

Out in the long grass. Shades,
Russian shades out of old slow novels,
Lengthened the afternoon.

G.M.B.
(10.7.77)

Old oak, old timber, sunk and rooted
 In the organic cancer
Of Devon soil, the need she had
 You could not answer.

Old wash and wump, the narrow seas
   Mindlessly breaking
She scanned lifelong; and yet the tide
   There's no mistaking

She mistook. She never thought,
   It seems, that the soft thunder
She heard nearby, the pluck and slide,
   Might tow her under.

I have as much to do with the dead
   And the dying, as with the living
Nowadays; and failing them is
   Past forgiving.

As soon be absolved for that, as if
   A tree, or a sea, should be shriven;
And yet the truth is, fail we must
   And be forgiven.

PHILIP LARKIN

The Explosion

On the day of the explosion
Shadows pointed towards the pithead:
In the sun the slagheap slept.

Down the lane came men in pitboots
Coughing oath-edged talk and pipe-smoke,
Shouldering off the freshened silence.

One chased after rabbits; lost them;
Came back with a nest of lark's eggs;
Showed them; lodged them in the grasses.

So they passed in beards and moleskins,
Fathers, brothers, nicknames, laughter,
Through the tall gates standing open.

At noon, there came a tremor; cows
Stopped chewing for a second; sun,
Scarfed as in a heat-haze, dimmed.

The dead go on before us, they
Are sitting in God's house in comfort,
We shall see them face to face—

Plain as lettering in the chapels
It was said, and for a second
Wives saw men of the explosion

Larger than in life they managed—
Gold as on a coin, or walking
Somehow from the sun towards them,

One showing the eggs unbroken.

Ambulances

Closed like confessionals, they thread
Loud noons of cities, giving back
None of the glances they absorb.
Light glossy grey, arms on a plaque,
They come to rest at any kerb:
All streets in time are visited.

Then children strewn on steps or road,
Or women coming from the shops
Past smells of different dinners, see
A wild white face that overtops
Red stretcher-blankets momently
As it is carried in and stowed,

And sense the solving emptiness
That lies just under all we do,
And for a second get it whole,
So permanent and blank and true.
The fastened doors recede. *Poor soul,*
They whisper at their own distress;

For borne away in deadened air
May go the sudden shut of loss
Round something nearly at an end,
And what cohered in it across
The years, the unique random blend
Of families and fashions, there

At last begin to loosen. Far
From the exchange of love to lie
Unreachable inside a room
The traffic parts to let go by
Brings closer what is left to come,
And dulls to distance all we are.

Posterity

Jake Balokowsky, my biographer,
Has this page microfilmed. Sitting inside
His air-conditioned cell at Kennedy
In jeans and sneakers, he's no call to hide
Some slight impatience with his destiny:
'I'm stuck with this old fart at least a year;

I wanted to teach school in Tel Aviv,
But Myra's folks'—he makes the money sign—
'Insisted I got tenure. When there's kids—'
He shrugs. 'It's stinking dead, the research line;
Just let me put this bastard on the skids,
I'll get a couple of semesters leave

To work on Protest Theater.' They both rise,
Make for the Coke dispenser. 'What's he like?
Christ, I just told you. Oh, you know the thing,
That crummy textbook stuff from Freshman Psych,
Not out of kicks or something happening—
One of those old-type *natural* fouled-up guys.'

Poetry of Departures

Sometimes you hear, fifth-hand,
As epitaph:
He chucked up everything
And just cleared off,
And always the voice will sound
Certain you approve
This audacious, purifying,
Elemental move.

And they are right, I think.
We all hate home
And having to be there:
I detest my room,
Its specially-chosen junk,
The good books, the good bed,
And my life, in perfect order:
So to hear it said

He walked out on the whole crowd
Leaves me flushed and stirred,
Like *Then she undid her dress*
Or *Take that you bastard*;
Surely I can, if he did?
And that helps me stay
Sober and industrious.
But I'd go today,

Yes, swagger the nut-strewn roads,
Crouch in the fo'c'sle
Stubbly with goodness, if
It weren't so artificial,
Such a deliberate step backwards
To create an object:
Books; china; a life
Reprehensibly perfect.

As Bad as a Mile

Watching the shied core
Striking the basket, skidding across the floor,
Shows less and less of luck, and more and more

Of failure spreading back up the arm
Earlier and earlier, the unraised hand calm,
The apple unbitten in the palm.

Mr Bleaney

'This was Mr Bleaney's room. He stayed
The whole time he was at the Bodies, till
They moved him.' Flowered curtains, thin and frayed,
Fall to within five inches of the sill,

Whose window shows a strip of building land,
Tussocky, littered. 'Mr Bleaney took
My bit of garden properly in hand.'
Bed, upright chair, sixty-watt bulb, no hook

Behind the door, no room for books or bags—
'I'll take it.' So it happens that I lie
Where Mr Bleaney lay, and stub my fags
On the same saucer-souvenir, and try

Stuffing my ears with cotton-wool, to drown
The jabbering set he egged her on to buy.
I know his habits—what time he came down,
His preference for sauce to gravy, why

He kept on plugging at the four aways—
Likewise their yearly frame: the Frinton folk
Who put him up for summer holidays,
And Christmas at his sister's house in Stoke.

But if he stood and watched the frigid wind
Tousling the clouds, lay on the fusty bed
Telling himself that this was home, and grinned,
And shivered, without shaking off the dread

That how we live measures our own nature,
And at his age having no more to show
Than one hired box should make him pretty sure
He warranted no better, I don't know.

Dublinesque

Down stucco sidestreets,
Where light is pewter
And afternoon mist
Brings lights on in shops
Above race-guides and rosaries,
A funeral passes.

The hearse is ahead,
But after there follows
A troop of streetwalkers
In wide flowered hats,
Leg-of-mutton sleeves,
And ankle-length dresses.

There is an air of great friendliness,
As if they were honouring
One they were fond of;
Some caper a few steps,
Skirts held skilfully
(Someone claps time),

And of great sadness also.
As they wend away
A voice is heard singing
Of Kitty, or Katy,
As if the name meant once
All love, all beauty.

The Card-Players

Jan van Hogspeuw staggers to the door
And pisses at the dark. Outside, the rain
Courses in cart-ruts down the deep mud lane.
Inside, Dirk Dogstoerd pours himself some more,
And holds a cinder to his clay with tongs,
Belching out smoke. Old Prijck snores with the gale,
His skull face firelit; someone behind drinks ale,
And opens mussels, and croaks scraps of songs
Towards the ham-hung rafters about love.
Dirk deals the cards. Wet century-wide trees
Clash in surrounding starlessness above
This lamplit cave, where Jan turns back and farts,
Gobs at the grate, and hits the queen of hearts.

Rain, wind and fire! The secret, bestial peace!

The Dedicated

Some must employ the scythe
Upon the grasses,
That the walks be smooth
For the feet of the angel.
Some keep in repair
The locks, that the visitor
Unhindered passes
To the innermost chamber.

Some have for endeavour
To sign away life
As lover to lover,
Or a bird using its wings
To fly to the fowler's compass,
Not out of willingness,
But being aware of
Eternal requirings.

And if they have leave
To pray, it is for contentment
If the feet of the dove
Perch on the scythe's handle,
Perch once, and then depart
Their knowledge. After, they wait
Only the colder advent,
The quenching of candles.

Days

What are days for?
Days are where we live.
They come, they wake us
Time and time over.
They are to be happy in:
Where can we live but days?

Ah, solving that question
Brings the priest and the doctor
In their long coats
Running over the fields.

Cut Grass

Cut grass lies frail:
Brief is the breath
Mown stalks exhale.
Long, long the death

It dies in the white hours
Of young-leafed June
With chestnut flowers,
With hedges snowlike strewn,

White lilac bowed,
Lost lanes of Queen Anne's lace,
And that high-builded cloud
Moving at summer's pace.

VERNON SCANNELL

The Old Books

They were beautiful, the old books, beautiful I tell you.
You've no idea, you young ones with all those machines;
There's no point in telling you; you wouldn't understand.
You wouldn't know what the word beautiful means.
I remember Mr Archibald—the old man, not his son—
He said to me right out: 'You've got a beautiful hand,
Your books are a pleasure to look at, real works of art.'
You youngsters with your ball-points wouldn't understand.
You should have seen them, my day book, and sales ledger:
The unused lines were always cancelled in red ink.
You wouldn't find better kept books in the City;
But it's no good talking: I know what you all think:
'He's old. He's had it. He's living in the past,
The poor old sod.' Well, I don't want your pity.
My forty-seventh Christmas with the firm. Too much to drink.
You're staring at me, pitying. I can tell by your looks.
You'll never know what it was like, what you've missed.
You'll never know. My God, they were beautiful, the old books.

The Moth

'The moth has got into it.'
I heard the woman speak from another room.
What the moth had entered I did not know,
Nor why that singular creature should own
The definite article before its name.
The woman said 'The moth' as she might say
'The dog', a minor member of the family,
Yet in my mind's commodious bestiary
There was no space for such a stray.
I knew that it was time for me to go.
I crept away. I left some clothes:
A sweater, vest, two pairs of socks with holes.

Sometimes I think of the moth in its cage,
Its great khaki wings heavy with dust
And the woman feeding it, pushing through the bars
The tasteless garments to assuage
An appetite that must
Make do with such rough food as she, too, must.

Dead Dog

One day I found a lost dog in the street.
The hairs about its grin were spiked with blood,
And it lay still as stone. It must have been
A little dog, for though I only stood
Nine inches for each one of my four years
I picked it up and took it home. My mother
Squealed, and later father spaded out
A bed and tucked my mongrel down in mud.

I can't remember any feeling but
A moderate pity, cool not swollen-eyed;
Almost a godlike feeling now it seems.
My lump of dog was ordinary as bread.
I have no recollection of the school
Where I was taught my terror of the dead.

Words and Monsters

When he was eight years old he had become
Hungry for words, and he would munch his way
Through comics, adverts, anything with some
Printed food to hold the pangs at bay.
His friends would hoard up birds' eggs, shells or stamps,
But he collected words. One day he saw—
As he walked lonely down the town's main street—
A poster done in thunderous colours, raw
And red as flesh of newly butchered meat:

A picture of a lady, mouth distressed,
Eyes wild and fat with fear; and, underneath,
These glaring words: *THE ABYSMAL BRUTE—The Best
Movie of the Year.* He felt his teeth
Bite on the word *abysmal* as you test
The goodness of a coin. This one was fine.
He took it home to add it to the rest
Of his collection. He liked its shape and shine
But did not know its worth. Inside his head
Its echo rang. He asked his mother what
Abysmal meant. 'Bottomless,' she said.

The Abysmal Brute was grunting in the hot
Dark outside, would follow him to bed.

Incendiary

That one small boy with a face like pallid cheese
And burnt-out little eyes could make a blaze
As brazen, fierce and huge, as red and gold
And zany yellow as the one that spoiled
Three thousand guineas' worth of property
And crops at Godwin's Farm on Saturday
Is frightening—as fact and metaphor:
An ordinary match intended for
The lighting of a pipe or kitchen fire
Misused may set a whole menagerie
Of flame-fanged tigers roaring hungrily.
And frightening, too, that one small boy should set
The sky on fire and choke the stars to heat
Such skinny limbs and such a little heart
Which would have been content with one warm kiss
Had there been anyone to offer this.

Six Reasons for Drinking

1

'It relaxes me,' he said,
Though no one seemed to hear.
He was relaxed: his head
Among fag-ends and spilt beer.
Free from all strain and care
With nonchalance he waved
Both feet in the pungent air.

2

'I drink to forget.'
But he remembers
Everything, the lot:
What hell war was,
Betrayal, lost
Causes best forgot.
The only thing he can't recall
Is how often before we've heard it all.

3

'It gives me the confidence I lack,'
He confided with a grin
Slapping down ten new pennies
For a pint and a double gin.

4

'It makes me witty fit to burst,'
He said from his sick-bed. 'There's nothing worse
Than seeing a man tongue-tied by thirst.
Hey! Bring me a bed-pun quickly, nurse!'

5

From behind a fierce imperialistic stare
He said, 'The reason's plain. Because it's there!'

6

'It releases your inhibitions,
Lets you be free and gay!'
The constable told him brusquely
To put it away.

Jailbird

His plumage is dun,
Talons long but blunt.
His appetite is indiscriminate.
He has no mate and sleeps alone
In a high nest built of brick and steel.
He sings at night
A long song, sad and silent.
He cannot fly.

The Discriminator

I can afford to discriminate
In the matter of female pulchritude,
Though I will readily admit
That, to many observers, my attitude
Must seem pernickety, even absurd.
This, of course, is not the way of it
Though I understand why the less fastidious
Call me poseur or hypocrite.
Take that girl over there—fine tits
I will concede, but her ankles are too thick.
Her eyes are pleasing, opalescent, dark
As a glass of stout held up to light,
But the mouth is so slack as to make you sick.
Her blonde companion, I must remark,
Is far too wide in the hips. She might
Be pretty enough, but in a style
So commonplace you must have seen
The same face in a hundred city streets.
I note your disbelieving smile.
Don't be deceived, young man; the time
Will come when you, too, will apply
The cool astringent judgement you observe
Me exercising now. Your eye
Will be, as mine, fastidious and cold,
And you will then display the fine
Wisdom and discernment of the old,

Enjoy the wages of experience,
Reject expediency and compromise
With the stern impartiality of age
And age's impotence.

Five Domestic Interiors

1

The lady of the house is on her benders;
She's scrubbed and mopped until her knees are sore.
She rests a second as her husband enters,
Then says, 'Look out! Don't walk on my clean floor.'
He looks up at the slick flies on the ceiling
And shakes his head, and goes back through the door.

2

She holds her chuckling baby to her bosom
And says, 'My honey-pie, my sugar bun,
Does Mummy love her scrumptious little darling?
You're lovely, yes, you are, my precious one!'
But when the little perisher starts bawling
She says, 'For God's sake listen to your son.'

3

Sandbagged by sleep at last the kids lie still.
The kitchen clock is nodding in warm air.
They spread the Sunday paper on the table
And each draws up a comfortable chair.
He turns the pages to the crossword puzzle,
Nonplussed they see a single large black square.

4

The radio is playing dated music
With lilac tune and metronomic beat.
She smiles and says, 'Remember that one, darling?
The way we used to foxtrot was a treat.'
But they resist the momentary temptation
To resurrect slim dancers on glib feet.

5

In bed his tall enthusiastic member
Receives warm welcome, and a moist one too.
She whispers, 'Do you love me? More than ever?'
And, panting, he replies, 'Of course I do.'
Then as she sighs and settles close for slumber
He thinks with mild surprise that it is true.

DANNIE ABSE

Down the M4

Me! dutiful son going back to South Wales, this time afraid
to hear my mother's news. Too often, now, her friends are disrobed,
and my aunts and uncles, too, go into the hole, one by one.
The beautiful face of my mother is in its ninth decade.

Each visit she tells me the monotonous story of clocks.
'Oh dear,' I say, or 'how funny,' till I feel my hair turning grey
for I've heard that perishable one two hundred times before—
like the rugby 'amateurs' with golden sovereigns in their socks.

Then the Tawe ran fluent and trout-coloured over stones stonier,
more genuine; then Annabella, my mother's mother, spoke Welsh
with such an accent the village said, 'Tell the truth, fach,
you're no Jewess. *They're* from the Bible. *You're* from Patagonia!'

I'm driving down the M4 again under bridges that leap
over me then shrink in my side mirror. Ystalyfera is farther
than smoke and God further than all distance known. I whistle
no hymn but an old Yiddish tune my mother knows. It won't keep.

Tales of Shatz

Meet Rabbi Shatz in his correct black homburg.
The cheder boys call him Ginger.
If taller than 5 foot you're taller than he;
also taller than his father,
grandfather, great grandfather.

Meet Ruth Shatz, née Ruth Pinsky,
short statured too, straight backed.
In her stockinged feet
her forehead against his,
her eyes smile into his.
And again on the pillow, later.
Ah those sexy red-headed Pinskys
of Leeds and Warsaw: her mother,
grandmother, great grandmother!

Mrs Shatz resembles Rabbi Shatz's mother.
Rabbi Shatz resembles Mrs Shatz's father.
Strangers mistake them for brother, sister.

At University, Solly Shatz, their morning star,
suddenly secular, all 6 foot of him—
a black-haired centre-forward on Saturdays—
switches studies from Theology to Genetics.

*

A certain matron of Golders Green,
fingering amber beads about her neck,
approaches Rabbi Shatz.
When I was a small child, she thrills,
once, just once, God the Holy One
came through the curtains of my bedroom.
What on earth has he been doing since?

Rabbi Shatz turns, he squints,
he stands on one leg
hoping for the inspiration of a Hillel.
The Holy One, he answers, blessed be He,
has been waiting, waiting patiently,
till you see Him again.

*

Consider the mazzle of Baruch Levy
who changed his name to Barry Lee,
who moved to Esher, Surrey,
who sent his four sons—Matthew, Mark,
Luke and John—to boarding school,
who had his wife's nose fixed,
who, blinking in the Gents,
turned from the writing on the wall
and later, still blinking, joined the golf club.

With new friend, Colonel Owen,
first game out, under vexed clouds,
thunder detonated without rain,
lightning stretched without thunder,
and near the 2nd hole,
where the darker green edged
to the shaved lighter green,
both looked up terrified.
Barbed fire zagged towards them
to strike dead instantly
Mostyn Owen, Barry Lee's opponent.
What luck that Colonel Owen
(as Barry discovered later)
once was known as Moshe Cohen.

Now, continued Rabbi Shatz,
recall how even the sorrows of Job
had a happy ending.

*

Being a religious man Shatz adored riddles.
Who? he asked his impatient wife.
Who like all men came into this world
with little fists closed, departed
with large hands open, yet on walking
over snow and away from sunsets
followed no shadow in front of him,
left no footprint behind him?

You don't know either, opined his wife.
You and your Who? Who?
Are you an owl?
Why do you always pester me with riddles
you don't know the answer of?

Rabbi Shatz for some reason wanted to cry.
If I knew the answers, he whispered,
would my questions still be riddles?
And he tiptoed away, closed the door
so softly behind him
as if on a sleeping dormitory.

Often when listening to music
before a beautiful slow movement
recaptured him, Shatz would blank out,
hear nothing. So now, too, in his lit study
as night rain tilted outside
across dustbins in the lane
he forgot why his lips moved, his body swayed.

Florida

Not one poem about an animal, she said,
in five, six volumes of poetry,
not one about The Peaceable Kingdom.
An accusation. Was she from the R.S.P.C.A.?
Your contemporaries have all composed
inspired elegies for expired beasts;
told of salmon flinging themselves up
the sheer waterfall; cold crows,
in black rags, loitering near motorways;
parables of foxes and pheasants,
owls and voles, mice and moles,
cats, bats, pigs, pugs, snails, quails;
so why can't you write one, just one *haiku*?
Oh, I said, Oh!—then wondered if she knew
the story of the starving dowager.

The lady looked as solemn as No.
Well, during the French Revolution,
the dowager, becoming thinner and thinner,
invited other lean aristocrats to dinner.
That night the guests saw (I continued)
slowly roasting on a rotating spit
the dowager's own poodle, Fido,
who proved to be most succulent.
So they made a feast of it.
Afterwards, the dowager sighed,
fingering the pearls about her neck,
sighed and said in noble French,
(I translate) What a damn shame Fido
isn't alive to eat up all those nice
crunchy bones left upon the plate.

My story over, I waited for applause. We'd
never cease from crying, she said,
if *one* insect could relate its misery.
Quite, I said, looking at my paws.
In Florida I saw a floating log
change and chase and swallow up
a barking dog. Hell, I said, an alligator?
A museum snake, too, in Gainesville,
Murder City, I can't forget,
poor black priapus in an empty case
lifting up its head for food not there.
With your gift I'd make a poem out of that.
So try, she said, do try and write
a creature poem and call it *Florida*.
I closed my eyes and she receded.

I thought of tigers and of Blake,
I thought of Fido and his bones.
No, no, she cried, think of Florida.
I saw the hotels of Miami Beach,
I heard waves collapsing ceaselessly.
No, no, she said, think again, think
of Florida, its creature kingdom.
Like a TV screen my imagination
lit up to startle the ghost of Blake
with my own eidetic ads for Florida:

first, that black frustrated snake erect,
then two grapefruit inside a brassière.
Open your eyes, the lady screamed, *wake up*.
I'm a poor bifurcated animal, I apologized.
Eagle beagle, bug grub, boar bear.

Public Library

Who, in the public library, one evening after rain,
amongst the polished tables and linoleum,
stands bored under blank light to glance at these pages?
Whose absent mood, like neon glowing in the night,
is conversant with wet pavements, nothing to do?

Neutral, the clock-watching girl stamps out the date,
a forced celebration, a posthumous birthday,
her head buttered by the drizzling library lamps;
yet the accident of words, too, can light the semi-dark
should the reader lead them home, generously journey,
later to return, perhaps leaving a bus ticket as a bookmark.

Who wrote in margins hieroglyphic notations,
that obscenity, deleted this imperfect line?
Read by whose hostile eyes, in what bed-sitting rooms,
in which rainy, dejected railway stations?

Peachstone

I do not visit his grave. He is not there.
Out of hearing, out of reach. I miss him here,
seeing hair grease at the back of a chair
near a firegrate where his spit sizzled,
or noting, in the cut-glass bowl, a peach.

For that night his wife brought him a peach,
his favourite fruit, while the sick light glowed,
and his slack, dry mouth sucked, sucked, sucked,
with dying eyes closed—perhaps for her sake—
till bright as blood the peachstone showed.

Watching a Cloud

A lacy mobile changing lazily
its animals, unstable faces, till
I imagine an angel, his vapours sailing
asleep at different speeds. My failing:

to see similes, cloud as something other.
Is all inspiration correspondences?
Machinery of cloud and angel both are silent,
both insubstantial. Neither violent.

And, truly, if one shining angel existed
what safer than the camouflage of a cloud?
There's deranged wind up there. God its power!
Let me believe in angels for an hour.

Let sunlight fade on walls and a huge blind
be drawn faster than a horse across this field.
I want to be theological, stare through
raw white angel-fabric at holy bits of blue.

Let long theatrical beams slant down
to stage-strike that hill into religion. Me too!
An angel drifts to the East, its edges burning;
sunny sunlight on stony stone returning.

ANTHONY HECHT

'It Out-Herods Herod.
Pray you, Avoid it.'

Tonight my children hunch
Toward their Western, and are glad
As, with a Sunday punch,
The Good casts out the Bad.

And in their fairy tales
The warty giant and witch
Get sealed in doorless jails
And the match-girl strikes it rich.

I've made myself a drink.
The giant and witch are set
To bust out of the clink
When my children have gone to bed.

All frequencies are loud
With signals of despair;
In flash and morse they crowd
The rondure of the air.

For the wicked have grown strong,
Their numbers mock at death,
Their cow brings forth its young,
Their bull engendereth.

Their very fund of strength,
Satan, bestrides the globe;
He stalks its breadth and length
And finds out even Job.

Yet by quite other laws
My children make their case;
Half God, half Santa Claus,
But with my voice and face,

A hero comes to save
The poorman, beggarman, thief,
And make the world behave
And put an end to grief.

And that their sleep be sound
I say this childermas
Who could not, at one time,
Have saved them from the gas.

Pig

In the manger of course were cows and the Child Himself
    Was like unto a lamb
Who should come in the fullness of time on an ass's back
    Into Jerusalem

And all things be redeemed—the suckling babe
    Lie safe in the serpent's home
And the lion eat straw like the ox and roar its love
    to Mark and to Jerome

And God's Peaceable Kingdom return among them all
    Save one full of offence
Into which the thousand fiends of a human soul
    Were cast and driven hence

And the one thus cured gone up into the hills
    To worship and to pray:
O Swine that takest away our sins
    That takest away

The Cost

'Why, let the stricken deer go weep,
    The hart ungallèd play ...'

Think how some excellent, lean torso hugs
    The brink of weight and speed,
Coasting the margins of those rival tugs
    Down the thin path of friction,
The athlete's dancing vectors, the spirit's need,
    And muscle's cleanly diction,

Clean as a Calder, whose interlacing ribs
    Depend on one another,
Or a keen heeling of tackle, fluttering jibs
    And slotted centreboards,
A fleet of breasting gulls riding the smother
    And puzzle of heaven's wards.

Instinct with joy, a young Italian banks
        Smoothly around the base
Of Trajan's column, feeling between his flanks
        That cool, efficient beast,
His Vespa, at one with him in a centaur's race,
        Fresh from a Lapith feast,

And his Lapith girl behind him. Both of them lean
        With easy nonchalance
Over samphire-tufted cliffs which, though unseen,
        Are known, as the body knows
New risks and tilts, terrors and loves and wants,
        Deeply inside its clothes.

She grips the animal-shouldered naked skin
        Of his fitted leather jacket,
Letting a wake of hair float out of the spin
        And dazzled rinse of air,
Yet for all their headlong lurch and flatulent racket
        They seem to loiter there,

Forever aslant in their moment and the mind's eye.
        Meanwhile, around the column
There also turn, and turn eternally,
        Two thousand raw recruits
And scarred veterans coiling the stone in solemn
        Military pursuits,

The heft and grit of the emperor's Dacian Wars
        That lasted fifteen years.
All of that youth and purpose is, of course,
        No more than so much dust.
And even Trajan, of his imperial peers
        Accounted 'the most just',

Honoured by Dante, by Gregory the Great
        Saved from eternal Hell,
Swirls in the motes kicked up by the cough and spate
        Of the Vespa's blue exhaust,
And a voice whispers inwardly, 'My soul,
        It is the cost, the cost,'

Like some unhinged Othello, who's just found out
      That justice is no more,
While Cassio, Desdemona, Iago shout
      Like true Venetians all,
'Go screw yourself; all's fair in love and war!'
      And the bright standards fall.

Better they should not hear that whispered phrase,
      The young Italian couple;
Surely the mind in all its brave assays
      Must put much thinking by,
To be, as Yeats would have it, free and supple
      As a long-legged fly.

Look at their slender purchase, how they list
      Like a blown clipper, brought
To the lively edge of peril, to the kissed
      Lip, the victor's crown,
The prize of life. Yet one unbodied thought
      Could topple them, bring down

The whole shebang. And why should they take thought
      Of all that ancient pain,
The Danube winters, the nameless young who fought,
      The blood's uncertain lease?
Or remember that that fifteen-year campaign
      Won seven years of peace?

The Ghost in the Martini

      Over the rim of the glass
Containing a good martini with a twist
I eye her bosom and consider a pass,
      Certain we'd not be missed

      In the general hubbub.
Her lips, which I forgot to say, are superb,
Never stop babbling once (Aye, there's the rub)
      But who would want to curb

Such delicious, artful flattery?
It seems she adores my work, the distinguished grey
Of my hair. I muse on the salt and battery
    Of the sexual clinch, and say

Something terse and gruff
About the marked disparity in our ages.
She looks like twenty-three, though eager enough.
    As for the famous wages

Of sin, she can't have attained
Even to union scale, though you never can tell.
Her waist is slender and suggestively chained,
    And things are going well.

The martini does its job,
God bless it, seeping down to the dark old id.
('Is there no cradle, Sir, you would not rob?'
    Says ego, but the lid

Is off. The word is Strike
While the iron's hot.) And now, ingenuous and gay,
She is asking me about what I was like
    At twenty. (Twenty, eh?)

You wouldn't have liked me then,
I answer, looking carefully into her eyes.
I was shy, withdrawn, awkward, one of those men
    That girls seemed to despise,

Moody and self-obsessed,
Unhappy, defiant, with guilty dreams galore,
Full of ill-natured pride, an unconfessed
    Snob and a thorough bore.

Her smile is meant to convey
How changed or modest I am, I can't tell which,
When I suddenly hear someone close to me say,
    'You lousy son-of-a-bitch!'

ANTHONY HECHT

A young man's voice, by the sound,
Coming, it seems, from the twist in the martini.
'You arrogant, elderly letch, you broken-down
    Brother of Apeneck Sweeney!

Thought I was buried for good
Under six thick feet of mindless self-regard?
Dance on my grave, would you, you galliard stud,
    Silenus in leotard?

Well, summon me you did,
And I come unwillingly, like Samuel's ghost.
"All things shall be revealed that have been hid."
    There's something for you to toast!

You only got where you are
By standing upon my ectoplasmic shoulders,
And wherever that is may not be so high or far
    In the eyes of some beholders.

Take, for example, me.
I have sat alone in the dark, accomplishing little,
And worth no more to myself, in pride and fee,
    Than a cup of luke-warm spittle.

But honest about it, withal ...'
('Withal,' forsooth!) 'Please not to interrupt.
And the lovelies went by, "the long and the short and the tall",
    Hankered for, but untupped.

Bloody monastic it was.
A neurotic mixture of self-denial and fear;
The verse halting, the cataleptic pause,
    No sensible pain, no tear,

But an interior drip
As from an ulcer, where, in the humid deep
Centre of myself, I would scratch and grip
    The wet walls of the keep,

Or lie on my back and smell
From the corners the sharp, ammoniac, urine stink.
"No light, but rather darkness visible."
    And plenty of time to think.

    In that thick, fetid air
I talked to myself in giddy recitative:
"I have been studying how I may compare
    This prison where I live

    Unto the world ..." I learned
Little, and was awarded no degrees.
Yet all that sunken hideousness earned
    Your negligence and ease.

    Nor was it wholly sick,
Having procured you a certain modest fame;
A devotion, rather, a grim device to stick
    To something I could not name.'

    Meanwhile, she babbles on
About men, or whatever, and the juniper juice
Shuts up at last, having sung, I trust, like a swan.
    Still given to self-abuse!

    Better get out of here;
If he opens his trap again it could get much worse.
I touch her elbow, and, leaning toward her ear,
    Tell her to find her purse.

A Letter

    I have been wondering
What you are thinking about, and by now suppose
    It is certainly not me.
But the crocus is up, and the lark, and the blundering
    Blood knows what it knows.
It talks to itself all night, like a sliding moonlit sea.

Of course, it is talking of you.
At dawn, where the ocean has netted its catch of lights,
The sun plants one lithe foot
On that spill of mirrors, but the blood goes worming through
Its warm Arabian nights,
Naming your pounding name again in the dark heart-root.

Who shall, of course, be nameless.
Anyway, I should want you to know I have done my best,
As I'm sure you have, too.
Others are bound to us, the gentle and blameless
Whose names are not confessed
In the ceaseless palaver. My dearest, the clear unquarried blue

Of those depths is all but blinding.
You may remember that once you brought my boys
Two little woolly birds.
Yesterday the older one asked for you upon finding
Your thrush among his toys.
And the tides welled about me, and I could find no words.

There is not much else to tell.
One tries one's best to continue as before,
Doing some little good.
But I would have you know that all is not well
With a man dead set to ignore
The endless repetitions of his own murmurous blood.

A Lot of Night Music

Even a Pyrrhonist
Who knows only that he can never know
(But adores a paradox)
Would admit it's getting dark. Pale as a wrist-
Watch numeral glow,
Fireflies build a sky among the phlox,

Imparting their faint light
Conservatively only to themselves.
　　　　Earthmurk and flowerscent
Sweeten the homes of ants. Comes on the night
　　　　When the mind rockets and delves
In blind hyperbolas of its own bent.

　　　　Above, the moon at large,
Muse-goddess, slightly polluted by the runs
　　　　Of American astronauts,
(Poor, poxed Diana, laid open to the charge
　　　　Of social Actaeons)
Mildly solicits our petty cash and thoughts.

　　　　At once with their votive mites,
Out of the woods and woodwork poets come,
　　　　Hauling their truths and booty,
Each one a Phosphor, writing by his own lights,
　　　　And with a diesel hum
Of mosquitoes or priests, proffer their wordy duty.

　　　　They speak in tongues, no doubt;
High glossolalia, runic gibberish.
　　　　Some are like desert saints,
Wheat-germ ascetics, draped in pelt and clout.
　　　　Some come in schools, like fish.
These make their litany of dark complaints;

　　　　Those laugh and rejoice
At liberation from the bonds of gender,
　　　　Race, morals and mind,
As well as metre, rhyme and the human voice.
　　　　Still others strive to render
The cross-word world in perfectly declined

　　　　Pronouns, starting with ME.
Yet there are honest voices to be heard:
　　　　The crickets keep their vigil
Among the grass; in some invisible tree
　　　　Anonymously a bird
Whistles a fioritura, a light, vestigial

Reminder of a time,
An Aesopic Age when all the beasts were moral
And taught their ways to men;
Some herbal dream, some chlorophyll sublime
In which Apollo's laurel
Blooms in a world made innocent again.

LOUIS SIMPSON

Things

A man stood in the laurel tree
Adjusting his hands and feet to the boughs.
He said, 'Today I was breaking stones
On a mountain road in Asia,

When suddenly I had a vision
Of mankind, like grass and flowers,
The same over all the earth.
We forgave each other; we gave ourselves
Wholly over to words.
And straightway I was released
And sprang through an open gate.'

I said, 'Into a meadow?'

He said, 'I am impervious to irony.
I thank you for the word....
I am standing in a sunlit meadow.
Know that everything your senses reject
Springs up in the spiritual world.'

I said, 'Our scientists have another opinion.
They say, you are merely phenomena.'

He said, 'Over here they will be angels
Singing, Holy holy be His Name!
And also, it works in reverse.
Things which to us in the pure state are mysterious,
Are your simplest articles of household use—
A chair, a dish, and meaner even than these,
The very latest inventions.
Machines are the animals of the Americans—
Tell me about machines.'

I said, 'I have suspected
The Mixmaster knows more than I do,
The air conditioner is the better poet.
My right front tyre is as bald as Odysseus—
How much it must have suffered!

Then, as things have a third substance
Which is obscure to both our senses,
Let there be a perpetual coming and going
Between your house and mine.'

Hubert's Museum

When I was young and used to wander
down to Times Square on a Saturday
to see a movie with social significance,
e.g., *The Battleship Potemkin*,

passing Hubert's Museum I'd look at pictures
of Ike and Mike, World Famous Midgets,
and Sahloo Snake Dancer,
and Princess Marie, the Ape with the Human Brain.

Now, looking back, it's not the crowd scene
on the steps that I remember—
'A marvel,' *New Masses*, 'of direction'—
nor the storming of the Winter Palace,

but the body of the Crocodile Man,
and the face of El Fusilado,
who 'faced a firing squad, received 8 bullets
through the body and head, yet LIVED!'

Summer Storm

In that so sudden summer storm they tried
Each bed, couch, closet, carpet, car-seat, table,
Both river banks, five fields, a mountain side,
Covering as much ground as they were able.

A lady, coming on them in the dark
In a white fixture, wrote to the newspapers
Complaining of the statues in the park.
By Cupid, but they cut some pretty capers!

The envious oxen in still rings would stand
Ruminating. Their sweet incessant ploughs
I think had changed the contours of the land
And made two modest conies move their house.

God rest them well, and firmly shut the door.
Now they are married Nature breathes once more.

Tonight the Famous Psychiatrist

Tonight the famous psychiatrist
Is giving a party.
There are figures from the sporting world
And flesh-coloured girls
Arriving straight from the theatre.

And many other celebrities ...
The Jew looks serious,
Questioning, always questioning, his liberal error;
The Negro laughs
Three times, like a trumpet.

The wife of the host enters slowly.
Poor woman!
She thinks she is still in Hungary,
And clings to her knitting needles.
For her the time passes slowly.

On the Lawn at the Villa

On the lawn at the villa—
That's the way to start, eh, reader?
We know where we stand—somewhere expensive—
You and I *imperturbes*, as Walt would say,
Before the diversions of wealth, you and I *engagés*.

On the lawn at the villa
Sat a manufacturer of explosives,
His wife from Paris,
And a young man named Bruno,

And myself, being American,
Willing to talk to these malefactors,
The manufacturer of explosives, and so on,
But somehow superior. By that I mean democratic.
It's complicated, being an American,
Having the money and the bad conscience, both at the same time.
Perhaps, after all, this is not the right subject for a poem.

We were all sitting there paralysed
In the hot Tuscan afternoon
And the bodies of the machine-gun crew were draped over the
   balcony.
So we sat there all afternoon.

A Son of the Romanovs

This is Avram the cello-mender,
the only Jewish sergeant
in the army of the Tsar.

One day he was mending cellos
when they shouted, 'The Tsar is coming,
everyone out for inspection!'
When the Tsar saw Avram marching
with Russians who were seven feet tall,
he said, 'He must be a genius.
I want that fellow at headquarters.'

Luck is given by God.
A wife you must find for yourself.

So Avram married a rich widow
who lived in a house in Odessa.
The place was filled with music ...
Yasnaya Polyana with noodles.

One night in the middle of a concert
they heard a knock at the door.
So Avram went. It was a beggar,
a Russian, who had been blessed
by God—that is, he was crazy.
And he said, 'I'm a natural son
of the Grand Duke Nicholas.'

And Avram said, 'Eat.
I owe your people a favour.'
And he said, 'My wife is complaining
we need someone to open the door.'
So Nicholas stayed with them for years.
Who ever heard of Jewish people
with a footman?

And then the Germans came. Imagine
the scene—the old people
holding on to their baggage,
and the children—they've been told it's a game,
but they don't believe it.
Then the German says, 'Who's this?'
pointing at Nicholas,
'he doesn't look like a Jew.'
And he said, 'I'm the natural son
of the Grand Duke Nicholas.'

And they saw he was feeble-minded,
and took him away too, to the death-chamber.

'He could have kept his mouth shut,'
said my Grandmother,
'but what can you expect.
All of those Romanovs were a little bit crazy.'

Before the Poetry Reading
Composition for Voices, Dutch Banjo, Sick Flute, and a Hair Drum

1

This is the poetry reading.
This is the man who is going to give the poetry reading.
He is standing in a street in which the rain is falling
With his suitcase open on the roof of a car for some reason,
And the rain falling into the suitcase,
While the people standing nearby say,
'If you had come on a Monday,
Or a Tuesday, or a Thursday,
If you had come on a Wednesday,
Or on any day but this,
You would have had an audience,
For we here at Quinippiac (Western, or Wretched State U.)
Have wonderful audiences for poetry readings.'
By this time he has closed the suitcase
And put it on the back seat, which is empty,
But on the front seat sit Saul Bellow,
James Baldwin, and Uncle Rudy and Fanya.
They are upright, not turning their heads, their fedoras straight on,
For they know where they are going,
And you should know, so they do not deign to answer
When you say, 'Where in Hell is this car going?'
Whereupon, with a leap, slamming the door shut,
Taking your suitcase with it, and your Only Available Manuscript,
And leaving you standing there,
The car leaps into the future,
Still raining, in which its tail-light disappears.
And a man who is still looking on
With his coat collar turned up, says

'If you had come on a Friday,
A Saturday or a Sunday,
Or if you had come on a Wednesday
Or a Tuesday, there would have been an audience.
For we here at Madagascar
And the University of Lost Causes
Have wonderful audiences for poetry readings.'

2

This is the man who is going to introduce you.
He says, 'Could you tell me the names
Of the books you have written.
And is there anything you would like me to say?'

3

This is the lady who is giving a party for you
After the poetry reading.
She says, 'I hope you don't mind, but
I have carefully avoided inviting
Any beautiful, attractive, farouche young women,
But the Vicar of Dunstable is coming,
Who is over here this year on an exchange programme,
And the Calvinist Spiritual Chorus Society,
And all the members of the Poetry Writing Workshop.'

4

This is the man who has an announcement to make.
He says, 'I have a few announcements.
First, before the poetry reading starts,
If you leave the building and walk rapidly
Ten miles in the opposite direction,
A concert of music and poetry is being given
By Wolfgang Amadeus Mozart and William Shakespeare.
Also, during the intermission
There is time for you to catch the rising
Of the Latter Day Saints at the Day of Judgement.
Directly after the reading,
If you turn left, past the Community Building,
And walk for seventeen miles,
There is tea and little pieces of eraser
Being served in the Gymnasium.

Last week we had a reading by Dante,
And the week before by Sophocles;
A week from tonight, Saint Francis of Assisi will appear in person—
But tonight I am happy to introduce
Mister Willoughby, who will make the introduction
Of our guest, Mr Jones.'

5

This has been the poetry reading.

Chocolates

Once some people were visiting Chekhov.
While they made remarks about his genius
the Master fidgeted. Finally
he said, 'Do you like chocolates?'

They were astonished, and silent.
He repeated the question,
whereupon one lady plucked up her courage
and murmured shyly, 'Yes.'

'Tell me,' he said, leaning forward,
light glinting from his spectacles,
'what kind? The light, sweet chocolate
or the dark, bitter kind?'

The conversation became general.
They spoke of cherry centres,
of almonds and Brazil nuts.
Losing their inhibitions
they interrupted one another.
For people may not know what they think
about politics in the Balkans,
or the vexed question of men and women,

but everyone has a definite opinion
about the flavour of shredded coconut.
Finally someone spoke of chocolates filled with liqueur,
and everyone, even the author of *Uncle Vanya*,
was at a loss for words.

When they were leaving he stood by the door
and took their hands.
                In the coach returning to Petersburg
they agreed that it had been a most
unusual conversation.

PATRICIA BEER

The Postilion has been Struck by Lightning

He was the best postilion
I ever had. That summer in Europe
Came and went
In striding thunder-rain.
His tasselled shoulders bore up
More bad days than he could count
Till he entered his last storm in the mountains.

You to whom a postilion
Means only a cocked hat in a museum
Or a light
Anecdote, pity this one
Burnt at milord's expense far from home
Having seen every sight
But never anyone struck by lightning.

Leaping into the Gulf

Children do not ask the proper questions
Of themselves, or so they come to think
Long afterwards. I do not feel I should
Have wondered who Curtius was, and why
He leaped and with what consequences.
Laziness and knowing that a painting
Was not a history lesson, absolved me then,
Forgive me now. But why did I not say:

A man who holds his shield up against nothing
Is mad, surely? A man who drops the reins
As though a horse needs no guidance through air
Has no sense of responsibility.
A horse that puts its head down, its behind up,
Like a dog trying to look harmless,
Can it be desperate? Should the hero wear
The artist's face without his spectacles?

A glare on paint was all I really saw,
Something inside a frame to goggle at,
A work of art. I certainly never laughed
At Haydon, as I hear so many did.
I simply stood there, well-grown for my age,
Bandaged and blindfolded and gagged,
Near a gulf, too, but very far from leaping.
I would as soon have answered my mother back.

Dilemma

Read about the Buddhist monk.
When seven brigands move through the still trees
To murder him he yells so loud
That businessmen in Peking
Look up, twenty miles away.
We must admire him.

But what a comfort
To see the Queen in corny historical plays
Pin up her hair, thank her ladies,
Forgive everybody and go
With only a sidelong glance
At the man with the axe.

Which ought I to be?

Birthday Poem from Venice

From this swaying city,
Luck. Red peppers bob in the canal,
Red ribbons on hats.

Holy gold is splashed
Everywhere, as if the first Wise Man
Had torn his moneybags.

Everyone fits in here,
Feels at home. One very hot afternoon
A ghost yawned.

We come across
Two slight acquaintances from NW3
Nuzzling at a Bellini.

Gimmicks as usual.
This year it is illuminated yo-yos,
A square full of fireflies.

Through the centuries
Untold valuable things have fallen
Into the water.

A column lies there idle
And leaves a gap-toothed church. One relic
A saint dived for,

Brought back to the shore
To everyone's amazement, doing breast stroke
With steady halo.

Today is paradisal.
A cat, five minutes created, sits with a pigeon.
Happy birthday.

Creed of Mr Nicholas Culpeper

Nothing grows in vain. Use plants to heal.
Self-centredly like animals they carry
A thick strong vein of health that can
Be tapped. To have no money
Is frightening, but disease kills fright and all.
Kick men when they come at you with a knife.
Easier to cheat a man out of his life
Than of a groat. Trust herbs. The King's Evil
Does not need a king, only some celandine.

Common sense and the planets both will help you.
If a herb is of the Sun and under
Leo, wait for them, for they
Must move, not you. And ponder
On the strength of the body that you give it to.
Knee-holly, for example, belongs to Mars
And can be much too gallant for our wars.
Mountain mint defies worms and the ague
But works on female subjects over-violently.

Beware of quacks. They tell you that a carrot
Helps to ease wind—which is certainly true—
But without saying that it can breed
Wind in the first place. Two
Uses of one plant is good. Wear it
As a poultice for the spleen—I speak of broom—
Or turn it upside down to sweep a room.
Colour must be appropriate. The merit
Of scarlet centaury is to reign over blood.

I did not grow in vain myself, for three
Hundred years hence you will still doubt the knife,
And root for remedies like mine.
Plants and eternal life
Have much in common, but remember me
Who show you the significance of time.
Death grew on purpose too, and in my prime
He picked me at full moon one January
And turned me into some concoction of his own.

Witch

I shall see justice done.
I shall protect time
From monkish, cowardly men
Who say this life is not all
And do not respect the clock.

On those who will not escape
I shall see justice done.
I have courage to use
Wax and the killing pin
On behalf of prisoners.

I cut off the pilot's thumb
Because his compass failed.
I shall see justice done
Whenever the homeward bound
Mistake their true home.

In my black pointed heart
I cherish the good of all.
With storms, potions and blood
I shall see justice done
For I know goodness well.

Never shall bogus love—
Habit, duty or weakness—
Win any mercy from me.
By the light of my long burning
I shall see justice done.

Gallery Shepherds

Shepherds on old hills, with robber
And wolf lurking
Think themselves not so much seers
As hard-working.

But in paintings the mother of a god
Often blesses
Those who tend wool bodies topped
By wasp faces.

And indeed shepherds are mostly shown
Simple and wise
In pictures, finding out things
Before spies.

Primed they come in from the country
To a small town
Thinking it glorious Gomorrah
That will burn.

Angels have spoken of a marvel
For countrymen
Who are portrayed as if gaping
At a con man.

The town needs them; they are followed
By knowing rich
Kings, entirely urban, whom the artist
Paints as such.

In the Cathedral

Together, fourteen years older
Back to Canterbury again
The same February day
As the first, but greyer, colder.

All the way east, snowmen
Hands stuck in their pockets.
Here the comfortless gloves
Of the serious foemen.

Vergers reverently freeze
With scarves on, underneath
Stained glass stories
Of cold babies on cold knees.

The pillars stutter
Into a fluent sentence
Of stone. Worn steps approach
The heart of the matter.

The mason's hand round the hammer
Must have been purple.
You take and hold my dead fingers
Declaring summer.

The Letter

I have not seen your writing
For ages, nor have been fretting
To see it. As once, darling.

This letter will certainly be
About some book, written by you or by me.
You turned to other ghosts. So did I.

It stopped raining long ago
But drops caught up in the bough
Fall murderously on me now.

Christmas Carols

They say a maiden conceived
Without so much as a kiss
At the time or afterwards.
Gloria in excelsis.

They name the eternal hall
Where we arrive to wine, fire,
Together and loving, but
Dead. *Quam dulcis est amor.*

Although in their description
Every midnight is clear
So that angels can be seen
Without peering, *hilariter,*

We know better in our fear
And avoid most carefully
David's city after dark.
Honor tibi, Domine.

JAMES K. BAXTER

Mandrakes for Supper

Memory feeds us on a prison diet
Of bits and scraps. 'Remember Mr X—,
That simple solemn man, so deathly quiet;

'And Sally Z—, compounded of raw sex
And circumstance'—'Ah yes, her corn-gold hair ...'
A land where roams Tyrannosaurus Rex,

The giant lizard, calloused by despair—
In Nowhere I received my education
(If memory can be trusted) mooching there

Like Dante's ghost, among a faceless nation.
The white antarctic Gorgon was my mentor:
Her cloudy arms, her eyes of desolation

Sisterly gazing from the whirlwind's centre,
Received, embraced my naked intuition.
The town of Nilburg too I shrank to enter

(If memory serves me right) and wept contrition
For indistinct all-but-committed crimes
In gelding-rooms and caves of parturition.

Yet undeniably I laughed at times
With those who shared my headless hullabaloo:
Fogeaters, Dwarfs, Green Quims and Paradigms.

Cellars of Nilburg! how I hated you,
Your Ixion wheels, hot frogs and icy toads,
Your existential climate where I grew

Into an adult mandrake. (Memory loads
My plate with mushrooms.) But I woke at length
And left you, travelling light by mountain roads
To Elsewhere; drank at desert wells; gained strength

A Family Photograph 1939

Waves bluster up the bay and through the throat
Of the one-span bridge. My brother shoots
The gap alone
Like Charon sculling in his boat
Above the squids and flounders. With the jawbone
Of a sperm whale he fights the town,
Dances on Fridays to the cello
With black-haired sluts. My father in his gumboots
Is up a ladder plucking down
The mottled autumn-yellow
Dangling torpedo clusters
Of passion fruit for home-made wine.
My mother in the kitchen sunshine
Tightens her dressing gown,
Chops up carrots, onions, leeks,
For thick hot winter soup. No broom or duster
Will shift the English papers piled on chairs
And left for weeks.
I, in my fuggy room at the top of the stairs,

A thirteen-year-old schizophrene,
Write poems, wish to die,
And watch the long neat mason-fly
Malignantly serene
Arrive with spiders dopier than my mind
And build his clay dungeons inside the roller blind.

To a Print of Queen Victoria

I advise rest; the farmhouse
we dug you up in has been
modernized, and the people
who hung you as their ikon
against the long passage wall
are underground—incubus

and excellent woman, we
inherit the bone acre
of your cages and laws. This
dull green land suckled at your
blood's *frigor Anglicanus*,
crowning with a housewife's tally

the void of Empire, does not
remember you—and certain
bloody bandaged ghosts rising
from holes of Armageddon
at Gallipoli or Sling
Camp, would like to fire a shot

through the gilt frame. I advise
rest, Madam; and yet the tomb
holds much that we must travel
barely without. Your print—'from
an original pencil
drawing by the Marchioness

'of Granby, March, eighteen nine-
ty-seven ...' Little mouth, strong
nose and hooded eye—they speak
of half-truths my type have slung
out of the window, and lack
and feel the lack too late. Queen,

you stand most for the time of
early light, clay roads, great trees
unfelled, and the smoke from huts
where girls in sack dresses
stole butter ... The small rain spits
today. You smile in your grave.

Evidence at the Witch Trials

No woman's pleasure did I feel
  Under the hazel tree
When heavy as a sack of meal
  The Black Man mounted me,
But cold as water from a dyke
  His seed that quickened me.

What his age I cannot tell;
  Foul he was, and fair.
There blew between us both from Hell
  A blast of grit and fire,
And like a boulder is the babe
  That in my womb I bear.

Though I was youngest in that band
  Yet I was quick to learn.
A red dress he promised me
  And red the torches burn.
Between the faggot and the flame
  I see his face return.

The Inflammable Woman

It was plain to see the sense of being a woman
Troubled her. She sat on the edge of the sofa
Holding a glass of gin and fizz
With seeds floating, trying to look at ease
Though the conversation about God and Kafka
Bored her to the core ... What core? What did she most
Regard herself as being? (Though no one
Bothered to find out)—a white rose? an old stocking?
An animal dying of hunger?
                              The host
Offered her another gin. He did not
Notice something rather shocking:
That the sofa was slowly turning to ash
Though keeping its shape. And then the leg of a table,
Part of the carpet, a corkscrew, went first red hot
Then a metallic grey. The toe of my shoe
Was nibbled away in a flash
(She, poor woman, all the while
Gripping her glass and hoping the party would not be long)—
I wondered what to do,
Whether to ring the Fire Brigade or smile
And put the whole occasion into a fable
As I finally did, being no longer young,
And carrying always a private bucket of sand. Thank you.

News from a Pacified Area

The day of anger after the holy night
Will bring down corpses from the broken hills

Rotating like rubber ducks. All corpses are the same.
These were villagers who preferred something

To something else, or had the lack of wisdom
Not to dig deeper than moles when men came

With gas and grenades. Death is a good master.
He pays us and does not expect us to learn

The difficult art of keeping sane. We heard
The raped girl yelling in the barn

And when their leader showed his head
It was our own troops. Her grandfather's dramatics

Were singularly useless. I have no interest
In bucking the odds. My sister who became

Different tells me you can grow fat as a hen
Scratching in the shadow of the guns. My father,

For the last time I put melons on your grave,
And promise—what? Vengeance? Hope?

To distinguish the assassin from the victim
Would take God's knowledge, and he is dead

Because he requires our love to keep him in life,
And love is not our talent. I have grown a face

Whitish and smooth, like new scar tissue, brother,
To hide the evidence I am no longer I.

A Dentist's Window

I, a boat with a bony keel,
Founder in waters of the afternoon,

Tilted back on the frightful chair
While Dr Gorodowski chooses

The perfect hornet drill.
High up on a pigeon-turded shelf

Above St Mary's canyon wall
Our Lady's concrete statue smiles

On floosies, taxi-drivers, psychopaths,
The whole rough stumble-footed town.

Lady, Lady, I am growing old,
My feathers moult, my prayers are cold,

Remember me today and when I die.
Take Dr Gorodowski by the hand,

Keep the drill's edge off the little nerve.
More than the rot of venial sin

I fear the stab, the graunch, the touch of metal.

The Apple Tree

From that high apple-tree, my love,
That somehow bent in Eden
Its branches down above the sleeping pair

(Mouth near to mouth, plaited together,
Bread newly baked in God's great oven)...
From that early happy grove

I think your fingers bring me
Leaves, your mouth air and water.
Through your kisses, I, time's prisoner,

Undo the stubborn bolts and enter
Where none have gone before. Your body
Is my wild apple-tree, my poor man's treasure.

The Buried Stream

Tonight our cat, Tahi, who lately lost
One eyebrow, yowls in the bush with another cat;

Our glass Tibetan ghost-trap has caught no ghost
Yet, but jangles suspended in the alcove that

We varnished and enlarged. Unwisely I have read
Sartre on Imagination—very dry, very French,

An old hound with noises in his head
Who dreams the hunt is on, yet fears the stench

Of action—he teaches us that human choice
Is rarely true or kind. My children are asleep.

Something clatters in the kitchen. I hear the voice
Of the buried stream that flows deep, deep,

Through caves I cannot enter, whose watery rope
Tugs my divining rod with the habit some call hope.

CHARLES TOMLINSON

Charlotte Corday

O Vertu! le poignard, seul espoir de la terre,
Est ton arme sacrée....   —Chénier

Courteously self-assured, although alone,
With voice and features that could do no hurt,
Why should she not enter? They let in
A girl whose reading made a heroine—
Her book was Plutarch, her republic Rome:
Home was where she sought her tyrant out.

The towelled head next, the huge batrachian mouth:
There was a mildness in him, even. He
Had never been a woman's enemy,
And time and sickness turned his stomach now
From random execution. All the same,
He moved aside to write her victims down,
And when she approached, it was to kill she came.

She struck him from above. One thrust. Her whole
Intent and innocence directing it
To breach through flesh and enter where it must,
It seemed a blow that rose up from within:
Tinville reduced it all to expertise:
—What, would you make of me a hired assassin?

—What did you find to hate in him?—His crimes.
Every reply was temperate save one
And that was human when all's said and done:
The deposition, read to those who sit
In judgement on her, 'What has she to say?'
'Nothing, except that I succeeded in it.'

—You think that you have killed all Marats off?
—I think perhaps such men are now afraid.
The blade hung in its grooves. How should she know
The Terror still to come, as she was led
Red-smocked from gaol out into evening's red?
It was to have brought peace, that faultless blow.

Uncowed by the unimaginable result,
She loomed by in the cart beneath the eye
Of Danton, Desmoulins and Robespierre,
Heads in a rabble fecund in insult:
She has remade her calendar, called this
The Fourth Day of the Preparation of Peace.

Greater than Brutus was what Adam Lux
Demanded for her statue's sole inscription:
His pamphlet was heroic and absurd
And asked the privilege of dying too:
Though the republic raised to her no statue,
The brisk tribunal took him at his word.

What haunted that composure none could fault?
For she, when shown the knife, had dropped her glance—
She 'who believed her death would raise up France'
As Chénier wrote who joined the later dead:
Her judge had asked: 'If you had gone uncaught,
Would you have then escaped?' 'I would,' she said.

A daggered Virtue, Clio's roll of stone,
Action unsinewed into statuary!
Beneath that gaze what tremor was willed down?
And, where the scaffold's shadow stretched its length,
What unlived life would struggle up against
Death died in the possession of such strength?

Perhaps it was the memory of that cry
That cost her most as Catherine Marat
Broke off her testimony ... But the blade
Inherited the future now and she
Entered a darkness where no irony
Seeps through to move the pity of her shade.

In Arden

'This is the forest of Arden ...'

Arden is not Eden, but Eden's rhyme:
   Time spent in Arden is time at risk
And place, also: for Arden lies under threat:
   Ownership will get what it can for Arden's trees:
No acreage of green-belt complacencies
   Can keep Macadam out: Eden lies guarded:
Pardonable Adam, denied its gate,
   Walks the grass in a less-than-Eden light
And whiteness that shines from a stone burns with his fate:
   Sun is tautening the field's edge shadowline
Along the wood beyond: but the contraries
   Of this place are contrarily unclear:
A haze beats back the summer sheen
   Into a chiaroscuro of the heat:
The down on the seeded grass that beards
   Each rise where it meets with sky,
Ripples a gentle fume: a fine
   Incense, smelling of hay smokes by:
Adam in Arden tastes its replenishings:
   Through its dense heats the depths of Arden's springs

Convey echoic waters—voices
  Of the place that rises through this place,
Overflowing, as it brims its surfaces
  In runes and hidden rhymes, in chords and keys
Where Adam, Eden, Arden run together
  And time itself must beat to the cadence of this river.

The Death of Will

The end was more of a melting:
as if frost turned heavily to dew
and the flags, dragged down by it,
clung to their poles: marble becoming glue.

Alive, no one had much cared
for Will: Will no sooner gone,
there was a *je ne sais quoi*, a *ton*
'fell from the air':

And how strange that, Will once dead,
Passion must die, too,
although they'd had nothing to do
with each other, so it was said:

It was then everyone stopped looking
for the roots of decay,
for curative spears and chapels perilous
and the etymology of 'heyday':

Parents supine, directionless,
looked to their wilful children now:
was this metempsychosis?
was Will reborn in them somehow?

Someone should record Will's story.
Someone should write a book on *Will and Zen*.
Someone should trace all those who
knew Will, to interview them. Someone

Macduff

This wet sack, wavering slackness
    They drew out silent through the long
Blood-edged incision, this black
    Unbreathing thing they must first
Hoist from a beam by its heels and swing
    To see whether it could yet expel
Death through each slimy nostril,
    This despaired-of, half-born mishap
Shuddered into a live calf, knew
    At a glance mother, udder and what it must do
Next and did it, mouthing for milk.
    The cow, too, her womb stitched back inside,
Her hide laced up, leans down untaught
    To lick clean her untimely firstborn:
'Pity it's a male.' She looms there innocent
    That words have meanings, but long ago
This blunt lapsarian instinct, poetry,
    Found life's sharpest, readiest
Rhyme, unhesitating—it was knife—
    By some farm-yard gate, perhaps,
That led back from nature into history.

Mr Brodsky

I had heard
before, of an
American who would have preferred
to be an Indian;
but not
until Mr Brodsky, of one
whose professed and long
pondered-on passion
was to become a Scot,
who even sent for haggis and oatcakes
across continent.

Having read him
in Cambridge English
a verse or two
from MacDiarmid,
I was invited
to repeat the reading
before a Burns Night Gathering
where the Balmoral Pipers
of Albuquerque would
play in the haggis
out of its New York tin.
Of course, I said
No. No. I could *not* go
and then
half-regretted I had not been.
But to console
and cure the wish, came
Mr Brodsky, bringing
his pipes and played
until the immense, distended
bladder of leather seemed
it could barely contain its water—
tears (idle
tears) for the bridal of Annie Laurie
and Morton J. Brodsky.
A bagpipe in a dwelling is
a resonant instrument
and there he stood
lost in the gorse
the heather or whatever
six thousand
miles and more
from the infection's source,
in our neo–New Mexican parlour
where I had heard
before of an
American who would have preferred
to be merely an Indian.

CHARLES TOMLINSON

A Dream
or the worst of both worlds

Yevtushenko, Voznesensky and I
are playing to a full house: I lack their verve
(I know) their red reserve
of Scythian corpuscles, to ride in triumph through
Indianapolis. They read. Libido roars
across the dionysian sluice of the applause
and the very caryatids lean down
to greet them: youth towers (feet
on shoulders) into instant acrobatic pyramids—
human triforia to shore up the roof
cheering. I come on
sorting my pages, searching for the one
I've failed to write. It's October
nineteen seventeen once more. But is it me
or Danton from the tumbril, stentoriously
starts delivering one by one my bits of ivory?
No matter. I still ride their tide of cheers
and I could read the whole sheaf
backwards, breasting effortlessly
the surge of sweat and plaudits to emerge
laurelled in vatic lather, brother, bard:
they hear me out who have not heard one word,
bringing us back for bows, bringing down the house
once more. The reds return to their homeground stadia,
their unforeseen disgraces; I
to the sobriety of a dawn-cold bed, to own
my pariah's privilege, my three-inch spaces,
the reader's rest and editor's colophon.

Civilities of Lamplight

Without excess (no galaxies
Gauds, illiterate exclamations)
It betokens haven,

An ordering, the darkness held
But not dismissed. One man
Alone with his single light
Wading obscurity refines the instance,
Hollows the hedge-bound track, a sealed
Furrow on dark, closing behind him.

THOM GUNN

The Wheel of Fortune

Strapped helpless, monarchs and prelates, round they swung.
O mutability they cried, O perfect Wheel!
  The bishop dreamt of ruin while he dozed,
  A lover that his secrets were exposed,
And Lambert Simnel that he stirred the king's porridge.

Deeper they dream, disorder comes: high, low, are flung
Faster, limbs spinning. As the great Hub cracks they peel
  From off the Felloe of that even round.
  Bishop and lover sprawl upon the ground,
And Lambert Simnel stirs the under-footman's porridge.

The Allegory of the Wolf Boy

The causes are in Time; only their issue
Is bodied in the flesh, the finite powers.
And how to guess he hides in that firm tissue
Seeds of division? At tennis and at tea
Upon the gentle lawn, he is not ours,
But plays us in a sad duplicity.

Tonight the boy, still boy open and blond,
Breaks from the house, wedges his clothes between
Two moulded garden urns, and goes beyond

His understanding, through the dark and dust:
Fields of sharp stubble, abandoned by machine
To the whirring enmity of insect lust.

As yet ungolden in the dense, hot night
The spikes enter his feet: he seeks the moon,
Which, with the touch of its infertile light,
Shall loose desires hoarded against his will
By the long urging of the afternoon.
Slowly the hard rim shifts above the hill.

White in the beam he stops, faces it square,
And the same instant leaping from the ground
Feels the familiar itch of close dark hair;
Then, clean exception to the natural laws,
Only to instinct and the moon being bound,
Drops on four feet. Yet he has bleeding paws.

Jesus and his Mother

My only son, more God's than mine,
Stay in this garden ripe with pears.
The yielding of their substance wears
A modest and contented shine:
And when they weep with age, not brine
But lazy syrup are their tears.
'I am my own and not my own.'

He seemed much like another man,
That silent foreigner who trod
Outside my door with lily rod:
How could I know what I began
Meeting the eyes more furious than
The eyes of Joseph, those of God?
I was my own and not my own.

And who are these twelve labouring men?
I do not understand your words:
I taught you speech, we named the birds,
You marked their big migrations then
Like any child. So turn again
To silence from the place of crowds.
'I am my own and not my own.'

Why are you sullen when I speak?
Here are your tools, the saw and knife
And hammer on your bench. Your life
Is measured here in week and week
Planed as the furniture you make,
And I will teach you like a wife
To be my own and all my own.

Who like an arrogant wind blown
Where he may please, needs no content?
Yet I remember how you went
To speak with scholars in furred gown.
I hear an outcry in the town;
Who carried that dark instrument?
'One all his own and not his own.'

Treading the green and nimble sward
I stare at a strange shadow thrown.
Are you the boy I bore alone,
No doctor near to cut the cord?
I cannot reach to call you Lord,
Answer me as my only son.
'I am my own and not my own.'

In Santa Maria Del Popolo

Waiting for when the sun an hour or less
Conveniently oblique makes visible
The painting on one wall of this recess
By Caravaggio, of the Roman School,

I see how shadow in the painting brims
With a real shadow, drowning all shapes out
But a dim horse's haunch and various limbs,
Until the very subject is in doubt.

But evening gives the act, beneath the horse
And one indifferent groom, I see him sprawl,
Foreshortened from the head, with hidden face,
Where he has fallen, Saul becoming Paul.
O wily painter, limiting the scene
From a cacophony of dusty forms
To the one convulsion, what is it you mean
In that wide gesture of the lifting arms?

No Ananias croons a mystery yet,
Casting the pain out under name of sin.
The painter saw what was, an alternate
Candour and secrecy inside the skin.
He painted, elsewhere, that firm insolent
Young whore in Venus' clothes, those pudgy cheats,
Those sharpers; and was strangled, as things went,
For money, by one such picked off the streets.

I turn, hardly enlightened, from the chapel
To the dim interior of the church instead,
In which there kneel already several people,
Mostly old women: each head closeted
In tiny fists holds comfort as it can.
Their poor arms are too tired for more than this
—For the large gesture of solitary man,
Resisting, by embracing, nothingness.

Breakfast

For two years I looked forward
only to breakfast. The night
was not night, it was tempered
by hotel signs opposite.

Yet I must have dozed, for all
at once I would distinguish
loaf and cup, monumental
on the sill's ginger varnish.

I do not mean that breakfast
was a remedy—still less
a ritual—but that toast
and coffee served as markers.

Unsour pungency, hot and
dark, sank down my throat. Dry rough
substance encountered the grind
of my teeth. These were enough,

were properties, as it were,
for a tenacity. I
would now get up from the chair,
to look for a job, or try

phoning my ex-wife. Without
future I had to keep on
—without love, without hope, but
without renunciation.

from *Misanthropos*

9

A serving man. Curled my hair,
wore gloves in my cap. I served
all degrees and both sexes.
But I gave readily from
the largess of high spirits,
a sturdy body and strong

fingers. Nor was I servile.
No passer-by could resist
the fragrant impulse nodding
upon my smile. I laboured
to become a god of charm,
an untirable giver.

Needing me, needing me, 'Quick!'
they would call: I came gladly.
Even as I served them sweets
I served myself a trencher
of human flesh in some dark
sour pantry, and munched from it.

My diet, now, is berries,
water, and the gristle of
rodents. I brought myself here,
widening the solitude
till it was absolute. But
at times I am ravenous.

Street Song

I am too young to grow a beard
But yes man it was me you heard
In dirty denim and dark glasses.
I look through everyone who passes
But ask him clear, I do not plead,
Keys lids acid and speed.

My grass is not oregano.
Some of it grew in Mexico.
You cannot guess the weed I hold,
Clara Green, Acapulco Gold,
Panama Red, you name it man,
Best on the street since I began.

My methedrine, my double-sun,
Will give you two lives in your one,
Five days of power before you crash.
At which time use these lumps of hash
—They burn so sweet, they smoke so smooth,
They make you sharper while they soothe.

Now here, the best I've got to show,
Made by a righteous cat I know.
Pure acid—it will scrape your brain,
And make it something else again.
Call it heaven, call it hell,
Join me and see the world I sell.

Join me, and I will take you there,
Your head will cut out from your hair
Into whichever self you choose.
With Midday Mick man you can't lose,
I'll get you anything you need.
Keys lids acid and speed.

Expression

For several weeks I have been reading
the poetry of my juniors.
Mother doesn't understand,
and they hate Daddy, the noted alcoholic.
They write with black irony
of breakdown, mental institution,
and suicide attempt, of which the experience
does not always seem first-hand.
It is very poetic poetry.

I go to the Art Museum
and find myself looking for something
though I'm not sure what it is.
I reach it, I recognize it,
seeing it for the first time.
An 'early Italian altar piece'.

The outlined Virgin, her lips
a strangely modern bow of red,
holds a doll-sized Child in her lap.
He has the knowing face of an adult,
and a precocious forelock curling
over the smooth baby forehead. She
is massive and almost symmetrical.
He does not wriggle, nor is he solemn.
The sight quenches, like water
after too much birthday cake.
Solidly there, mother and child
stare outward, two pairs of matching eyes
void of expression.

PETER PORTER

An Exequy

In wet May, in the months of change,
In a country you wouldn't visit, strange
Dreams pursue me in my sleep,
Black creatures of the upper deep—
Though you are five months dead, I see
You in guilt's iconography,
Dear Wife, lost beast, beleaguered child,
The stranded monster with the mild
Appearance, whom small waves tease,
(Andromeda upon her knees
In orthodox deliverance)
And you alone of pure substance,
The unformed form of life, the earth
Which Piero's brushes brought to birth
For all to greet as myth, a thing
Out of the box of imagining.

This introduction serves to sing
Your mortal death as Bishop King
Once hymned in tetrametric rhyme
His young wife, lost before her time;
Though he lived on for many years
His poem each day fed new tears
To that unreaching spot, her grave,
His lines a baroque architrave
The Sunday poor with bottled flowers
Would by-pass in their mourning hours,
Esteeming ragged natural life
('Most dearly loved, most gentle wife'),
Yet, looking back when at the gate
And seeing grief in formal state
Upon a sculpted angel group,
Were glad that men of god could stoop
To give the dead a public stance
And freeze them in their mortal dance.

The words and faces proper to
My misery are private—you
Would never share your heart with those
Whose only talent's to suppose,
Nor from your final childish bed
Raise a remote confessing head—
The channels of our lives are blocked,
The hand is stopped upon the clock,
No one can say why hearts will break
And marriages are all opaque:
A map of loss, some posted cards,
The living house reduced to shards,
The abstract hell of memory,
The pointlessness of poetry—
These are the instances which tell
Of something which I know full well,
I owe a death to you—one day
The time will come for me to pay
When your slim shape from photographs
Stands at my door and gently asks
If I have any work to do
Or will I come to bed with you.

O scala enigmatica,
I'll climb up to that attic where
The curtain of your life was drawn
Some time between despair and dawn—
I'll never know with what halt steps
You mounted to this plain eclipse
But each stair now will station me
A black responsibility
And point me to that shut-down room,
'This be your due appointed tomb.'

I think of us in Italy:
Gin-and-chianti-fuelled, we
Move in a trance through Paradise,
Feeding at last our starving eyes,
Two people of the English blindness
Doing each masterpiece the kindness
Of discovering it—from Baldovinetti
To Venice's most obscure jetty.
A true unfortunate traveller, I
Depend upon your nurse's eye
To pick the altars where no Grinner
Puts us off our tourists' dinner
And in hotels to bandy words
With Genevan girls and talking birds,
To wear your feet out following me
To night's end and true amity,
And call my rational fear of flying
A paradigm of Holy Dying—
And, oh my love, I wish you were
Once more with me, at night somewhere
In narrow streets applauding wines,
The moon above the Apennines
As large as logic and the stars,
Most middle-aged of avatars,
As bright as when they shone for truth
Upon untried and avid youth.

The rooms and days we wandered through
Shrink in my mind to one—there you
Lie quite absorbed by peace—the calm
Which life could not provide is balm

In death. Unseen by me, you look
Past bed and stairs and half-read book
Eternally upon your home,
The end of pain, the left alone.
I have no friend, or intercessor,
No psychopomp or true confessor
But only you who know my heart
In every cramped and devious part—
Then take my hand and lead me out,
The sky is overcast by doubt,
The time has come, I listen for
Your words of comfort at the door,
O guide me through the shoals of fear—
'Fürchte dich nicht, ich bin bei dir.'

Non Piangere, Liù

A card comes to tell you
you should report
to have your eyes tested.

But your eyes melted in the fire
and the only tears, which soon dried,
fell in the chapel.

Other things still come—
invoices, subscription renewals,
shiny plastic cards promising credit—
not much for a life spent
in the service of reality.

You need answer none of them.
Nor my asking you for one drop
of succour in my own hell.

Do not cry, I tell myself,
the whole thing is a comedy
and comedies end happily.

The fire will come out of the sun
and I shall look in the heart of it.

May, *1945*

As the Allied tanks trod Germany to shard
and no man had seen a fresh-pressed uniform
for six months, as the fire storm
bit out the core of Dresden yard by yard,

as farmers hid turnips for the after-war,
as cadets going to die passed Waffen SS
tearing identifications from their battledress,
the Russians only three days from the Brandenburger Tor—

in the very hell of sticks and blood and brick dust
as Germany the phoenix burned, the wraith
of History pursed its lips and spoke, thus:

To go with teeth and toes and human soap,
the radio will broadcast Bruckner's Eighth
so that good and evil may die in equal hope.

Mort aux chats

There will be no more cats.
Cats spread infection,
cats pollute the air,
cats consume seven times
their own weight in food a week,
cats were worshipped in
decadent societies (Egypt
and Ancient Rome), the Greeks
had no use for cats. Cats
sit down to pee (our scientists
have proved it). The copulation
of cats is harrowing; they
are unbearably fond of the moon.

Perhaps they are all right in
their own country but their
traditions are alien to ours.
Cats smell, they can't help it,
you notice it going upstairs.
Cats watch too much television,
they can sleep through storms,
they stabbed us in the back
last time. There have never been
any great artists who were cats.
They don't deserve a capital C
except at the beginning of a sentence.
I blame my headache and my
plants dying on to cats.
Our district is full of them,
property values are falling.
When I dream of God I see
a Massacre of Cats. Why
should they insist on their own
language and religion, who
needs to purr to make his point?
Death to all cats! The Rule
of Dogs shall last a thousand years!

Gertrude Stein at Snails Bay

I am Miss Stein
and this bay is mine

I am Miss Stein (pronounced Steen)
and this sea is green

Americans do not like
European pronunciation

I live in Europe because Americans
do not like Europeans

I do not live in America
because Europeans do not like Americans

I am in Australia because
I hear you have an opera
and I am searching for snails

I am not here to buy your paintings

I am in Snails Bay to find snails

Although there are no snails in Snails Bay
there are buses behind me
and children in front of me
and sea in front of the children

They tell me this is Arbor Day

No, I do not drop my aitches

Nothing can be done in the face
of ordinary unhappiness

Above all, there is nothing to do in words

I have written a dozen books
to prove nothing can be done in words

A great artist may fall off an inner alp
but I will not roll down this gentle bank

I would not give a cook book for his alp

I have a message for the snails
of New South Wales

You will never know
which of you is Shakespeare

Yes, I am a disagreeable old woman
who talks selfishly and strangely
and writes down words in a peculiar order

It is to prevent unhappiness escaping
and poisoning the world

How do you define
the truth, Miss Stein?

A snail has not the right to say
it will or won't: it must obey

With the buses and the children and the sea
I have nothing to do

I am an observer,
I observe the blue and you

I see an immense rain
washing pebbles up the beach
and evacuating misery

The plane for America is a sort of star

A. K. RAMANUJAN

Some Indian Uses of History
on a Rainy Day

1

Madras,
            1965, and rain.
Head clerks from city banks
curse, batter, elbow
in vain the patchwork gangs
of coolies in their scramble
for the single seat
in the seventh bus:

they tell each other how
Old King Harsha's men
beat soft gongs
to stand a crowd of ten
thousand monks

in a queue, to give them
and the single visiting Chinaman
a hundred pieces of gold,
a pearl, and a length of cloth;

so, miss another bus, the eighth,
and begin to walk, for King Harsha's
monks had nothing but their own two feet.

2

Fulbright Indians, tiepins of ivory,
colour cameras for eyes, stand every July
in Egypt among camels,

faces pressed against the past
as against museum glass,
tongue tasting dust,

amazed at pyramidfuls
of mummies swathed in millennia
of Calicut muslin.

3

1935. Professor of Sanskrit
on cultural exchange;
                              passing through; lost
in Berlin rain; reduced
to a literal, turbanned child,
spelling German signs on door, bus, and shop,
trying to guess *go* from *stop*;
                              desperate
for a way of telling apart
a familiar street from a strange,
or east
from west at night,
the brown dog that barks
from the brown dog that doesn't,

memorizing a foreign paradigm
of lanterns, landmarks,
a gothic lotus on the iron gate;

suddenly comes home
in English, gesture, and Sanskrit,
assimilating
   the swastika
on the neighbour's arm
in that roaring bus from a grey
nowhere to a green.

The Hindoo: he doesn't Hurt a Fly or a Spider either

It's time I told you why
I'm so gentle, do not hurt a fly.

Why, I cannot hurt a spider
either, not even a black widow,

for who can tell Who's Who?
Can you? Maybe it's once again my

great swinging grandmother,
and that other (playing at

patience centred in his web)
my one true ancestor,

the fisherman lover who waylaid her
on the ropes in the Madras harbour,

took her often from behind
imprinting on her face and body

(not to speak of family tree
or gossip column)

lasting impressions of his net:
till, one day, spider-

fashion, she clamped down and bit
him while still inside her,

as if she'd teeth down there—
they'd a Latin name for it,

which didn't help the poor man one bit.

And who can say I do not bear,
as I do his name, the spirit

of Great Grandfather, that still man,
untimely witness, timeless eye,

perpetual outsider,
watching as only husbands will

a suspense of nets vibrate
under wife and enemy

with every move of hand or thigh:
watching, watching, like some

spider-lover a pair
of his Borneo specimens mate

in murder, make love with hate,
or simply stalk a local fly.

Small-scale Reflections on a Great House

Sometimes I think that nothing
that ever comes into this house
goes out. Things come in every day

to lose themselves among other things
lost long ago among
other things lost long ago;

lame wandering cows from nowhere
have been known to be tethered,
given a name, encouraged

to get pregnant in the broad daylight
of the street under the elders'
supervision, the girls hiding

behind windows with holes in them.

Unread library books
usually mature in two weeks
and begin to lay a row

of little eggs in the ledgers
for fines, as silverfish
in the old man's office room

breed dynasties among long legal words
in the succulence
of Victorian parchment.

Neighbours' dishes brought up
with the greasy sweets they made
all night the day before yesterday

for the wedding anniversary of a god,

never leave the house they enter,
like the servants, the phonographs,
the epilepsies in the blood,

sons-in-law who quite forget
their mothers, but stay to check
accounts or teach arithmetic to nieces,

or the women who come as wives
from houses open on one side
to rising suns, on another

to the setting, accustomed
to wait and to yield to monsoons
in the mountains' calendar

beating through the hanging banana leaves.

And also, anything that goes out
will come back, processed and often
with long bills attached,

like the hooped bales of cotton
shipped off to invisible Manchesters
and brought back milled and folded

for a price, cloth for our days'
middle-class loins, and muslin
for our richer nights. Letters mailed

have a way of finding their way back
with many re-directions to wrong
addresses and red ink marks

earned in Tiruvella and Sialkot.

And ideas behave like rumours,
once casually mentioned somewhere
they come back to the door as prodigies

born to prodigal fathers, with eyes
that vaguely look like our own,
like what Uncle said the other day:

that every Plotinus we read
is what some Alexander looted
between the malarial rivers.

A beggar once came with a violin
to croak out a prostitute song
that our voiceless cook sang

all the time in our backyard.

Nothing stays out: daughters
get married to short-lived idiots;
sons who run away come back

in grandchildren who recite Sanskrit
to approving old men, or bring
betelnuts for visiting uncles

who keep them gaping with
anecdotes of unseen fathers,
or to bring Ganges water

in a copper pot
for the last of the dying
ancestors' rattle in the throat.

And though many times from everywhere,

recently only twice:
once in nineteen forty-three
from as far away as the Sahara,

half-gnawed by desert foxes,
and lately from somewhere
in the north, a nephew with stripes

on his shoulder was called
an incident on the border
and was brought back in plane

and train and military truck
even before the telegrams reached,
on a perfectly good

chatty afternoon.

A. K. RAMANUJAN

The Last of the Princes

They took their time to die, this dynasty
falling in slow motion from Aurangzeb's time:
some of bone TB,
others of a London fog that went to their heads,

some of current trends, imported wine and women,
one or two heroic in war or poverty,
with ballads
to their name. Father, uncles, seven

folklore brothers, sister so young so lovely
that snakes loved her and hung dead,
ancestral
lovers, from her ceiling; brothers' many

wives, their unborn stillborn babies, numberless
cousins, royal mynahs and parrots
in the harem;
everyone died, to pass into his slow

conversation. He lives on, heir to long
fingers, faces in paintings, and a belief
in auspicious
snakes in the skylight: he lives on, to cough,

remember and sneeze, a balance of phlegm
and bile, alternating loose bowels and hard
sheep's pellets.
Two girls, Honey and Bunny, go to school

on half fees. Wife, heirloom pearl in her nose-ring,
pregnant again. His first son, trainee
in telegraphy,
has telegraphed thrice already for money.

TED HUGHES

Wilfred Owen's Photographs

When Parnell's Irish in the House
Pressed that the British Navy's cat-
O'-nine-tails be abolished, what
Shut against them? It was
Neither Irish nor English nor of that
Decade, but of the species.

Predictably, Parliament
Squared against the motion. As soon
Let the old school tie be rent
Off their necks, and give thanks, as see gone
No shame but a monument—
Trafalgar not better known.

'To discontinue it were as much
As ship not powder and cannonballs
But brandy and women' (Laughter). Hearing which
A witty profound Irishman calls
For a 'cat' into the House, and sits to watch
The gentry fingering its stained tails.

Whereupon ...
               quietly, unopposed,
The motion was passed.

Her Husband

Comes home dull with coal-dust deliberately
To grime the sink and foul towels and let her
Learn with scrubbing brush and scrubbing board
The stubborn character of money.

And let her learn through what kind of dust
He has earned his thirst and the right to quench it
And what sweat he has exchanged for his money
And the blood-weight of money. He'll humble her

With new light on her obligations.
The fried, woody chips, kept warm two hours in the oven,
Are only part of her answer.
Hearing the rest, he slams them to the fire back

And is away round the house-end singing
'Come back to Sorrento' in a voice
Of resounding corrugated iron.
Her back has bunched into a hump as an insult.

For they will have their rights.
Their jurors are to be assembled
From the little crumbs of soot. Their brief
Goes straight up to heaven and nothing more is heard of it.

Examination at the Womb-door

Who owns these scrawny little feet?   *Death*.
Who owns this bristly scorched-looking face?   *Death*.
Who owns these still-working lungs?   *Death*.
Who owns this utility coat of muscles?   *Death*.
Who owns these unspeakable guts?   *Death*.
Who owns these questionable brains?   *Death*.
All this messy blood?   *Death*.
These minimum-efficiency eyes?   *Death*.
This wicked little tongue?   *Death*.
This occasional wakefulness?   *Death*.

Given, stolen, or held pending trial?
Held.

Who owns the whole rainy, stony earth?   *Death*.
Who owns all of space?   *Death*.

Who is stronger than hope?   *Death*.
Who is stronger than the will?   *Death*.
Stronger than love?   *Death*.
Stronger than life?   *Death*.

But who is stronger than death?
                                    Me, evidently.

Pass, Crow.

A Childish Prank

Man's and woman's bodies lay without souls,
Dully gaping, foolishly staring, inert
On the flowers of Eden.
God pondered.

The problem was so great, it dragged him asleep.

Crow laughed.
He bit the Worm, God's only son,
Into two writhing halves.

He stuffed into man the tail half
With the wounded end hanging out.

He stuffed the head half headfirst into woman
And it crept in deeper and up
To peer out through her eyes
Calling its tail-half to join up quickly, quickly
Because O it was painful.

Man awoke being dragged across the grass.
Woman awoke to see him coming.
Neither knew what had happened.

God went on sleeping.

Crow went on laughing.

Esther's Tomcat

Daylong this tomcat lies stretched flat
As an old rough mat, no mouth and no eyes,
Continual wars and wives are what
Have tattered his ears and battered his head.

Like a bundle of old rope and iron
Sleeps till blue dusk. Then reappear
His eyes, green as ringstones: he yawns wide red,
Fangs fine as a lady's needle and bright.

A tomcat sprang at a mounted knight,
Locked round his neck like a trap of hooks
While the knight rode fighting its clawing and bite.
After hundreds of years the stain's there

On the stone where he fell, dead of the tom:
That was at Barnborough. The tomcat still
Grallochs odd dogs on the quiet,
Will take the head clean off your simple pullet,

Is unkillable. From the dog's fury,
From gunshot fired point-blank he brings
His skin whole, and whole
From owlish moons of bekittenings

Among ashcans. He leaps and lightly
Walks upon sleep, his mind on the moon.
Nightly over the round world of men,
Over the roofs go his eyes and outcry.

A Dove

Snaps its twig-tether—mounts—
Free
Dream-yanked up into vacuum
Wings snickering.

Another, in a shatter, hurls dodging away up.

They career through tree-mazes
Nearly uncontrollable love-weights.

And now
Temple-dancers, possessed, and steered
By solemn powers,
Through insane stately convulsions.

Porpoises
Of dove-lust and blood-splendour
With arcs
And plungings, and spray-slow explosions.

Now violently gone
Riding the snake of the long love-whip
Among flarings of mares and stallions.

Now staying
Coiled on a bough
Bubbling molten, wobbling top-heavy
Into one and many.

The River in March

Now the river is rich, but her voice is low.
It is her Mighty Majesty the sea
Travelling among the villages incognito.

Now the river is poor. No song, just a thin mad whisper.
The winter floods have ruined her.
She squats between draggled banks, fingering her rags and rubbish.

And now the river is rich. A deep choir.
It is the lofty clouds, that work in heaven,
Going on their holiday to the sea.

The river is poor again. All her bones are showing.
Through a dry wig of bleached flotsam she peers up ashamed
From her slum of sticks.

Now the river is rich, collecting shawls and minerals.
Rain brought fatness, but she takes ninety-nine per cent
Leaving the fields just one per cent to survive on.

And now she is poor. Now she is East wind sick.
She huddles in holes and corners. The brassy sun gives her a headache.
She has lost all her fish. And she shivers.

But now once more she is rich. She is viewing her lands.
A hoard of king-cups spills from her folds, it blazes, it cannot be
  hidden.
A salmon, a sow of solid silver,

Bulges to glimpse it.

Leaves

Who's killed the leaves?
Me, says the apple, I've killed them all.
Fat as a bomb or a cannonball
I've killed the leaves.

Who sees them drop?
Me, says the pear, they will leave me all bare
So all the people can point and stare.
I see them drop.

Who'll catch their blood?
Me, me, me, says the marrow, the marrow.
I'll get so rotund that they'll need a wheelbarrow.
I'll catch their blood.

Who'll make their shroud?
Me, says the swallow, there's just time enough
Before I must pack all my spools and be off.
I'll make their shroud.

Who'll dig their grave?
Me, says the river, with the power of the clouds
A brown deep grave I'll dig under my floods.
I'll dig their grave.

Who'll be their parson?
Me, says the Crow, for it is well-known
I study the bible right down to the bone.
I'll be their parson.

Who'll be chief mourner?
Me, says the wind, I will cry through the grass
The people will pale and go cold when I pass.
I'll be chief mourner.

Who'll carry the coffin?
Me, says the sunset, the whole world will weep
To see me lower it into the deep.
I'll carry the coffin.

Who'll sing a psalm?
Me, says the tractor, with my gear grinding glottle
I'll plough up the stubble and sing through my throttle.
I'll sing the psalm.

Who'll toll the bell?
Me, says the robin, my song in October
Will tell the still gardens the leaves are over.
I'll toll the bell.

Full Moon and Little Frieda

A cool small evening shrunk to a dog bark and the clank of a bucket—

And you listening.
A spider's web, tense for the dew's touch.
A pail lifted, still and brimming—mirror
To tempt a first star to a tremor.

Cows are going home in the lane there, looping the hedges with their
   warm wreaths of breath—
A dark river of blood, many boulders,
Balancing unspilled milk.

'Moon!' you cry suddenly, 'Moon! Moon!'

The moon has stepped back like an artist gazing amazed at a work
That points at him amazed.

DEREK WALCOTT

Volcano

Joyce was afraid of thunder,
but lions roared at his funeral
from the Zürich zoo.
Was it Zürich or Trieste?
No matter. These are legends, as much
as the death of Joyce is a legend,
or the strong rumour that Conrad
is dead, and that VICTORY is ironic.
On the edge of the night-horizon
from this beach house on the cliffs
there are now, till dawn,
two glares from the miles-out-
at-sea derricks; they are like
the glow of the cigar
and the glow of the volcano
at VICTORY's end.
One could abandon writing
for the slow-burning signals
of the great, to be, instead
their ideal reader, ruminative,
voracious, making the love of masterpieces
superior to attempting
to repeat or outdo them,
and be the greatest reader in the world.

At least it requires awe,
which has been lost to our time,
so many people have seen everything,
so many people can predict,
so many refuse to enter the silence
of victory, the indolence
that burns at the core,
so many are no more than
erect ash, like the cigar,
so many take thunder for granted.
How common is the lightning,
how lost the leviathans
we no longer look for!
There were giants in those days.
In those days they made good cigars.
I must read more carefully.

New World

Then after Eden,
was there one surprise?
O yes, the awe of Adam
at the first bead of sweat.

Thenceforth, all flesh
had to be sown with salt,
to feel the edge of seasons,
fear and harvest,
joy, that was difficult,
but was, at least, his own.

The snake? It would not rust
on its forked tree.
The snake admired labour,
it would not leave him alone.

And both would watch the leaves
silver the alder,
oaks yellowing October,
everything turning money,

so when Adam was exiled
to our New Eden, in the ark's gut,
the coined snake coiled there for good
fellowship also; that was willed.

Adam had an idea.
He and the snake would share
the loss of Eden for a profit.
So both made the New World. And it looked good.

The Virgins

Down the dead streets of sun-stoned Frederiksted,
the first freeport to die for tourism,
strolling at funeral pace, I am reminded
of life not lost to the American dream,
but my small-islander's simplicities
can't better our new empire's civilized
exchange of cameras, watches, perfumes, brandies
for the good life, so cheaply underpriced
that only the crime rate is on the rise
in streets blighted with sun, stone arches
and plazas blown dry by the hysteria
of rumour. A condominium drowns
in vacancy; its bargains are dusted,
but only a jewelled housefly drones
over the bargains. The roulettes spin
rustily to the wind; the vigorous trade
that every morning would begin afresh
by revving up green water round the pierhead
heading for where the banks of silver thresh.

Nights in the Gardens of Port of Spain

Night, our black summer, simplifies her smells
into a village; she assumes the impenetrable

musk of the Negro, grows secret as sweat,
her alleys odorous with shucked oyster shells,

coals of gold oranges, braziers of melon.
Commerce and tambourines increase her heat.

Hellfire or the whorehouse: crossing Park Street,
a surf of sailors' faces crests, is gone

with the sea's phosphorescence; the bôites de nuit
twinkle like fireflies in her thick hair.

Blinded by headlamps, deaf to taxi klaxons,
she lifts her face from the cheap, pitch-oil flare

towards white stars, like cities, flashing neon,
burning to be the bitch she will become.

As daylight breaks the Indian turns his tumbril
of hacked, beheaded coconuts towards home.

The Whale, His Bulwark

To praise the blue whale's crystal jet,
To write, 'O fountain!' honouring a spout
Provokes this curse:
        'The high are humbled yet'
From those who humble Godhead, beasthood, verse.

Once, the Lord raised this bulwark to our eyes,
Once, in our seas, whales threshed,
The harpooner was common. Once, I heard
Of a baleine beached up the Grenadines, fleshed
By derisive, antlike villagers: a prize
Reduced from majesty to pygmy-size.
Salt-crusted, mythological,
And dead.

The boy who told me couldn't believe his eyes,
And I believed him. When I was small
God and a foundered whale were possible.
Whales are rarer, God as invisible.
Yet, through His gift, I praise the unfathomable,
Though the boy may be dead, the praise unfashionable,
The tale apocryphal.

A Country Club Romance

The summer slams the tropic sun
Around all year, and Miss Gautier
Made, as her many friends had done,
Of tennis, her deuxième-métier.

Her breathless bosom rose
As proud as Dunlop balls;
She smelled of the fresh rose
On which the white dew falls.

Laburnum-bright her hair,
Her eyes were blue as ponds,
Her thighs, so tanned and bare,
Sounder than Government bonds.

She'd drive to the Country Club
For a set, a drink, and a tan;
She smoked, but swore never to stub
Herself out on any young man.

The Club was as carefree as Paris,
Its lawns, Arcadian;
Until at one tournament, Harris
Met her, a black Barbadian.

He worked in the Civil Service,
She had this job at the Bank;
When she praised his forearm swerve, his
Brain went completely blank.

O love has its revenges,
Love whom man has devised;
They married and lay down like Slazengers
Together. She was ostracized.

Yet she bore her husband a fine set
Of doubles, twins. And her thanks
Went up to her God that
Her children would not work in banks.

She took an occasional whisky;
Mr Harris could not understand.
He said, 'Since you so damn frisky,
Answer this backhand!'

Next she took pills for sleeping,
And murmured lost names in the night;
She could not hear him weeping:
'Be Jeez, it serve us right.'

Her fleet life ended anno
domini 1947,
From Barclay's D.C.&O.
Her soul ascends to heaven.

To Anglo Catholic prayers
Heaven will be pervious,
Now may Archdeacon Mayers
Send her a powerful service.

Now every afternoon
When tennis soothes our hates,
Mr Harris and his sons,
Drive past the C.C. gates.

While the almonds yellow the beaches,
And the breezes pleat the lake,
And the blondes pray God to 'teach us
To profit from her mistake'.

Force

Life will keep hammering the grass blades into the ground.

I admire this violence;
love is iron. I admire

the brutal exchange between breaker and rock.
They have an understanding.

I may even understand the contract
between the galloping lion and the stunned doe,
there is some yes to terror in her eyes

what I will never understand
is the beast who writes this
and claims the centre of life.

GEOFFREY HILL

Genesis

1

Against the burly air I strode,
Where the tight ocean heaves its load,
Crying the miracles of God.

And first I brought the sea to bear
Upon the dead weight of the land;
And the waves flourished at my prayer,
The rivers spawned their sand.

And where the streams were salt and full
The tough pig-headed salmon strove,
Curbing the ebb and the tide's pull,
To reach the steady hills above.

2

The second day I stood and saw
The osprey plunge with triggered claw,
Feathering blood along the shore,
To lay the living sinew bare.

And the third day I cried: 'Beware
The soft-voiced owl, the ferret's smile,
The hawk's deliberate stoop in air,
Cold eyes, and bodies hooped in steel,
Forever bent upon the kill.'

3

And I renounced, on the fourth day,
This fierce and unregenerate clay,

Building as a huge myth for man
The watery Leviathan,

And made the glove-winged albatross
Scour the ashes of the sea
Where Capricorn and Zero cross,
A brooding immortality—
Such as the charmed phoenix has
In the unwithering tree.

4

The phoenix burns as cold as frost;
And, like a legendary ghost,
The phantom-bird goes wild and lost,
Upon a pointless ocean tossed.

So, the fifth day, I turned again
To flesh and blood and the blood's pain.

5

On the sixth day, as I rode
In haste about the works of God,
With spurs I plucked the horse's blood.

By blood we live, the hot, the cold,
To ravage and redeem the world:
There is no bloodless myth will hold.

And by Christ's blood are men made free
Though in close shrouds their bodies lie
Under the rough pelt of the sea;

Though Earth has rolled beneath her weight
The bones that cannot bear the light.

Picture of a Nativity

Sea-preserved, heaped with sea-spoils,
Ribs, keels, coral sores,
Detached faces, ephemeral oils,
Discharged on the world's outer shores,

A dumb child-king
Arrives at his right place; rests,
Undisturbed, among slack serpents; beasts
With claws flesh-buttered. In the gathering

Of bestial and common hardship
Artistic men appear to worship
And fall down; to recognize
Familiar tokens; believe their own eyes.

Above the marvel, each rigid head,
Angels, their unnatural wings displayed,
Freeze into an attitude
Recalling the dead.

The White Ship

Where the living with effort go,
Or with expense, the drowned wander
Easily: seaman
And king's son also

Who, by gross error lost,
Drift, now, in salt crushed
Polyp- and mackerel-fleshed
Tides between coast and coast,

Submerge or half-appear.
This does not much matter.
They are put down as dead. Water
Silences all who would interfere;

Retains, still, what it might give
As casually as it took away:
Creatures passed through the wet sieve
Without enrichment or decay.

'Domaine Public'

i.m. Robert Desnos, died Terezin Camp, 1945

For reading I can recommend
   the Fathers. How they
cultivate the corrupting flesh:

toothsome contemplation: cleanly
   maggots churning spleen
to milk. For exercise, prolonged

suppression of much improper
   speech from proper tombs.
If the ground opens, should men's mouths

open also? 'I am nothing
   if not saved now!' or
'Christ, what a pantomime!' The days

of the week are seven pits. Look,
   Seigneur, again we
resurrect and the judges come.

GEOFFREY HILL

In Piam Memoriam

1

Created purely from glass the saint stands,
Exposing his gifted quite empty hands
Like a conjurer about to begin,
A righteous man begging of righteous men.

2

In the sun lily-and-gold-coloured,
Filtering the cruder light, he has endured,
A feature for our regard; and will keep;
Of worldly purity the stained archetype.

3

The scummed pond twitches. The great holly-tree,
Emptied and shut, blows clear of wasting snow,
The common, puddled substance: beneath,
Like a revealed mineral, a new earth.

Two Chorale-Preludes
on melodies by Paul Celan

1 Ave Regina Coelorum
Es ist ein Land Verloren...

There is a land called Lost
at peace inside our heads.
The moon, full on the frost,
vivifies these stone heads.

Moods of the verb 'to stare',
split selfhoods, conjugate
ice-facets from the air,
the light glazing the light.

Look at us, Queen of Heaven!
Our solitudes drift by
your solitudes, the seven
dead stars in your sky.

2 Te Lucis Ante Terminum

Wir gehen dir, Heimat, ins Garn...

Centaury with your staunch bloom
you there alder beech you fern,
midsummer closeness my far home,
fresh traces of lost origin.

Silvery the black cherries hang,
the plum-tree oozes through each cleft
and horse-flies siphon the green dung,
glued to the sweetness of their graft:

immortal transience, a 'kind
of otherness', self-understood,
BE FAITHFUL grows upon the mind
as lichen glimmers on the wood.

A Short History of British India

1

Make miniatures of the once-monstrous theme:
the red-coat devotees, mêlées of wheels,
Jagannath's lovers. With indifferent aim
unleash the rutting cannon at the walls

of forts and palaces; pollute the wells.
Impound the memoirs for their bankrupt shame,
fantasies of true destiny that kills
'under the sanction of the English name'.

Be moved by faith, obedience without fault,
the flawless hubris of heroic guilt,
the grace of visitation; and be stirred

by all her god-quests, her idolatries,
in conclave of abiding injuries,
sated upon the stillness of the bride.

2

Suppose they sweltered here three thousand years
patient for our destruction. There is a greeting
beyond the act. Destiny is the great thing,
true lord of annexation and arrears.

Our law-books overrule the emperors.
The mango is the bride-bed of light. Spring
jostles the flame-tree. But new mandates bring
new images of faith, good subahdars!

The flittering candles of the wayside shrines
melt into dawn. The sun surmounts the dust.
Krishna from Radha lovingly untwines.

Lugging the earth, the oxen bow their heads.
The alien conscience of our days is lost
among the ruins and on endless roads.

3

Malcolm and Frere, Colebrooke and Elphinstone,
the life of empire like the life of the mind
'simple, sensuous, passionate', attuned
to the clear theme of justice and order, gone.

Gone the ascetic pastimes, the Persian
scholarship, the wild boar run to ground,
the watercolours of the sun and wind.
Names rise like outcrops on the rich terrain,

like carapaces of the Mughal tombs
lop-sided in the rice-fields, boarded-up
near railway-sidings and small aerodromes.

'India's a peacock-shrine next to a shop
selling mangola, sitars, lucky charms,
heavenly Buddhas smiling in their sleep.'

PETER REDGROVE

Christiana

That day in the Interpreter's house, in one of his Significant Rooms,
There was naught but an ugly spider hanging by her hands on the wall,
And it was a spacious room, the best in all the house.
'Is there but one spider in all this spacious room?'
And then the water stood in my eyes
And I thought how like an ugly creature I looked
In what fine room soever I was,
And my heart crept like a spider.

And my heart crept like a spider into the centre of my web
And I sat bell-tongued there and my sound
Was the silvery look of my rounds and radii,
And I bent and sucked some blood, but I did it
With care and elegance like a crane unloading vessels;
I set myself on damask linen and I was lost to sight there,
And I hugged my legs astride it, wrapping the pearl-bunch round;
I skated on the water with legs of glass, and with candystriped legs
Ran through the dew like green racks of glass cannonball;
And I saw myself hanging with trustful hands
In any room in every house, hanging on by faith
Like wolfhounds that were dwarfs, or stout shaggy oats,
And I wept to have found so much of myself ugly
In the trustful beasts that are jewel-eyed and full of clean machinery,
And thought that many a spacious heart was ugly
And empty without its tip-toe surprise of spiders
Running like cracks in the universe of a smooth white ceiling,
And how a seamless heart is like a stone.

And the Interpreter saw
The stillness of the water standing in her eyes,
And said,
Now you must work on Beelzebub's black flies for Me.

The Curiosity-Shop

It was a Borgia-pot, he told me,
A baby had been distilled alive into the pottery,
He recommended the cream, it would make a mess of anybody's face;
My grief moved down my cheeks in a slow mass like ointment.

Or there was this undine-vase, if you shook it
The spirit made a silvery tinkling inside;
Flat on the table, it slid so that it pointed always towards the sea.
A useful compass, he said.
I could never unseal this jar, tears would never stop flowing towards
    the sea.

Impatiently he offered me the final item, a ghoul-sack,
I was to feed it with rats daily unless I had a great enemy
Could be persuaded to put his head inside;
That's the one! I said,
That's the sackcloth suit sewn for the likes of me
With my one love's grief, and my appetite for curiosity.

Intimate Supper

He switched on the electric light and laughed,
He let light shine in the firmament of his ceiling,
He saw the great light shine around and it was good,
The great light that rilled through its crystalline pendentives,
And marvelled at its round collection in a cheval glass,
And twirled the scattered crystal rays in his champagne glass.
He spun the great winds through his new hoover
And let light be in the kitchen and that was good too
For he raised up the lid of the stock-pot
And dipped a deep spoon in the savours that were rich
And swarming, and felt the flavours live in his mouth
Astream with waters. He danced to the fire and raked it and created
    red heat
And skipped to the bathroom and spun the shining taps
Dividing air from the deep, and the water, good creature,
Gave clouds to his firmament for he had raked the bowels

Of the seamy coal that came from the deep earth.
And he created him Leviathan and wallowed there,
Rose, and made his own image in the steamy mirrors
Having brooded over them, wiping them free
Again from steamy chaos and the mist that rose from the deep,
But the good sight faded
For there was no help, no help meet for him at all,
And he set his table with two stars pointed on wax
And with many stars in the cutlery and clear crystal
And he set thereon fruits of the earth, and thin clean bowls
For the clear waters of the creatures of earth that love to be cooked,
And until the time came that he had appointed
Walked in his garden in the cool of the evening, waited.

The Million

The number one is a good clean number;
It is like the first bold finger-stroke down a stranger's spine;
It is also a black obelisk with sealed doors:
On the stroke of one they open.

The number ten winks at us all
And its lids open sideways
Like certain other lips, and it is not an impossible number.

The number one hundred
Is like three people in front of a firing-squad;
Two have already fallen, collapsed.

The number one thousand is a cheap funeral
With a tricycle lugging the coffin;
The number one thousand is not large enough, even for a dead man.

The number ten thousand however
Begins to lean with its dark tunnel
Against its closed door;
I lean on its door to keep it shut; like an inheritance, it scares me.

The number one hundred thousand seems to be better
Since it immediately converts itself to a sum of money in a newspaper
And then to a lower figure which is the simple interest
And a very comfortable income.

But the horror of the number a million
Wipes his one long lip with her knickers
Free from the grease of the last massacred lady
Where he squats with the bones

On the glittering desert island of far greater numbers than he,
Circled by seas of numbers greater and more traitless than they.

I return to the first number, one, which is the prime candle
Muting a gracious hollow upward flame.

Dog Prospectus

The dog must see your corpse. The last thing that you feel
Must be the dog's warm-tufa licking of your hand,
Its clear gaze on your trembling lips, then
Snapping at flies, catches the last breath in its teeth,
And trots off with you quickly to the Judge,
Your advocate and friend. The corpse a dog has not seen
Pollutes a thousand men; the Bishop's hound
Tucked like a cushion at his tombstone feet
Once through the door carries a helix staff
And looks like Hermes on that side, the Bishop tumbling
On the puppy-paws of death . . .
          as a temporary Professor at this U
I practise, when the campus swarms with them,
Focusing out the students, so the place
Is amply empty, except for a few dogs.
They should study here, the U enrol them
And take more fees, at agreed standards teaching
Elementary Urinology, and Advanced
Arboreal Urinology: The Seasons and their Smells;
Freshman Osteology: The Selection and Concealment
Of Bones; Janitology: The Budding Watchdog, with
Fawning, a two-semester course. Lunar Vocalization,

Or Baying at the Moon; the 'lame-dog bid for sympathy
With big sad eyes and hanging tongue'. which is
Cosmetic Ophthalmology with Intermittent Claudication
In the Rhetorical Physiognomy Gym. Shit and Its Meaning;
Coprology: the Dog-Turd and Modern Legislation; The
Eating of Jezebel, or Abreactive Phantasising; The Black Dog,
Or Studies in Melancholy; The Age of Worry:
An Era Favourable to Dogs .... How to Beg:
A Long-Term Economic Good; with How to Fuck,
Or Staggering in Six-Legged Joy; Fleas,
A Useful Oracle, and in this same last year
The Dedicated Castrate or God's Eunuch,
The Canine Celibate as Almost-Man;
And finally how, if uncastrated,
To change places and become Master-Dog,
The Palindromic Homocane and Goddog-Doggod,
Wise Hermes of the Intelligent Nose,

Leading to the Degree of Master of Hounds.
The campus throngs with hounds, this degree
Is very popular, alas—
I focus them out: in ample emptiness
A few humans hurry to their deep study
Without prospectus, without University.
This one is desirous of becoming a perfect scribe:
He knows vigilance, ferocity, and how to bark;
This one studies gazing as the dogs used to
On the images of the gods, as prophets should.
What gods, what images?

Those glorious trees, trilling with birds, cicadas,
Pillars of the sky, our books and ancestors;
I piss my tribute here, I cannot help it;
The few humans left, noble as dogs once were,
Piss on this university.

Design

The designer sits, head in hand.
What costume could be better for battle, the more sensible?
Why, one blood won't mar.
I'll score it with scarlet.

But often men outlast deep wounds.
Some blood is old, and black.
Let's have a tatter, then, I slash scarlet black.

And here is a master-stroke. Let it be random tatter.
Random tables fed into the looms.
Thus as they advance none perhaps are wounded,

Or all are, mortally, and ripped from the field.
Horrible half-dry men.
Yes. Let them advance as though ripped from the clay.
One of the many patterns of battle.
And pipeclay features with blacking sockets, General.

Red Indian Corpse

Deer-of-the-Waters: he laboured hard on his grammar
And learnt to say John Doe; his coat of arms of a deer
Went back to the Stone Age: the family mark,
The dodaim or totem which was his true father
And everyone's true father, since the pregnant women
Fed on venison, and this built his body; the red flesh
Of all his ancestors was this same totem venison.
Then they did the Italian Pope Trick on him:
Confessed him, shot him, and as one might say
John O'Woman, called him after the totem: Doe,
Typed on a tag-label tied to his left big toe.

PETER REDGROVE

Serious Readers

All the flies are reading microscopic books;
They hold themselves quite tense and silent
With shoulders hunched, legs splayed out
On the white formica table-top, reading.
With my book I slide into the diner-booth;
They rise and circle and settle again, reading
With hunched corselets. They do not attempt to taste
Before me my fat hamburger-plate, but wait,
Like courteous readers until I put it to one side,
Then taste briefly and resume their tomes
Like reading-stands with horny specs. I
Read as I eat, one fly
Alights on my book, the size of print;
I let it be. Read and let read.

JON STALLWORTHY

A Letter from Berlin

My dear,
    Today a letter from Berlin
where snow—the first of '38—flew in,
settled and shrivelled on the lamp last night,
broke moth wings mobbing the window. Light
woke me early, but the trams were late:
I had to run from the Brandenburg Gate
skidding, groaning like a tram, and sodden
to the knees. Von Neumann operates at 10
and would do if the sky fell in. They lock
his theatre doors on the stroke of the clock—
but today I was lucky: found a gap
in the gallery next to a chap
I knew just as the doors were closing. Last,
as expected, on Von Showmann's list

the new vaginal hysterectomy
that brought me to Berlin.
                    Delicately
he went to work, making from right to left
a semi-circular incision. Deft
dissection of the fascia. The blood-
blossoming arteries nipped in the bud.
Speculum, scissors, clamps—the uterus
cleanly delivered, the pouch of Douglas
stripped to the rectum, and the cavity
closed. Never have I seen such masterly
technique. 'And so little bleeding!' I said
half to myself, half to my neighbour.
                    'Dead,'
came his whisper. 'Don't be a fool'
I said, for still below us in the pool
of light the marvellous unhurried hands
were stitching, tying the double strands
of catgut, stitching, tying. It was like
a concert, watching those hands unlock
the music from their score. And at the end
one half expected him to turn and bend
stiffly towards us. Stiffly he walked out
and his audience shuffled after. But
finishing my notes in the gallery
I saw them uncover the patient: she
was dead.
                    I met my neighbour in the street
waiting for the same tram, stamping his feet
on the pavement's broken snow, and said:
'I have to apologize. She was dead,
but how did you know?' Back came his voice
like a bullet '—saw it last month, twice.'

Returning your letter to an envelope
yellower by years than when you sealed it up,
darkly the omens emerge. A ritual wound
yellow at the lip yawns in my hand;
a turbulent crater; a trench, filled
not with snow only, east of Buchenwald.

JON STALLWORTHY

Miss Lavender

Miss Lavender taught us to ride
clamping halfcrowns between saddle and knee
on Sunday afternoons
in a watermeadow one mile wide:
and the hot halfcrowns
she would keep, after an hour, for her fee.

Her horses stepped like a king's own
always to imperatives of Spanish drill.
Miss Lavender said,
'A horseman has to be thrown
ten times.' From thoroughbred
to exploding grass we headoverheeled; until

that March the watermeadow froze
and Miss Lavender died, consumptive
on a stable floor
among motionless horses. Those
died after for no reason, or
for want of a Spanish imperative.

A Question of Form and Content

I owe you an apology,
love my love, for here you are
in a school anthology
without so much as a bra
between your satin self and those
who come upon us in crisp sheets.
What they will make of us, God knows,
but no harm's done if it's
what we make of each other. Let
them observe, love, our *enjambement*.
They shall be guests at the secret
wedding of form and content.

JON STALLWORTHY

The Beginning of the End

1

Passing the great plane tree in the square—
and noticing me noticing
the railing's sawn-off arrowhead
ingrown too many rings deep there
in 1940 to be shifted—
you ask me what I am thinking,
and wish the words unsaid.

2

'Our' café

since a morning
not to be talked about
these mornings

has put out

its tulip awning,
and the bell above the door
like a clockwork canary
sings its one song.

As we
crossed this chequerboard floor

'Buon giorno'

affable
as if we were regulars.
Setting down our saucers
on the glass-topped table

'Due grandi neri—
this morning, please,
you are my guests. The lease
finito. I shall be
with the vino rosso
next month in Tuscany.
No more grandi neri,
no more espresso.'

Spilt coffee
           spelt my name
           and your name, linked, on this
           glass table—our knees kiss-
           ing under it.
                The same
finger writes TUSCANY
and rubs it out. We have
run out of words
           like love.
Next month where shall we be?

                3

Getting up to go.
'My gloves!' Floor, seat,
handbag—'oh no, no,
not in the street!'

        My first present. It
        seemed right and proper
        enough. 'A perfect fit'
        said the girl in the shop
        as one hand pushed
        the other, finger by
        finger, home; and you blushed
        to meet my eye.

Stripped of their shadows,
disconsolate hands stare
at each other and those
inert elsewhere—
the warmth and scent
of their fingers failing,
trampled on the pavement,
impaled on a railing.

Walking against the Wind

'*Roast chestnuts, a shilling*
a bag.' Shilling and bag
change hands by brazier light.
And there they stand shelling
plump kernels to plug
each other's mouth as tight

as with a kiss. She wears
his blue coat, but the wind
cannot touch him with that
hot nut in his hand
and her thawing fingers
moving towards his mouth.

They shelter in my mind
at midnight, as the brilliant
mosaic towers black out.
Walking against the wind
I wish them a blue coat
for coverlet; jubilant

knowledge of each other;
ignorance that it blows
nowhere on earth so cold
as nightly between those
whom God hath joined together
to have and not to hold.

Again

I have been there again, and seen the backs
convulsing at the heart of the bazaar,
spasmed with laughter and the lunging jar
of shoulders as the fruit is thrown. A crack

in the crowd wall brought me to the ring
where, linked so one at first could not tell which
was which, the pie-dog and his trembling bitch
suffered the tribesmen's pitiless pelting.

Though terrible their straining from each other,
her crying and his scabbed flanks shaken
with hurt and terror—worse to waken
from that harsh sobbing to the bed's shudder.

War Story

of one who grew up at Gallipoli
not over months and miles, but in the space
of feet and half a minute. Wading shoreward
with a plague of bullets pocking the sea
he tripped, as it seemed to him over his scabbard,
and stubbed his fingers on a dead man's face.

Sindhi Woman

Barefoot through the bazaar,
and with the same undulant grace
as the cloth blown back from her face,
she glides with a stone jar
high on her head
and not a ripple in her tread.

Watching her cross erect
stones, garbage, excrement, and crumbs
of glass in the Karachi slums,
I, with my stoop, reflect
they stand most straight
who learn to walk beneath a weight.

SEAMUS HEANEY

Death of a Naturalist

All year the flax-dam festered in the heart
Of the townland; green and heavy-headed
Flax had rotted there, weighted down by huge sods.
Daily it sweltered in the punishing sun.
Bubbles gargled delicately, bluebottles
Wove a strong gauze of sound around the smell.
There were dragon-flies, spotted butterflies,
But best of all was the warm thick slobber
Of frogspawn that grew like clotted water
In the shade of the banks. Here, every spring
I would fill jampotfuls of the jellied
Specks to range on window-sills at home,
On shelves at school, and wait and watch until
The fattening dots burst into nimble-
Swimming tadpoles. Miss Walls would tell us how
The daddy frog was called a bullfrog
And how he croaked and how the mammy frog
Laid hundreds of little eggs and this was
Frogspawn. You could tell the weather by frogs too
For they were yellow in the sun and brown
In rain.

    Then one hot day when fields were rank
With cowdung in the grass the angry frogs
Invaded the flax-dam; I ducked through hedges
To a coarse croaking that I had not heard
Before. The air was thick with a bass chorus.
Right down the dam gross-bellied frogs were cocked
On sods; their loose necks pulsed like sails. Some hopped:
The slap and plop were obscene threats. Some sat
Poised like mud grenades, their blunt heads farting.
I sickened, turned, and ran. The great slime kings
Were gathered there for vengeance and I knew
That if I dipped my hand the spawn would clutch it.

The Outlaw

Kelly's kept an unlicensed bull, well away
From the road: you risked fine but had to pay

The normal fee if cows were serviced there.
Once I dragged a nervous Friesian on a tether

Down a lane of alder, shaggy with catkin,
Down to the shed the bull was kept in.

I gave Old Kelly the clammy silver, though why
I could not guess. He grunted a curt 'Go by

Get up on that gate.' And from my lofty station
I watched the business-like conception.

The door, unbolted, whacked back against the wall.
The illegal sire fumbled from his stall

Unhurried as an old steam-engine shunting.
He circled, snored and nosed. No hectic panting,

Just the unfussy ease of a good tradesman;
Then an awkward, unexpected jump, and

His knobbled forelegs, straddling her flank,
He slammed life home, impassive as a tank,

Dropping off like a tipped-up load of sand.
'She'll do,' said Kelly and tapped his ash-plant

Across her hindquarters. 'If not, bring her back.'
I walked ahead of her, the rope now slack

While Kelly whooped and prodded his outlaw
Who, in his own time, resumed the dark, the straw.

Rite of Spring

So winter closed its fist
And got it stuck in the pump.
The plunger froze up a lump

In its throat, ice founding itself
Upon iron. The handle
Paralysed at an angle.

Then the twisting of wheat straw
Into ropes, lapping them tight
Round stem and snout, then a light

That sent the pump up in flame.
It cooled, we lifted her latch,
Her entrance was wet, and she came.

A Drink of Water

She came every morning to draw water
Like an old bat staggering up the field:
The pump's whooping cough, the bucket's clatter
And slow diminuendo as it filled,
Announced her. I recall
Her grey apron, the pocked white enamel
Of the brimming bucket, and the treble
Creak of her voice like the pump's handle.
Nights when a full moon lifted past her gable
It fell back through her window and would lie
Into the water set out on the table.
Where I have dipped to drink again, to be
Faithful to the admonishment on her cup,
Remember the Giver fading off the lip.

Limbo

Fishermen at Ballyshannon
Netted an infant last night
Along with the salmon.
An illegitimate spawning,

A small one thrown back
To the waters. But I'm sure
As she stood in the shallows
Ducking him tenderly

Till the frozen knobs of her wrists
Were dead as the gravel,
He was a minnow with hooks
Tearing her open.

She waded in under
The sign of her cross.
He was hauled in with the fish.
Now limbo will be

A cold glitter of souls
Through some far briny zone.
Even Christ's palms, unhealed,
Smart and cannot fish there.

The Skunk

Up, black, striped and damasked like the chasuble
At a funeral mass, the skunk's tail
Paraded the skunk. Night after night
I expected her like a visitor.

The refrigerator whinnied into silence.
My desk light softened beyond the verandah.
Small oranges loomed in the orange tree.
I began to be tense as a voyeur.

After eleven years I was composing
Love-letters again, broaching the word 'wife'
Like a stored cask, as if its slender vowel
Had mutated into the night earth and air

Of California. The beautiful, useless
Tang of eucalyptus spelt your absence.
The aftermath of a mouthful of wine
Was like inhaling you off a cold pillow.

And there she was, the intent and glamorous,
Ordinary, mysterious skunk,
Mythologized, demythologized,
Snuffing the boards five feet beyond me.

It all came back to me last night, stirred
By the sootfall of your things at bedtime,
Your head-down, tail-up hunt in a bottom drawer
For the black plunge-line nightdress.

Whatever You Say Say Nothing

1

I'm writing just after an encounter
With an English journalist in search of 'views
On the Irish thing'. I'm back in winter
Quarters where bad news is no longer news,

Where media-men and stringers sniff and point,
Where zoom lenses, recorders and coiled leads
Litter the hotels. The times are out of joint
But I incline as much to rosary beads

As to the jottings and analyses
Of politicians and newspapermen
Who've scribbled down the long campaign from gas
And protest to gelignite and sten,

Who proved upon their pulses 'escalate',
'Backlash' and 'crack down', 'the provisional wing',
'Polarization' and 'long-standing hate'.
Yet I live here, I live here too, I sing,

Expertly civil tongued with civil neighbours
On the high wires of first wireless reports,
Sucking the fake taste, the stony flavours
Of those sanctioned, old, elaborate retorts:

'Oh, it's disgraceful, surely, I agree,'
'Where's it going to end?' 'It's getting worse.'
'They're murderers.' 'Internment, understandably...'
The 'voice of sanity' is getting hoarse.

2

Men die at hand. In blasted street and home
The gelignite's a common sound effect:
As the man said when Celtic won, 'The Pope of Rome
's a happy man this night.' His flock suspect

In their deepest heart of hearts the heretic
Has come at last to heel and to the stake.
We tremble near the flames but want no truck
With the actual firing. We're on the make

As ever. Long sucking the hind tit
Cold as a witch's and as hard to swallow
Still leaves us fork-tongued on the border bit:
The liberal papist note sounds hollow

When amplified and mixed in with the bangs
That shake all hearts and windows day and night.
(It's tempting here to rhyme on 'labour pangs'
And diagnose a rebirth in our plight,

But that would be to ignore other symptoms.
Last night you didn't need a stethoscope
To hear the eructation of Orange drums
Allergic equally to Pearse and Pope.)

On all sides 'little platoons' are mustering—
The phrase is Cruise O'Brien's via that great
Backlash, Burke—while I sit here with a pestering
Drouth for words at once both gaff and bait

To lure the tribal shoals to epigram
And order. I believe any of us
Could draw the line through bigotry and sham
Given the right line, *aere perennius*.

3

'Religion's never mentioned here,' of course.
'You know them by their eyes,' and hold your tongue.
'One side's as bad as the other,' never worse.
Christ, it's near time that some small leak was sprung

In the great dykes the Dutchman made
To dam the dangerous tide that followed Seamus.
Yet for all this art and sedentary trade
I am incapable. The famous

Northern reticence, the tight gag of place
And times: yes, yes. Of the 'wee six' I sing
Where to be saved you only must save face
And whatever you say, you say nothing.

Smoke-signals are loud-mouthed compared with us:
Manoeuvrings to find out name and school,
Subtle discrimination by addresses
With hardly an exception to the rule

That Norman, Ken and Sidney signalled Prod
And Seamus (call me Sean) was sure-fire Pape.
O land of password, handgrip, wink and nod,
Of open minds as open as a trap,

Where tongues lie coiled, as under flames lie wicks,
Where half of us, as in a wooden horse
Were cabin'd and confined like wily Greeks,
Besieged within the siege, whispering morse.

4

This morning from a dewy motorway
I saw the new camp for the internees:
A bomb had left a crater of fresh clay
In the roadside, and over in the trees

Machine-gun posts defined a real stockade.
There was that white mist you get on a low ground
And it was déjà-vu, some film made
Of Stalag 17, a bad dream with no sound.

Is there a life before death? That's chalked up
In Ballymurphy. Competence with pain,
Coherent miseries, a bite and sup,
We hug our little destiny again.

DEREK MAHON

I Am Raftery

I am Raftery, hesitant and confused among
the cold-voiced graduate students and inter-
changeable instructors. Were it not for the
nice wives who do the talking I would have
run out of hope some time ago, and of love.
I have traded-in the 'simplistic maunderings'
that made me famous, for a wry dissimulation,
an imagery of adventitious ambiguity dredged
from God knows what polluted underground spring.
Death is near, I have come of age, I doubt if
I shall survive another East Anglian winter.
Scotch please, plenty of water. I am reading
Joyce by touch and it's killing me. Is it
empty pockets I play to? Not on your life,
they ring with a bright inflationary music—
two seminars a week and my own place reserved
in the record library. Look at me now,
my back to the wall, taking my cue
from an idiot disc-jockey between commercials.

Grandfather

They brought him in on a stretcher from the world,
Wounded but humorous. And he soon recovered.
Boiler-rooms, row upon row of gantries rolled
Away to reveal the landscape of a childhood
Only he can recapture. Even on cold
Mornings he is up at six with a block of wood
Or a box of nails, discreetly up to no good
Or banging round the house like a four-year-old—

Never there when you call. But after dark
You hear his great boots thumping in the hall
And in he comes, as cute as they come. Each night
His shrewd eyes bolt the door and set the clock
Against the future, then his light goes out.
Nothing escapes him; he escapes us all.

My Wicked Uncle

His was the first corpse I had ever seen,
Untypically silent in the front room.
Death had deprived him of his moustache,
His thick horn-rimmed spectacles,
The easy corners of his salesman dash—
Those things by which I had remembered him—
And sundered him behind a sort of gauze.
His hair was badly parted on the right
As if for Sunday School. That night
I saw my uncle as he really was.

The stories he retailed were mostly
Wicked-avuncular fantasy;
He went in for waistcoats and Brylcreem.
But something about him
Demanded that you picture the surprise
Of the Chairman of the Board, when to
'What will you have with your whisky?' my uncle replies,
'Another whisky please.'

He claimed to have been arrested in New York
Twice on the same day—
The crookedest chief steward in the Head Line.
And once, so he would say,
Sailing from San Francisco to Shanghai,
He brought a crew of lascars out on strike
In protest at the loss of a day's pay
Crossing the International Dateline.

He was buried on a blustery day above the sea,
The young Presbyterian minister
Tangled and wind-swept in the sea air.
I saw sheep huddled in the long wet grass
Of the golf course, and the empty freighters
Sailing for ever down Belfast Lough
In a fine rain, their sirens going,
As the gradual graph of my uncle's life
And times dipped precipitately
Into the black earth of Carnmoney Cemetery.

His teenage kids are growing horns and claws—
More wicked already than ever my uncle was.

The Banished Gods

Near the headwaters of the longest river
        There is a forest clearing,
            A dank, misty place
        Where light stands in columns
And birds sing with a noise like paper tearing.

Far from land, far from the trade routes,
        In an unbroken dream-time
            Of penguin and whale,
        The seas sigh to themselves
Reliving the days before the days of sail.

Where the wires end the moor seethes in silence,
  Scattered with scree, primroses,
    Feathers and faeces.
  It shelters the hawk and hears
In dreams the forlorn cries of lost species.

It is here that the banished gods are in hiding,
  Here they sit out the centuries
    In stone, water
    And the hearts of trees,
Lost in a reverie of their own natures—

Of zero-growth economics and seasonal change
  In a world without cars, computers
    Or chemical skies,
  Where thought is a fondling of stones
And wisdom a five-minute silence at moonrise.

A Disused Shed in Co. Wexford

'Let them not forget us, the weak souls among the asphodels'—
                            Seferis, *Mythistorema*

  Even now there are places where a thought might grow—
  Peruvian mines, worked out and abandoned
  To a slow clock of condensation,
  An echo trapped for ever, and a flutter
  Of wildflowers in the lift-shaft,
  Indian compounds where the wind dances
  And a door bangs with diminished confidence,
  Lime crevices behind rippling rainbarrels,
  Dog corners for bone burials;
  And in a disused shed in Co. Wexford,

  Deep in the grounds of a burnt-out hotel,
  Among the bathtubs and the washbasins
  A thousand mushrooms crowd to a keyhole.
  This is the one star in their firmament
  Or frames a star within a star.

What should they do there but desire?
So many days beyond the rhododendrons
With the world waltzing in its bowl of cloud,
They have learnt patience and silence
Listening to the rooks querulous in the high wood.

They have been waiting for us in a foetor
Of vegetable sweat since civil war days,
Since the gravel-crunching, interminable departure
Of the expropriated mycologist.
He never came back, and light since then
Is a keyhole rusting gently after rain.
Spiders have spun, flies dusted to mildew,
And once a day, perhaps, they have heard something—
A trickle of masonry, a shout from the blue
Or a lorry changing gear at the end of the lane.

There have been deaths, the pale flesh flaking
Into the earth that nourished it;
And nightmares, born of these and the grim
Dominion of stale air and rank moisture.
Those nearest the door grow strong—
'Elbow room! Elbow room!'
The rest, dim in a twilight of crumbling
Utensils and broken flower-pots, groaning
For their deliverance, have been so long
Expectant that there is left only the posture.

A half century, without visitors, in the dark—
Poor preparation for the cracking lock
And creak of hinges. Magi, moonmen,
Powdery prisoners of the old regime,
Web-throated, stalked like triffids, racked by drought
And insomnia, only the ghost of a scream
At the flash-bulb firing squad we wake them with
Shows there is life yet in their feverish forms.
Grown beyond nature now, soft food for worms,
They lift frail heads in gravity and good faith.

They are begging us, you see, in their wordless way,
To do something, to speak on their behalf
Or at least not to close the door again.
Lost people of Treblinka and Pompeii!
'Save us, save us,' they seem to say,
'Let the god not abandon us
Who have come so far in darkness and in pain.
We too had our lives to live.
You with your light meter and relaxed itinerary,
Let not our naïve labours have been in vain!'

The Snow Party

Bashō, coming
To the city of Nagoya,
Is asked to a snow party.

There is a tinkling of china
And tea into china;
There are introductions.

Then everyone
Crowds to the window
To watch the falling snow.

Snow is falling on Nagoya
And farther south
On the tiles of Kyōto.

Eastward, beyond Irago,
It is falling
Like leaves on the cold sea.

Elsewhere they are burning
Witches and heretics
In the boiling squares,

Thousands have died since dawn
In the service
Of barbarous kings;

But there is silence
In the houses of Nagoya
And the hills of Ise.

DOUGLAS DUNN

The Patricians

In small backyards old men's long underwear
Drips from sagging clotheslines.
The other stuff they take in bundles to the Bendix.

There chatty women slot their coins and joke
About the grey unmentionables absent.
The old men weaken in the steam and scratch at their rough chins.

Suppressing coughs and stiffnesses, they pedal bikes
On low gear slowly, in their faces
The effort to be upright, the dignity

That fits inside the smell of aromatic pipes.
Walking their dogs, the padded beats of pocket watches
Muffled under ancient overcoats, silences their hearts.

They live watching each other die, passing each other
In their white scarves, too long known to talk,
Waiting for the inheritance of the oldest, a right to power.

The street patricians, they are ignored.
Their anger proves something, their disenchantments
Settle round me like a cold fog.

They are the individualists of our time.
They know no fashions, copy nothing but their minds.
Long ago, they gave up looking in mirrors.

Dying in their sleep, they lie undiscovered.
The howling of their dogs brings the sniffing police,
Their middle-aged children from the new estates.

A Removal from Terry Street

On a squeaking cart, they push the usual stuff,
A mattress, bed ends, cups, carpets, chairs,
Four paperback westerns. Two whistling youths
In surplus U.S. Army battle-jackets
Remove their sister's goods. Her husband
Follows, carrying on his shoulders the son
Whose mischief we are glad to see removed,
And pushing, of all things, a lawnmower.
There is no grass in Terry Street. The worms
Come up cracks in concrete yards in moonlight.
That man, I wish him well. I wish him grass.

Glasgow Schoolboys, Running Backwards

High wind ... They turn their backs to it, and push.
Their crazy strides are chopped in little steps.
And all their lives, like that, they'll have to rush
Forwards in reverse, always holding their caps.

After the War

The soldiers came, brewed tea in Snoddy's field
Beside the wood from where we watched them pee
In Snoddy's stagnant pond, small boys hidden
In pines and firs. The soldiers stood or sat
Ten minutes in the field, some officers apart
With the select problems of a map. Before,
Soldiers were imagined, we were them, gunfire
In our mouths, most cunning local skirmishers.
Their sudden arrival silenced us. I lay down
On the grass and saw the blue shards of an egg
We'd broken, its warm yolk on the green grass,
And pine cones like little hand grenades.

One burst from an imaginary Browning,
A grenade well thrown by a child's arm,
And all these faces like our fathers' faces
Would fall back bleeding, trucks would burst in flames,
A blood-stained map would float on Snoddy's pond.
Our ambush made the soldiers laugh, and some
Made booming noises from behind real rifles
As we ran among them begging for badges,
Our plimsolls on the fallen May-blossom
Like boots on the faces of dead children.
But one of us had left. I saw him go
Out through the gate, I heard him on the road
Running to his mother's house. They lived alone,
Behind a hedge round an untended garden
Filled with broken toys, abrasive loss;
A swing that creaked, a rusted bicycle.
He went inside just as the convoy passed.

Warriors

'O arms that arm, for a child's wars, the child!'—Randall Jarrell

Though never in the wards of the hospital for
Disabled servicemen at Erskine—First World War—
I saw an old man wheelchaired through its park one night
By an old man who was blind. The candles were alight
On chestnut trees, a lame destroyer on the Clyde
Was being nursed by tugs against the highest tide
Of May to its dismantlement. The wheelchaired man
Was watching, too, telling his friend, that veteran
And blinded one, all that was going on. No shock
Of pride or pity moved me then. Dumbarton Rock
Rose in the dusk, my own Gibraltar. History
Was everywhere as forts and battles, conscripting me.

My mother went to Erskine once with ladies from
Inchinnan Women's Guild. In bed when she came home,
I heard her tell my father how moved she'd been by these
Blinded basketweavers and nimble amputees.
In my imagination, there is a special place
For that night, for that Park, and for the expert face

Of the man in the wheelchair, and his friend who was blind.
If that is wrong, or nearly patriotic, I don't mind.
To me it's neither. For they had suffered all that gore
We played at, and made me see that as a guilty war,
A childhood. Neither willingness nor wounds would lead
Me to them from the field. In no war would I bleed.

Remembering Lunch

Noticing from what they talk about, and how they stand, or walk,
That my friends have lost the ability or inclination to wander
Along the shores of an estuary or sea in contented solitude,
Disturbs me on the increasingly tedious subject of myself.
I long for more chances to walk along depopulated shores,
For more hours dedicated to fine discriminations of mud
As it shades from grey to silver or dries into soft pottery;
Discriminations of wind, sky, rough grasses and water-birds,
And, above all, to be well-dressed in tweeds and serviceable shoes
Although not like an inverted popinjay of the demented gentry
But as a schoolmaster of some reading and sensibility
Circa 1930 and up to his eccentric week-end pursuits, noticing,
Before the flood of specialists, the trace of lost peoples
In a partly eroded mound, marks in the earth, or this and that
Turned over with the aforementioned impermeable footwear.
Describing this to my strangely sophisticated companions
Is to observe them docket it for future reference in
A pigeon-hole of the mind labelled *Possible Satires*.
We are far gone in our own decay. I admit it freely,
Longing no more for even the wherewithal of decent sufficiency
Or whatever hypothetical brilliance makes it possible.
Whatever my friends long for, they no longer confess it
In the afternoon twilight of a long lunch in London
After that moment when the last carafe has been ordered.
Such delicate conversations of years gone by! You would think
Perceptions of this sort best left for approaching senility,
Especially as, in my case, I was not born ever to expect
To enjoy so long-drawn-out a lunchtime at steep prices
Among tolerant waiters resigned to our lasting presences
As if they could sense a recapitulation by young men of young men
In that fine hour of Edwardian promise at the *Tour Eiffel*

Or expatriate Americans and Irishmen in 'twenties Paris.
It is pretty well standard among literary phenomena.
Whether in the Rome of Martial Martialis or London ordinaries
Favoured by roaring playwrights and poets destined for
Future righteousness or a destructive addiction to sack,
Lunch, lunch is a unitary principle, as Balzac would tell you
And as any man of letters consulting his watch towards noon
Would undoubtedly endorse. Lunch is the business of capitals,
Whether in *L'Escargot Bienvenu*, *Gobbles*, or the cheap Italian joint.
Impoverished or priggish in the provinces, where talent is born,
The angry poets look towards London as to a sea of restaurants,
Cursing the overpriced establishments of where they live
And the small scatter of the like-minded not on speaking terms.
But even this pleasure has waned, and its sum of parts—
People shaking hands on the pavement, a couple entering
A taxi bright in the London rain, the red tears on a bottle
And the absorbing conspiracies and asserted judgements
Of young men in the self-confident flush of their promise—
Its sum of parts no longer presents a street of epiphanies.
Too much now has been spoken, or published, or unpublished.
Manias without charm, cynicism without wit, and integrity
Lying around so long it has begun to stink, can be seen and heard,
And to come south from the country in a freshly pressed suit
Is no longer the exercise in youthful if gauche dignity
It once was in days of innocent enthusiasm without routine.
And so I look forward to my tweed-clad solitude, alone
Beside the widening estuary, the lighthoused island appearing
Where waves of the sea turmoil against the river's waters
Baring their salty teeth and roaring. And here I can stand
In a pretence of being a John Buchan of the underdog—
Forgive me my fantasies as, Lord, I surely forgive you yours—
With my waistcoated breast puffed against the wind. What do they
    long for?
Propping up bars with them, I can pretend to be as they are
Though I no longer know what they are thinking, if ever I did,
And, raising this civil if not entirely sympathetic interest
In what they feel, I know it contributes little to them,
Adding, as it does, to a change in myself they might not notice,
Causing me this pain as I realize the way I must change
Is to be different from friends I love and whose company—
When the last carafe was ordered, an outrageous remark spoken,
Or someone announced his plan for an innovating stanza

Or a new development in his crowded sex-life—whose company
Was a landmark in my paltry accumulation of knowledge.
Perhaps, after all, this not altogether satisfactory
Independence of mind and identity before larger notions
Is a better mess to be in, with a pocketful of bread and cheese,
My hip-flask, and the *Poésie* of Philippe Jaccottet,
Listening to the sea compose its rhythms of urbanity,
Although it is a cause for fear to notice that only my footprints
Litter this deserted beach with signs of human approach,
Each squelch of leather on mud complaining, '*But where are you going?*'

The House Next Door

    Old dears gardening in fur coats
    And 'Hush Puppies', though it's a mild July,
    Once met Freddie Lonsdale at John o' Groat's.
    Their keyboard's Chopin and their humour's wry.
        There's no one I'd rather be called 'famous' by.
        They have an antique goldfish, a cat called Sly.

    They live in my unpublished play
    For two sad characters. Their Chippendale
    Haunts England's salesrooms, their silver tray
    That brought Victoria's breakfast and her mail.
        I visit their house—its coffee aroma,
        The cat out cold in its afternoon coma!

    I watch them watching for the post,
    Wondering who writes. In *my* play, no one writes,
    They are alone, together, and have lost
    Our century by being old. Their nights
        Are spent rehearsing through Irving Berlin;
        The gardens turn to stage-sets when they begin.

    My best times with them are 'Chopin
    Mornings'. They smile vainly at my small applause—
    No one plays the Pole as badly as they can—
    And Sly stands up, and purrs, stretching his claws,
        Playing his cat's piano on the cushions,
        And called by pianist sisters, Perfect Nuisance.

There garage is pronounced gar*age*,
Strawberries never known as strawbs, but *fraises*,
And cheddar is called cheese, the rest *fromage*,
And all life is a lonely Polonaise.
     Why do I love them, that milieu not mine,
     The youngest, laughingly, 'last of the line'?

No answers. They have given me
Too much for answering. I am their pet,
Like Sly. They have defied me, cutting free
From my invention. 'Let us live. Forget
     You made us up for money. We'll give you tea,
And you shall drive our ancient crock down to the sea.'

A Dream of Judgement

Posterity, thy name is Samuel Johnson.
You sit on a velvet cushion on a varnished throne
Shaking your head sideways, saying No,
Definitely no, to all the books held up to you.
Licking your boots is a small Scotsman
Who looks like Boswell, but is really me.
You go on saying No, quite definitely no,
Adjusting the small volume of Horace
Under your wig and spitting in anger
At the portrait of Blake Swift is holding up.
Quite gently, Pope ushers me out into the hell
Of forgotten books. Nearby, teasingly,
In the dustless heaven of the classics,
There is singing of morals in Latin and Greek.

ACKNOWLEDGEMENTS

The editor is particularly grateful for assistance received from Mr Jonathan Barker, of the Arts Council Poetry Library, and from Mrs Jacqueline Simms, of Oxford University Press, as also from those others concerned in the making of books who by tradition go unnamed.

The editor and publishers gratefully acknowledge permission to use copyright poems in this book:

Dannie Abse: From *Collected Poems* (Hutchinson, 1977). Reprinted by permission of Anthony Sheil Associates Ltd.

Kingsley Amis: From *Collected Poems 1944–1979* (1979). Reprinted by permission of Hutchinson Publishing Group.

James K. Baxter: 'Evidence at the Witch Trials', 'A Dentist's Window' and 'The Apple Tree' from *Howrah Bridge and Other Poems* (Oxford University Press, 1961). Reprinted by permission of Oxford University Press. 'The Inflammable Woman' from *Collected Poems* (1980), 'Mandrakes for Supper', and 'The Buried Stream' from *The Bone Chanter* (1976), 'A Family Photograph 1939' and 'To A Print of Queen Victoria' from *The Rock Woman: Selected Poems* (1969), 'News from a Pacified Area' from *The Labyrinth* (1974). Reprinted by permission of Oxford University Press, New Zealand.

Patricia Beer: From *Selected Poems* (Hutchinson, 1980). Reprinted by permission of the author.

John Berryman: 'A Professor's Song' from *Homage to Mistress Bradstreet* (1959). 'King David Dances', and 'Certainty Before Lunch' from *Delusions, Etc.* (1972), and 'Eleven Addresses to the Lord' from *Love and Fame* (1971). Reprinted by permission of Faber and Faber Ltd.

Earle Birney: From *The Bear on the Delhi Road* (1973). Reprinted by permission of Chatto & Windus Ltd.

Elizabeth Bishop: '12 O'Clock News' from *Geography III* (1977). Reprinted by permission of Chatto & Windus Ltd. 'Seascape', 'Large Bad Picture', 'The Shampoo', 'Arrival at Santos', 'A Summer's Dream' and 'Manners' from *The Complete Poems* (1970). Copyright © 1941, 1946, 1948, 1952, 1955, 1969 by Elizabeth Bishop. Copyright renewed © 1974, 1976 by Elizabeth Bishop. Reprinted by permission of Farrar, Straus and Giroux, Inc. 'Large Bad Picture' and 'A Summer's Dream' originally appeared in *The New Yorker*.

George Mackay Brown: 'Old Fisherman with Guitar', 'Trout Fisher' and 'Beachcomber' from *Selected Poems* (1977). Reprinted by permission of The Hogarth Press. 'The Desertion of the Women and Seals', 'Carpenter', 'Tea Poems' and 'The Keeper of the Midnight Gate' from *Winterfold* (1976). Reprinted by permission of Chatto & Windus Ltd.

Charles Causley: 'Loss of an Oil Tanker', 'Infant Song', and 'Ten Types of Hospital Visitor' from *Collected Poems 1971–75* (Macmillan, 1975). 'At the British War Cemetery, Bayeux' from *Union Street* (Hart-Davis, 1957) and

ACKNOWLEDGEMENTS

'For an Ex-Far East Prisoner of War' from *Johnny Alleluia* (Hart-Davis Ltd., 1961). Reprinted by permission of David Higham Associates Ltd.

Robert Conquest: '747 (London-Chicago)', 'To Be a Pilgrim', 'Appalachian Convalescence' from *Forays* (1979). Reprinted by permission of Chatto & Windus Ltd. 'Excerpt from Report to the Galactic Council' and 'Generalities' from *Between Mars and Venus* (Hutchinson, 1962). Reprinted by permission of Curtis Brown Ltd. 'Guided Missiles Experimental Range' and 'Lake Success' from *Poems* (1955). Reprinted by permission of Macmillan, London and Basingstoke.

Donald Davie: 'A Christening', 'The Priory of St Saviour, Glendalough', 'Barnsley and District' and 'A Meeting of Cultures' from *Collected Poems, 1950–1970* (1972). Reprinted by permission of Routledge & Kegan Paul Ltd. 'To a Teacher of French' from *In The Stopping Train* (1977). Reprinted by permission of Carcanet Press Ltd. 'G.M.B.' first appeared in *The Times Literary Supplement* and is reprinted by permission of the author.

Douglas Dunn: 'The Patricians', 'A Removal from Terry Street' and 'A Dream of Judgement' from *Terry Street* (1969). 'Glasgow Schoolboys, Running Backwards' and 'Warriors' from *Barbarians* (1978). 'After the War' from *The Happier Life* (1972), and 'The House Next Door' from *Love or Nothing* (1974). All reprinted by permission of Faber and Faber Ltd. 'Remembering Lunch' first appeared in *Encounter* January 1979. Reprinted by permission of the author.

D. J. Enright: 'The Verb "To Think"' and 'History of World Languages' from *Paradise Illustrated* (Chatto & Windus, 1978), 'In Cemeteries', 'R-and-R Centre: An Incident from the Vietnam War' from *Sad Ires* (Chatto & Windus, 1975), 'Poet Wondering What He Is Up To' from *Selected Poems* (Chatto & Windus, 1968). 'Anecdote from William IV Street' first appeared in *The Times Literary Supplement*. 'Guest' first appeared in *The Listener* 20/27 December 1979. All reprinted by permission of Bolt & Watson Ltd Authors' Agents. 'Midstream' is printed by permission of the author.

Gavin Ewart: 'The Dell', 'Fiction: A Message' and 'From V.C. (a Gentleman of Verona)' from *Be My Guest* (Trigram Press Ltd., 1975). 'An Exeter Riddle' first appeared in *The Times Literary Supplement* 27 January 1978. 'The Lovesleep' first appeared in *The Listener* 20 July 1978. 'Prayer' first appeared in *The Listener* 27 October 1977. 'They flee from me that sometime did me seek' first appeared in *Encounter* January 1979. All reprinted by permission of the author. 'On the Tercentenary of Milton's Death' and 'Pastoral' from *Or Where a Young Penguin Lies Screaming* (1977). Reprinted by permission of Victor Gollancz Ltd.

Roy Fuller: 'The Unremarkable Year', 'Edmond Halley', 'Outside the Supermarket' from *Tiny Tears* (1972). 'Autobiography of a Lungworm' and 'The Family Cat' from *Collected Poems* (1962). 'Consolations of Art', 'Reading in the Night', 'The Other Side' and 'From the Joke Shop' from *From The Joke Shop* (1975). Reprinted by permission of André Deutsch Ltd. 'Shop Talk' is printed by permission of the author.

ACKNOWLEDGEMENTS

Thom Gunn: 'The Wheel of Fortune', 'The Allegory of the Wolf Boy' and 'Jesus and his Mother' from *The Sense of Movement* (1957). 'In Santa Maria del Popolo' from *My Sad Captains* (1961). 'Breakfast' and 'Misanthropos (section 9)' from *Touch* (1967). 'Street Song' from *Moly* (1971). Reprinted by permission of Faber and Faber Ltd. 'Expression' first appeared in *The Listener* 18 January 1979. Reprinted by permission of the author.

Seamus Heaney: 'Death of a Naturalist' from *Death of a Naturalist* (1966). 'The Outlaw' and 'Rite of Spring' from *Door into the Dark* (1969). 'Limbo' from *Wintering Out* (1972). 'Whatever You Say Say Nothing' from *North* (1975). 'A Drink of Water' and 'The Skunk' from *Field Work* (1979). Reprinted by permission of Faber and Faber Ltd.

John Heath-Stubbs: 'Preliminary Poem', 'Virgin Martyrs', 'Not Being Oedipus', 'The Unpredicted' and 'Carol for Advent' from *Selected Poems* (Oxford University Press, 1965). 'Send for Lord Timothy', 'The Gifts' and 'To a Poet a Thousand Years Hence' from *The Watchman's Flute* (Carcanet Press, 1979). Reprinted by permission of David Higham Associates Ltd.

Anthony Hecht: 'It Out-Herods Herod. Pray you, Avoid it', 'Pig' and 'A Letter' from *The Hard Hours*, © Anthony E. Hecht 1967. 'The Cost', 'The Ghost in the Martini' and 'A Lot of Night Music' from *Millions of Strange Shadows*, © Anthony E. Hecht 1977. Reprinted by permission of Oxford University Press.

Geoffrey Hill: 'Genesis', 'Picture of a Nativity', 'The White Ship', and 'In Piam Memoriam' from *For the Unfallen* (1959). 'Domaine Public' from *King Log* (1968). 'Two Chorale-Preludes' and 'A Short History of British India (1, 2 and 3)' from *Tenebrae* (1978). Reprinted by permission of André Deutsch Ltd.

A. D. Hope: 'Tiger', 'Paradise Saved', 'Prometheus Unbound', 'E questo il nido in che la mia fenice?', 'The House of God', 'The Bed' and 'On Shakespeare Critics' (from *Dunciad Minor*: Book V) from *Collected Poems, 1930–1970* (1972). Reprinted by permission of Angus and Robertson Publishers. 'The Female Principle' from *New Poems 1976–77* (Hutchinson, 1976). Reprinted by permission of Curtis Brown (Aust.) Pty. Ltd.

Ted Hughes: 'Wilfred Owen's Photographs' and 'Esther's Tomcat' from *Lupercal* (1960). 'Her Husband' and 'Full Moon and Little Frieda' from *Wodwo* (1968). 'Examination at the Womb-door' and 'A Childish Prank' from *Crow* (1972). 'The River in March' and 'Leaves' from *Season Songs* (1976). Reprinted by permission of Faber and Faber Ltd. 'A Dove' first appeared in *The Listener* 15 March 1979. Reprinted by permission of Olwyn Hughes on behalf of the author.

Randall Jarrell: 'A Lullaby', 'The Truth', 'A Front', 'A Camp in the Prussian Forest', 'Protocols', 'The Woman at the Washington Zoo', 'A Sick Child', 'The Lonely Man' and 'The Author to the Reader' from *The Complete Poems* (1971). Reprinted by permission of Faber and Faber Ltd. 'In Nature There Is Neither Right nor Left nor Wrong' from 'Lost World', a section from *Complete Poems*. Reprinted by permission of Eyre & Spottiswoode (Publishers) Ltd.

ACKNOWLEDGEMENTS

Philip Larkin: 'The Explosion', 'Posterity', 'Dublinesque', 'The Card-Players' and 'Cut Grass' from *High Windows* (1974). 'Ambulances', 'As Bad as a Mile', 'Mr Bleaney' and 'Days' from *The Whitsun Weddings* (1964). Reprinted by permission of Faber and Faber Ltd. 'Poetry of Departures' from *The Less Deceived* (1955). Reprinted by permission of The Marvell Press. 'The Dedicated' from *XX Poems* (1951). Reprinted by permission of the author.

Robert Lowell: 'The Dead in Europe', 'The Holy Innocents' from *Poems 1938–1949* (1950). 'A Mad Negro Soldier Confined at Munich' and 'Skunk Hour' from *Life Studies* (1959). 'Waking Early Sunday Morning' from *Near the Ocean* (1967). 'Ford Madox Ford' and 'Identification in Belfast (I.R.A. Bombing)' from *History* (1973). Reprinted by permission of Faber and Faber Ltd.

Norman MacCaig: 'Fetching Cows', 'Movements', 'Sheep Dipping', 'Flooded Mind', 'Orgy', 'In My Mind', 'Old Maps and New', 'Ringed Plover by a Water's Edge' and 'Gone are the Days' from *Old Maps and New:Selected Poems* (1978). Reprinted by permission of The Hogarth Press Ltd. 'Close-ups of Summer' and 'The Drowned' from *Tree of Strings* (1977), and 'Cock before Dawn' from *The Equal Skies* (1980). Reprinted by permission of Chatto & Windus Ltd.

Derek Mahon: 'I am Raftery', 'Grandfather', 'My Wicked Uncle', 'The Banished Gods', 'A Disused Shed in Co. Wexford' and 'The Snow Party' from *Poems 1962–1978*, © Derek Mahon 1979. Reprinted by permission of Oxford University Press.

Howard Nemerov: 'To the Rulers' and 'The Backward Look' from *The Western Approaches* (1975). 'September, the First Day of School', 'Extract from Memoirs', 'The Death of God' and 'On Being Asked for a Peace Poem' from *Gnomes and Occasions* (1973). 'A Picture' from *The Next Room of the Dream* (1962), 'Money' from *The Blue Swallows* (1967) and 'On Certain Wits' from *New and Selected Poems* (1960), University of Chicago Press. Reprinted by permission of the author.

Peter Porter: 'An Exequy', 'Non Piangere, Liù' and 'Gertrude Stein at Snails Bay' from *The Cost of Seriousness*, © Peter Porter 1978. 'May, 1945' and 'Mort aux chats' from *Preaching to the Converted*, © Oxford University Press, 1972. Reprinted by permission of Oxford University Press.

A. K. Ramanujan: 'Some Indian Uses of History on a Rainy Day', 'The Hindoo: he doesn't Hurt a Fly or a Spider either', 'Small-scale Reflections on a Great House' and 'The Last of the Princes' from *Relations*, © Oxford University Press, 1971. Reprinted by permission of Oxford University Press.

Peter Redgrove: 'Christiana', 'The Curiosity-Shop', 'Intimate Supper' and 'The Million' from *Dr Faust's Sea-Spiral Serpent* (1972). 'Dog Prospectus' and 'Serious Readers' from *Every Chink of the Ark* (1977). 'Design' from *The Force* (1966). 'Red Indian Corpse' from *The Weddings at Nether Powers* (1979). Reprinted by permission of Routledge & Kegan Paul Ltd.

Vernon Scannell: 'The Old Books', 'The Moth', 'Dead Dog' and 'Incendiary' from *Selected Poems* (1971). 'Words and Monsters', 'Six Reasons for Drinking', 'The Discriminator' and 'Five Domestic Interiors' from *The Winter Man* (1973). Reprinted by permission of Allison & Busby Ltd. 'Jailbird' from *Mastering the Craft* (1970). Reprinted by permission of Pergamon Press Ltd.

Louis Simpson: 'Things' and 'Tonight the Famous Psychiatrist' from *Selected Poems*, © Louis Simpson 1966. 'Hubert's Museum' and 'Before the Poetry Reading' from *Searching for the Ox*, © Louis Simpson 1976. 'A Son of the Romanovs' from *Adventures of the Letter I*, © Louis Simpson 1971. Reprinted by permission of Oxford University Press. 'Summer Storm' and 'On the Lawn at the Villa' from *At the End of the Open Road* (1963), © 1949, 1963 by Louis Simpson. Reprinted by permission of Wesleyan University Press. 'Chocolates' first appeared in *The Listener* 26 October 1978. Reprinted by permission of the author.

C. H. Sisson: 'Family Fortunes', 'The Queen of Lydia', 'A and B' and 'At First' from *In the Trojan Ditch* (1974). 'Marcus Aurelius' and 'Over the Wall: Berlin, May 1975' from *Anchises* (1976). Reprinted by permission of Carcanet Press Ltd.

Stevie Smith: From *Collected Poems* (Allen Lane 1975). Reprinted by permission of James MacGibbon as executor.

Jon Stallworthy: 'A Letter from Berlin' from *Root and Branch* (1969) and 'A Question of Form and Content', 'The Beginning of the End', 'Walking against the Wind' and 'Again' from *Hand in Hand* (1974). Reprinted by permission of Chatto & Windus Ltd. 'Miss Lavender', 'War Story' and 'Sindhi Woman' from *The Apple Barrel*, © Oxford University Press, 1963. Reprinted by permission of Oxford University Press.

R. S. Thomas: 'Aside', 'Lore', 'The One Furrow', 'A Welshman to Any Tourist' and 'Poetry for Supper' from *Selected Poems 1946–1968* (Hart-Davis, 1973) and 'Pisces' from *Song at the Year's Turning* (Hart-Davis, 1955). Reprinted by permission of Granada Publishing Ltd. 'The Woman', 'After Jericho' and 'At It' from *Frequencies* (1978), 'The Hand' from *Laboratories of the Spirit* (1975) and 'Postscript' from *H'm* (1972). Reprinted by permission of Macmillan, London and Basingstoke. 'At It' first appeared in *Encounter* March 1978 under the title 'The Verdict'.

Charles Tomlinson: 'Charlotte Corday', 'In Arden', 'The Death of Will' and 'Macduff' from *The Shaft*, © Charles Tomlinson 1978, and 'Mr Brodsky', 'A Dream' and 'Civilities of Lamplight' from *Selected Poems, 1951–1974*, © Charles Tomlinson 1978. Reprinted by permission of Oxford University Press.

Derek Walcott: 'Volcano', 'New World', 'The Virgins' and 'Force' from *Sea Grapes* (1976). 'Nights in the Gardens of Port of Spain' and 'The Whale, His Bulwark' from *The Castaway* (1965), and 'A Country Club Romance' from *In A Green Night* (1962). Reprinted by permission of Jonathan Cape Ltd.

Richard Wilbur: 'Advice to a Prophet', 'Loves of the Puppets', 'Shame', 'The Undead' and 'Pangloss's Song: A Comic-Opera Lyric' from *Advice to a Prophet* (1962). 'For the Student Strikers', 'The Writer' and 'John Chap-

ACKNOWLEDGEMENTS

man' from *The Mind-Reader* (1977). Reprinted by permission of Faber and
Faber Ltd. 'John Chapman' first appeared in *The New Yorker*. 'To the
Etruscan Poets' from *The Mind-Reader* reprinted by permission of *The
Ontario Review*.

While every effort has been made to secure permission, we may have failed
in a few cases to trace the copyright holder. We apologize for any apparent
negligence.

INDEX OF FIRST LINES

The numbers refer to pages

291

INDEX OF FIRST LINES

INDEX OF FIRST LINES

INDEX OF FIRST LINES

INDEX OF AUTHORS

The numbers refer to pages

OXFORD

MORE OXFORD PAPERBACKS

This book is just one of nearly 1000 Oxford Paperbacks currently in print. If you would like details of other Oxford Paperbacks, including titles in the World's Classics, Oxford Reference, Oxford Books, OPUS, Past Masters, Oxford Authors, and Oxford Shakespeare series, please write to:

UK and Europe: Oxford Paperbacks Publicity Manager, Arts and Reference Publicity Department, Oxford University Press, Walton Street, Oxford OX2 6DP.

Customers in UK and Europe will find Oxford Paperbacks available in all good bookshops. But in case of difficulty please send orders to the Cash-with-Order Department, Oxford University Press Distribution Services, Saxon Way West, Corby, Northants NN18 9ES. Tel: 0536 741519; Fax: 0536 746337. Please send a cheque for the total cost of the books, plus £1.75 postage and packing for orders under £20; £2.75 for orders over £20. Customers outside the UK should add 10% of the cost of the books for postage and packing.

USA: Oxford Paperbacks Marketing Manager, Oxford University Press, Inc., 200 Madison Avenue, New York, N.Y. 10016.

Canada: Trade Department, Oxford University Press, 70 Wynford Drive, Don Mills, Ontario M3C 1J9.

Australia: Trade Marketing Manager, Oxford University Press, G.P.O. Box 2784Y, Melbourne 3001, Victoria.

South Africa: Oxford University Press, P.O. Box 1141, Cape Town 8000.

OXFORD POETS

A PORTER SELECTED

Peter Porter

This selection of about one hundred of Porter's best poems is chosen from all his works to date, including his latest book, *Possible Worlds*, and *The Automatic Oracle*, which won the 1988 Whitbread Prize for Poetry.

What the critics have said about Peter Porter:

'I can't think of any contemporary poet who is so consistently entertaining over such a variety of material.' John Lucas, *New Statesman*

'an immensely fertile, lively, informed, honest and penetrating mind.' Stephen Spender, *Observer*

'He writes vigorously, with savage erudition and wonderful expansiveness . . . No one now writing matches Porter's profoundly moral and cultured overview.' Douglas Dunn, *Punch*

OXFORD BOOKS

THE NEW OXFORD BOOK OF
IRISH VERSE

Edited, with Translations, by Thomas Kinsella

Verse in Irish, especially from the early and medieval periods, has long been felt to be the preserve of linguists and specialists, while Anglo-Irish poetry is usually seen as an adjunct to the English tradition. This original anthology approaches the Irish poetic tradition as a unity and presents a relationship between two major bodies of poetry that reflects a shared and painful history.

'the first coherent attempt to present the entire range of Irish poetry in both languages to an English-speaking readership' *Irish Times*

'a very satisfying and moving introduction to Irish poetry' *Listener*

OXFORD REFERENCE

THE CONCISE OXFORD COMPANION TO ENGLISH LITERATURE

Edited by Margaret Drabble and Jenny Stringer

Based on the immensely popular fifth edition of the *Oxford Companion to English Literature* this is an indispensable, compact guide to the central matter of English literature.

There are more than 5,000 entries on the lives and works of authors, poets, playwrights, essayists, philosophers, and historians; plot summaries of novels and plays; literary movements; fictional characters; legends; theatres; periodicals; and much more.

The book's sharpened focus on the English literature of the British Isles makes it especially convenient to use, but there is still generous coverage of the literature of other countries and of other disciplines which have influenced or been influenced by English literature.

From reviews of *The Oxford Companion to English Literature*:

'a book which one turns to with constant pleasure ... a book with much style and little prejudice' Iain Gilchrist, *TLS*

'it is quite difficult to imagine, in this genre, a more useful publication' Frank Kermode, *London Review of Books*

'incarnates a living sense of tradition ... sensitive not to fashion merely but to the spirit of the age' Christopher Ricks, *Sunday Times*